GREECE & ROME STUDIES

VOLUME III

D0206901

GREECE & ROME STUDIES

# WOMEN IN ANTIQUITY

*Edited by*

IAN McAUSLAN

*and*

PETER WALCOT

Published by
OXFORD UNIVERSITY PRESS

on behalf of
THE CLASSICAL ASSOCIATION
1996

UNIVERSITY OF TULSA-MCFARLIN LIBRARY

*Oxford University Press, Walton Street, Oxford* OX2 6DP
*Oxford New York*
*Athens Auckland Bangkok Bombay*
*Calcutta Cape Town Dar es Salaam Delhi*
*Florence Hong Kong Istanbul Karachi*
*Kuala Lumpur Madras Madrid Melbourne*
*Mexico City Nairobi Paris Singapore*
*Taipei Tokyo Toronto*
*and associated companies in*
*Berlin Ibadan*

*Oxford is a trade mark of Oxford University Press*

*Published in the United States*
*by Oxford University Press Inc., New York*

© *The Individual Contributors 1996*

*All rights reserved. No part of this publication may be reproduced, stored in a retrieval system, or transmitted, in any form or by any means, without the prior permission in writing of Oxford University Press. Within the UK, exceptions are allowed in respect of any fair dealing for the purpose of research or private study, or criticism or review, as permitted under the Copyright, Designs and Patents Act, 1988, or in the case of reprographic reproduction in accordance with the terms of the licences issued by the Copyright Licensing Agency. Enquiries concerning reproduction outside these terms and in other countries should be sent to the Rights Department, Oxford University Press, at the address above*

*British Library Cataloguing in Publication Data*
*Data available*

*Library of Congress Cataloging in Publication Data*

*Women in antiquity / edited by Ian McAuslan and Peter Walcot.*
*—(Greece & Rome studies : v. 3)*
*Includes indexes.*
*1. Women—History—To 500. 2. Women—Greece—History. 3. Women–*
*–Rome—History. I. McAuslan, Ian. II. Walcot, Peter.*
*III. Series.*
*HQ1127.W64 1995*
*305.4'09'01—dc20 95–9278*
*ISBN 0–19–920302-–4*
*ISBN 0–19–920303–2 (Pbk)*

1 3 5 7 9 10 8 6 4 2

*Typeset by Regent Typesetting, London*
*Printed and bound on acid-free paper by*
*Biddles Ltd,*
*Guildford and King's Lynn*

HQ1127
.W64
1996

# CONTENTS

# NOTES ON CONTRIBUTORS

GILLIAN CLARK: Lecturer in Classics, University of Liverpool.

ANTHONY J. MARSHALL: Professor of Classics, Queen's University at Kingston, Ontario.

AVERIL CAMERON: Warden, Keble College, Oxford.

DOUGLAS M. MACDOWELL: Professor of Greek, University of Glasgow.

MARY R. LEFKOWITZ: Andrew W. Mellon Professor in the Humanities, Wellesley College, Massachusetts.

THOMAS E. J. WIEDEMANN: Reader in the History of the Roman Empire, University of Bristol.

PETER WALCOT: Professor in the School of History and Archaeology, University of Wales College of Cardiff.

SHELLEY P. HALEY: Associate Professor, Department of Classics, Hamilton College, New York.

DAVID COHEN: Associate Professor, Department of Rhetoric, University of California, Berkeley.

JANE F. GARDNER: Professor of Ancient History, Department of Classics, University of Reading.

LORNA HARDWICK: Staff Tutor and Senior Lecturer in Classical Studies, the Open University.

A. T. FEAR: Lecturer in Ancient History, University of Keele.

H. S. VERSNEL: Professor of Ancient History, University of Leiden.

# INTRODUCTION

*By* GILLIAN CLARK

These papers from *Greece & Rome* reflect twenty years of scholarship on women in Graeco-Roman antiquity, from the first cautious mention of feminist approaches to the confident deployment of techniques and assumptions which would once have prompted incredulity. The first paper in the collection, published in 1975, followed twenty years of silence about women. (There had been a few papers before that: the original selection considered by the Board of Management included one from 1945, F. E. Adcock's 'Women in Roman Life and Letters', and one from 1955, Charles Seltman's 'The Status of Women at Athens'. These are recommended reading for anyone who is interested in seeing how much society and scholarship have changed in this half-century.) In 1995, after twenty very productive years of work on women's history and on the representation of women in art and literature, we may be entering a new phase of scholarship. Work on women has been merging into work on gender, that is, on femaleness and maleness in relation to each other and in the context of the society which interpreted what it was to be male or female. This may mean that, in the long term, the history of women and the history of men are integrated rather than separated.

'Women in Antiquity' is a controversial subject. It is bound up with the experiences of individual researchers and readers, and with their beliefs about human relationships and about the study of past societies. Interpretations change not only when new evidence is discovered but also when new perspectives are found, and it is very easy to be surprised, or even shocked, at what other people think they recognize. One scholar sees, in the surviving texts and works of art, competent and respected wives and mothers who leave politics to the men. Another sees, in the very same texts and works of art, women denied the freedom and the education to say what they want from life, and categorized as inferior and irrational. This raises the problem of 'respecting the evidence'. The first scholar could argue that we must listen to what the evidence says instead of imposing our own beliefs upon it, or taking it out of context, or going beyond the conclusions it allows. The second could argue that listening to the evidence should not mean accepting the agenda of the men who provided almost all of it: it includes what can be inferred by reading between the lines and against the grain of the texts (that is, not how the author expected to be read), and also by thinking about what the texts do not say.

Again, the first scholar may think that his or her task is to explain, as clearly and fully as possible, what exactly is the evidence we have, and how some kinds of evidence may relate to others: his or her personal life and beliefs should be kept distinct from this intellectual task. Another scholar may think that intellectual honesty requires acknowledgement of 'where you are coming from' in seeking to interpret the surviving evidence: perhaps a description of personal history and reactions to the problem discussed, perhaps an account of where a piece of work stands in relation to particular theories about gender or about literature. Ideally, each scholar will think of the other as a fellow human being with a history and with a concern for the subject, but this does not always happen.

Given the diversity, and the very wide range, of the subject, the obvious way to advance discussion is by collections of papers. An assemblage of topics and viewpoints is more appropriate than a unified history: thus the first volume of *A History of Women in the West*[1] is a collection, and there have been several others. The papers in *Greece & Rome Studies III* vary in range and approach, but they have some common characteristics which result from the intended audience of the journal. *Greece & Rome* was founded (in 1931) with the modest intention of being useful to people, not necessarily professional academics and teachers, who were interested in the classics. It has become much more a professional journal—two of the latest papers in this collection, by Lorna Hardwick (1990) and H. S. Versnel (1992), are noticeably more difficult reading than the earlier papers—but it still aims to be usable by sixth-formers and university students, by their teachers, and by friends of classics generally. So one common characteristic of these papers is a focus on classical Greece and Rome. By contrast, many collections on women in antiquity take 'antiquity' to mean ancient cultures in the widest sense, and make use of comparisons between cultures to sharpen perceptions of women's lives in any particular culture. One of the earliest collections, *Images of Women in Antiquity*,[2] included papers on Egyptian, Hittite, Babylonian, and Celtic women, and one of the most recent, *Women in Ancient Societies*,[3] includes only five papers out of fourteen on classical Greece and Rome. This contrast does not mean that *Studies III* has a narrowly classical focus: several papers use a 'comparativist' approach, but the comparison is rather with patterns of thought and behaviour which survive in present-day Mediterranean cultures, or which are, perhaps, recurrent in human nature.

The second common characteristic is an interest in reading social history out of written and visual texts, especially those which are part of the main classical curriculum. (It may seem strange to call a picture, or a sculpture, a 'text'. The point is that we cannot just look at it and see what it is: we interpret or 'read' it.) The central questions of these papers are those which most often interest sixth-formers and undergraduates: what did women do, what was life like for them, and was it like what poets say and artists show? The favoured tactic for answering the questions is to read the texts in the light of new expectations about how people behave. These new expectations may derive from the changed social position of women in the later twentieth century, or from general theories about human motivations, or from anthropological study of societies in which people are, apparently, behaving and thinking like the people represented in the texts. The papers vary in the extent to which they discuss method or acknowledge the problems of using texts as evidence, but none of them starts from the assumption that texts do not tell the reader anything about life. By contrast, it can be argued that we have no information about women: what we have is man-made images of women or representations of women. (These are the titles of two of the first collections of papers, *Representations of Women in Antiquity*,[4] and *Images of Women in Antiquity*.[5]) If that is right, we can study 'constructs' of women, that is, fantasies about women or theories about what it is to be a woman, and this may be instructive, but it tells us about the making of images and not about women. There is also a more far-reaching argument, derived from critical theory: that reading texts teaches us about the activity of reading, about the relationship of texts to readers and to other texts, about how what we read shapes us and how we use it to give shape to our own experience—but not about anything 'outside the text', such as the lives of women (or, for that matter, men) in antiquity.

It is difficult to sell this idea to school and university students: teachers are more likely to be working at the other end of the range and trying to persuade them out of the 'biographical fallacy', the conviction that creative writers and artists almost always depict their own experiences of life. Moreover, critical theory is often very difficult to read, even for professional academics working in the same discipline, and it is fair to ask whether this is necessary. Classicists, especially if they were trained to write proses, often suspect that obscurity results from not thinking out what you want to say; classicists who are interested in the sociology of knowledge may suspect that obscurity results (as in Alexandrian poetry) from a wish to defend the territory of a cultural élite. But the questions remain as a much-needed warning against naïve reading. The classics of art and literature have survived as classics because they are very impressive works, and it is genuinely difficult to keep in mind that the heroines of Athenian tragedy, or of Latin love-poetry, are literary creations, which may or may not tell us something about the social experience of the men who invented them or the social context in which they were produced.

Thirdly, the papers have something of a common tone: moderate or wryly resigned rather than polemic, and optimistic about ordinary human relations in the ancient world. They discuss, or at least mention, most of the constraints on women's lives, and most of the negative associations of femaleness. Readers are reminded that many women married very early and without being able to choose their partner, that child-bearing was dangerous and that husbands could opt not to rear a child, that there were social limitations on where a woman could go and whom she could meet, that there were very few options for women other than marriage and domestic life, the most obvious being life as an 'entertainer', that women took no official part in politics, law, and government, and that some women had, in theory, no property of their own. Readers are also reminded that women were associated with weakness, incompetence, unreason, untamed nature, and uncontrollable desires, and were suspected of lying, stealing, infidelity, and dominating their sons. Nevertheless, there is in these papers a recurrent confidence that women had in practice some freedom of action, or at least that they did not mind too much about the constraints on their lives because they did not miss what they had never known, and because there was a difference between what men thought (or at least said) about women in general and what they thought about their own wives, sisters, and daughters.

Before I turn to the individual papers, there is an explanation, even an apology, due to their authors. None of them expected their work (including footnotes and incidental remarks) to be used as an illustration of what was happening at a particular time in a particular subject-area: all of them wrote on topics which they found interesting and which they thought would interest the readers of *Greece & Rome*. The editors invited the authors to update their papers: those who responded have usually done so by adding bibliography or modifying points they made, rather than by commenting on the way they wrote the paper or on how the subject has changed. Style is often (not always) revealing, but the experience of reading a paper is quite different when one knows its author or has, at least, heard his or her living voice, and I have not heard four of these authors (Marshall, Haley, Cohen, Versnel). Publication dates can also be misleading: the author of a paper which appeared later than some important work may not have known about that work when the paper was in preparation. (Or the converse may apply: for instance, Roger Just's invaluable *Women in Athenian Law and Life* finally appeared in 1989, but the typescript of an article he wrote in 1978 had been in circulation for some years; and Susan Treggiari had worked since the mid-1970s on the subject-matter of her *Roman Marriage*, which came out in 1991.) The comments which follow are, I hope, useful in that I have worked in this area for most of the twenty years covered by these papers, and have several times revised my ideas about how to do it or (more often) wondered after the event why I had not seen some obvious point. I have no notion of sitting in judgement, only of trying to provide a context.

The first paper in *Studies III*, Anthony Marshall's 'Tacitus and the

Governor's Lady', was originally published in 1975. Its main concern is the purpose of Tacitus in narrating a debate of A.D. 21 on whether the wives of Roman governors should accompany them to their provinces. The question arose because a governor's wife was inevitably a person of influence in the province, and it was not thought appropriate for women to have public status; on the other hand, Roman governors might prefer to have the company of their wives or (more cynically) to know what they were doing. Early in his paper, Marshall points out that this debate has been used, out of context, as evidence (*a*) for the good sense and beneficent influence of Roman women, (*b*) for their moral decline in the Early Empire, and (*c*) for a long-term effort to repress the emancipation of Roman women. The dates are significant. (*a*) and (*b*) belong to the early years of the twentieth century, and the scholars who advanced the arguments were most concerned with the morals of women in general (or even Woman, as in the splendid title of J. Donaldson's book of 1907: *Woman: Her Position and Influence in Ancient Greece and Rome, and among the Early Christians*). (*c*) belongs to 1964, and reflects the Women's Movement of the 1960s. Marshall was unconvinced by Claudine Herrmann's attempt, in *Le Rôle judiciaire et politique des femmes sous la République romaine*,[6] to argue for an ongoing feminist movement in republican Rome: it seemed to him another case of imposing anachronistic concerns on the evidence, ignoring the specific historical context and the diversity of individual and political motives. He comments, in a footnote, that 'not one gleam of humour appears to lighten this fanciful exegesis', to which one might be tempted to reply that the oppression of women is not funny, and that feminist activism is not fanciful. But the underlying argument is, again, that it is a failure of historical awareness to imagine women of the Middle Republic behaving like Sixties activists. ('What do we want?' 'Marriage without *manus*!' 'When do we want it?' 'Now!')

Marshall's paper raises important questions about 'respecting the evidence'. He takes the purpose of the author as central, and he argues that Tacitus was interested not in the status of women, but in the competence of the senate. But readers who are interested in the status of women may want to ask their own questions, not the questions which interest Tacitus; and readers who have known women campaigning for increased opportunities may think they have seen something which Tacitus did not see or refused to acknowledge. The Women's Movement made women realize how much inequality and prejudice they still had to contend with and how many assumptions they had made about themselves. It also made classical scholars think about women in antiquity, the inequality and prejudice from which they had suffered, and the assumptions about them which scholars (male and female) had taken over from writings almost invariably by men.

In North America, the 1973 issue of *Arethusa* recognized 'Women in Antiquity' as a field of scholarship, and the 1978 issue was also about women. The preface to *Women in the Ancient World: The Arethusa Papers*[7] remarks that the authors of the 1973 papers had to struggle to get their subject accepted as a legitimate concern of classical scholars. Sarah Pomeroy's pioneering survey, *Goddesses, Whores, Wives and Slaves*[8] came out in the same year as Anthony Marshall's paper. Her title (startling at the time) confronted the reader with what had happened to women in the ancient world. She explained (p. ix) that 'this book was conceived when I asked myself what women were doing while men were active in all the areas traditionally emphasized by modern scholars' and when she found that standard works on economy and social history did not help her to answer the question. Worse, the kind of discrimination that women were identifying in their own lives appeared to have its roots in classical literature and philosophy. Feminist classicists, in the 1970s, found that their subject was not remote from the struggle, but had a political agenda. If there was evidence for matriarchies and mother goddesses in early Greek history, this would show that patriarchal society and the male-dominated Olympian religion were latecomers, and that male-dominated societies are not universal. Even if there was no such evidence, it could at least be argued that western culture had been brainwashed on the subject of women, and that the brainwashing began with the classics, which had been produced by a slave-owning male élite and perpetuated by an élitist male-dominated profession. So work was done to document misogyny, male dominance, and the oppression of women in classical culture, and to find examples of women who had escaped from the domestic stereotype.

The papers in this collection do not include a representative of this phase, but they do show reactions to it—not least in the sudden increase of papers about women in *Greece & Rome* from 1980 on. Averil Cameron notes, in her update to 'Neither Male nor Female' (1980), that work inspired by the Women's Movement was only just beginning to appear when her paper was in its first version, in 1976. Her bibliography includes work which was of great importance in the 1970s: *Arethusa* (1973) and Pomeroy for classics, Rosemary Ruether's collection *Religion and Sexism*[9] for Judaeo-Christian theology, and Juliet Mitchell and Ann Oakley for sociology and the history of feminism. I have only two comments to add to Cameron's own assessment of her paper and of changes since it was written. One is a further update: the Church of England now has women priests. It also has clergy and laity who are still unable to accept them, for a variety of reasons which (for some) include beliefs about the nature and social role of women. The other comment is that the paper makes an important point about differentiating social, cultural, and economic backgrounds instead of generalizing about 'Christian women' (or Jewish, or Greek, or Roman women). This has become easier, and more obvious, as more work has been done; one could not now write an article, or even a book, blithely entitled 'Roman Women' (unless, of course, it was a collection).

The range of my 'Roman Women' (1981) now seems absurdly wide. There are, now, detailed studies of the subject-matter of almost every sentence: it is quite hard to remember how little was available at the time of writing. The paper came out of the culture shock of domesticity, and asks a series of important, but perhaps unanswerable, questions about what Roman women did with their lives and how they could stand it. I still think that we should not underrate the economic and social contribution of women whose main concern was (or is) with household and family, and I am still not prepared to say that we know nothing about them from the material which survives. But this paper is too 'positivist' in that it tries to answer questions by accumulating items of source material, and it does not do enough to acknowledge the diversity of the material it uses. The first footnote, interestingly, mentions the first North American edition of the source collection by Mary Lefkowitz and Maureen Fant, *Women's Life in Greece and Rome*.[10] Source collections have their problems, in particular that they necessarily take their material away from its context. This is why *Women in the Classical World*[11] opts for discursive essays with extensive quotations and illustrations. But the great advantage of source collections is that students are not told what to think, and it became very much easier to teach 'Women in Antiquity' when the first UK edition of Lefkowitz and Fant appeared in 1982, offering not only literary sources but also legal, medical, and epigraphic material which had previously been scattered through various technical works. The revised edition of 1992 included much more material: not new discoveries, but material now seen to be relevant.

Douglas MacDowell's 'Love versus the Law: An Essay on Menander's *Aspis*' (1982) uses some genuinely new discoveries (new fragments of plays by Menander) and, as he says, draws on legal studies which would not normally be read by non-specialists. It is a technical, but very clear, discussion of Athenian law on inheritance where there was no son. Because Athenian women were not recognized as the legal owners of property, an Athenian *epiklēros*, a daughter who at her father's death had no surviving brothers, was not strictly speaking an heiress. But she and her father's property went together: it could not be claimed by another relative unless he also took responsibility for her by marrying her. Her father's closest male relative had the first claim to do so (and might even divorce for the purpose), but she herself could not choose whom to marry. The situation of the *epiklēros* has provoked mixed reactions. Some people think it is a brutal demonstration that the nuclear family is (as Engels, a classicist by training, argued) a device for transmitting property in the male line, and that Athenian men and Athenian law were interested only in the continuation of the property-owning household. Others point out that it ensured protection for an *epiklēros* who inherited nothing but claims against her father's property, and argue that it shows Athenian men, and Athenian law, to be concerned for the well-being of women.

MacDowell suggests that Menander is challenging the legal rules because he wants his audience to take love (specifically, romantic love) into account. The paper uses Menander's plays as evidence for Athenian law, on the grounds that they tell stories which could have happened in late fourth-century Athens. MacDowell's update, responding to a challenge from P. G. McC. Brown, argues in more detail that the plot had to be credible to the men in the audience who had sat on juries—and one could add that many women, although they did not sit on juries, would be just as concerned about inheritance. But questions remain both about law and about love. MacDowell takes Athenian law to be similar to classical Roman law: a detailed set of rules, composed by legal experts, which can be (partially) reconstructed from the surviving evidence. So a newly discovered play by Menander can be used to supply some missing pieces of the jigsaw. Recent work on Athenian law (for instance, Stephen Todd, *The Shape of Athenian Law*)[12] has been influenced by studies of social systems in which law is not a neutral device for the resolution of conflict, but is rather one of the arenas in which families can compete. In these circumstances, a detailed set of binding legal rules is less likely than a mixture of basic rules, social assumptions, and decisions in particular cases which did not necessarily create a precedent. If that is right, Menander need not be making a revolutionary suggestion that it is wrong to act in accordance with the law on 'heiresses': rather, he is saying that a decent man would not assert some of the claims which a lawcourt would probably allow. As for love, it is indeed remarkable that Menander's plots rely on the love, leading to or expressed in marriage, of a young man and a young woman. This seems so obvious a theme that it is easy to forget the contrast with other kinds of writing (both ancient and modern) about male–female relations in fourth-century Athens, and the question of whether this kind of love is a universal human experience, or whether the felt emotion derives from particular ways of thinking about human relationships. Michel Foucault's *History of Sexuality*[13] drew attention to this problem, and recent work has explored changing presentations of romantic, sexual, marital, and extramarital love.[14]

Mary Lefkowitz's 'Wives and Husbands' (1983) is concerned with marital relationships over almost a millennium, from Homer to the late fourth century A.D. She remarks on the state of the question: before the Women's Movement, there had been a tendency to assume that women were generally contented with their domestic role, or at least did not complain about it; after, there was a tendency to assume that women were generally frustrated, and would have liked to do what the few exceptional women did. Lefkowitz draws attention to the problem which is sometimes called 'presentism', that is, judging past societies and past lives by present-day standards of achievement. She asks what satisfaction women could have found in married domestic life, and her tactic is to imagine the aims and the responses of women whose lives (as she warns) are reported or imagined by male authors. Her main sources are Athenian tragedy and comedy, and epitaphs both from Athens and from Rome; and she sometimes writes as if Penelope and Alcestis were real people. This (like Gillian Clark's 'Roman Women' of 1981) is a very wide-ranging paper, and there has since been a great output of work on family relationships, on the various kinds of source-material used, and on the general problems of using literature as a source of information about the lives of women. Lefkowitz notes especially an important paper by John Gould, 'Law, Custom and Myth: Aspects of the Social Position of Women in Classical Athens', which appeared in the *Journal of Hellenic Studies* in 1980. It was a careful documentation, making use of anthropology as well as classical scholarship, of the truths (often affirmed and often forgotten) that our evidence offers only the men's perspective, even though it may have been accepted by some women, and that the use of different kinds of evidence produces quite different accounts of Athenian attitudes to women. He also, in a final comment, noted that 'love' is not a simple concept. But Lefkowitz's main concern is to show the persistence over time, and in different kinds of evidence, of a particular set of values: those of a traditional marriage with clear gender-roles.

Thomas Wiedemann, in a paper also from 1983, is also concerned with gender-roles, but from a quite different perspective. The title of his 'Thucydides, Women, and the Limits of Rational Analysis' in fact begins with a brief Greek citation, which means 'least … renown among males'. This phrase comes from the Funeral Speech which, according to Thucydides, Pericles delivered in praise of Athens at the first ever state funeral for the war dead, in 431 B.C. Wiedemann does not spell out the citation, because the sentence in which it occurs had for many years been notorious as an expression of Athenian attitudes to women. In the long and imposing speech, one brief paragraph, almost at the end, is addressed to women, who are offered advice in a deliberate paradox: they will be most renowned if they are not mentioned among men. This apparently spectacular example of 'social muting' has (as Wiedemann notes in his update) been gradually defused. The advice is addressed specifically to young widows, a dangerous social category because they are neither in the charge of a husband nor old enough to be sexless; the occasion was particularly difficult, because a state funeral made public what was usually a family event in which women were expected to display strong emotion; and it was Thucydides, not Pericles, who wrote the speech.

This last point is the important one for Wiedemann: Thucydides rarely mentions women. This may be because Athenian democracy, in its early years, was struggling to make a distinction between the public world of debate and decision (by adult free Athenian-born males) and the private concerns of Athenian households. On the other hand, we may have this impression of Athenian democracy because Thucydides is the dominant historian of the late fifth century. Wiedemann argues that Thucydides uses the presence or absence of women in his narrative as a signal that he is dealing with, or rejecting, a particular kind of historical explanation. His predecessor Herodotus prefers to offer stories about individuals as an explanation of events, and of course women feature in these stories. But in Thucydides' history, women mark the non-rational and uncontrollable aspects of what happens in history. This association of rationality and male control has been called the 'gendering of reason'. It is a powerful theme of Greek moral philosophy, which Foucault characterized as a pre-occupation, even an obsession, with the 'autonomous male subject' who can control both his own desires (often personified as feminine) and his responses to events.

Peter Walcot's 1984 paper is concerned with the failure of male control. 'Greek Attitudes towards Women: The Mythological Evidence' uses mythology to illustrate fear of female sexuality. Walcot offers two possible (and compatible) interpretations of myths: they may explain particular customs or beliefs, and they may manifest deep-seated human fears which are also expressed in dreams. He provides examples of stories about dangerously seductive or destructive females, discussing especially the Amazons as 'reversal myth', that is, a story which explains a custom by presenting its opposite: this is what happens when women are warriors like men instead of wives and mothers. (This argument is developed in Hardwick's paper.) He also suggests that Greek men had a particular devotion to safely sexless females, the virgin goddesses and the virtuous 'bee' wife who is bee-like not in that she collects honey but in that she dislikes sex. (Bees recur in Versnel's paper of 1992.)

Walcot's introduction remarks on the spectacular growth of interest in women's studies in the early 1980s. Perhaps there is a subtext here: given this seemingly uncontrollable demand, there may be safety in separation, in assigning it to distinct courses on women. Walcot also comments on increased understanding, though he duly puts 'facts' into scare quotes when he says that we are now reasonably clear about conditions of life for women in classical Athens. The interpretation he offers depends on comparative anthropology. Mediterranean peasant societies (in particular the Sarakatsani shepherds of northern Greece) had been found to show a concern for honour, and a deep distrust of women as possible threats to honour, which could make sense of classical Greek patterns of behaviour. These patterns (ancient or modern) are of course seen from the perspective of the men concerned, but anthropologists have sometimes been disheartened to find that women say very much the same about the dangerous nature of women. It depends who is asking and who else is listening. Walcot suggests that fear is the key: Athenian girls were married at puberty in order to give their sexuality a safe expression, dowries acted as an incentive for girls to behave well and make a good marriage, and restriction of movement safeguarded women's reputations so that their menfolk did not need to avenge their honour. More briefly, he suggests that this was not so grim as we might think, because (an important point developed by David Cohen in his paper from 1989) the social ideal that women stay at home might not have corresponded to the reality, because women did not have twentieth-century expectations and therefore did not suffer from the frustration of such expectations, and because women and men expected, and even preferred, to lead separate lives.

Shelley Haley's paper of 1985, 'The Five Wives of Pompey the Great', intervenes, as it happens, in a sequence of papers (Walcot 1984 and 1987, Cohen 1989, Gardner 1989, and Hardwick 1990) which variously use anthropology to illuminate women's lives, and anxious fantasies about women, in classical Greece. The imbalance between Greece and Rome in this collection of papers is typical of the subject before the late 1980s. The Greek material was perhaps more exciting precisely because there was less individual detail, so there was more scope for analysing and constructing unfamiliar structures of thought. Haley's paper focuses on the individual, discussing Roman political marriages with a deliberate shift of perspective away from their political purpose. The five marriages of Pompey are used to illustrate women's concerns and the private life of a Roman public man. Haley reads between the lines of her sources to find distinct individual characters for the wives and to speculate (like Lekfowitz in her paper from 1983) on what satisfaction they may have found in their marriages. The problem here is that almost all the evidence comes from Plutarch. Recent work (again drawing on Foucault) has emphasized Plutarch's distinctive interest in marital and family relationships, and the question arises, as it did for Menander, whether Plutarch gives expression to a universal awareness which had simply not been mentioned, or whether he manifests a new concern for personal relations which results from a sense of loss. Members of traditionally powerful families, in Rome and Italy as well as the provinces, experienced a loss of political power once Rome had an emperor, and Plutarch wrote about adjusting to the new role of loyal subject and local patriot. He may have misinterpreted, or overinterpreted, the feelings of extremely powerful Romans a century before his time. (Present-day British readers may be tempted to misinterpret the suggestion that Pompey wanted to spend more time with his family.) One other interesting aspect of this paper is that Shelley Haley, who wrote it in the impersonal and moderately optimistic manner of most of these papers, has recently described her experience as a black woman classicist encountering the conventions of classical scholarship.[15]

Peter Walcot's second paper, 'Plato's Mother and Other Terrible Women' (1987), confronts another kind of fear provoked by women: fear of the dominant mother. His devastating epigraph from Freud observes that 'a mother can transfer to her son the ambition which she has been obliged to suppress in herself'. Here again is the problem of the human reaction which (like romantic love) may be universal or may be culture-dependent. Seneca, as Walcot observes, noticed the phenomenon of mothers transferring their ambitions to their sons, but, unlike Freud, he considered it to be a typical vice of women, not the sign of a perfect, non-ambivalent relationship. Freud, who is still thought by some people to have illuminated the basic workings of human nature, has been under attack from others for forcing his own interpretations on the experience of his patients, and especially for his characterization of the experience of women. It has been argued that Freudian psychology is culturally dependent, and has more to do with the social patterns of nineteenth-century Vienna than with the universal human condition. For instance, 'Oedipal' dreams are reported from the ancient world, but the intercourse of son with mother is interpreted as intercourse with Mother Earth signifying either death or conquest. Some people conclude that the ancient world repressed the true significance of Oedipal dreams, others that the Oedipus complex is an invention of Freud and of nineteenth-century Vienna. John J. Winkler, in *The Constraints of Desire: The Anthropology of Sex and Gender in Ancient Greece*,[16] uses reports of sexual dreams as a further argument that it is culture, not nature, which determines the significance of sexual relationships.

Walcot discusses, with a range of examples from Achilles to Augustine, the temptations and hazards of 'psychohistory', the interpretation of Greeks and Romans in terms of modern speculation on the effects of childhood. It is an important difference between ancient and modern biography that there is usually very little information on the childhood of famous men. (Augustine is the great exception, and is therefore the classic example of Freudian categories applied to a different culture; but it needs to be remembered that Augustine's account of his own childhood serves a specific theological purpose, to show that human desire to possess is inherent in human nature from the beginning of life.) Walcot's final suggestion draws on anthropology rather than psychology: in societies which restrict the activities of women, the influence of mothers on sons is likely to be powerful. He notes in his update some recent work on Greek and Roman childhood, which documents the standard expectation that sons show deference to mothers and that mothers are concerned for the moral qualities of their sons. This makes the 'terrible' mother somewhat less alarming: Ambrose, bishop of Milan, congratulated Augustine on his mother's devotion. Another shift in perspective may also be relevant. Plato's account of the developing 'timocrat' under pressure from his mother, which is Walcot's starting-point, reads differently if the mother is not a frustrated housewife seeking an outlet in her son, but an active participant in the competition between households who expects her menfolk to be the household's public face. This picture of classical Athens cannot be read out of the extant sources any more than frustrated housewives can, but it can be supported by comparison with other cultures in which the public role belongs to men.

David Cohen's 'Seclusion, Separation, and the Status of Women in Classical Athens', one of two papers on women in the April 1989 issue, offers an important contribution from comparative anthropology. He distinguishes ideological statements, such as 'a woman's place is in the home', from social reality, and argues (as Walcot briefly suggests in his 1984 paper) that separation of male and female roles need not imply seclusion of women from all activity outside the home. Anthropologists have realized that what they are told, or allowed to see, depends on who they are: man or woman, married or unmarried, with or without children, young or old, with or without connections to particular members of the society they study. Women anthropologists may form a quite different understanding of a society previously known to men anthropologists; Cohen gives the example of work by Mary Clark on Methana, which contradicted her own expectation of finding powerless women who believed themselves to be inferior to men. Anthropologists have also realized that 'informants' do not always set out to inform. They say what they want you to know, or even what they want you (if you are a polite person) politely to acknowledge, even though you both know it is not the case. These assertions are sometimes called 'protocols', things that need to be affirmed: for instance, that women never leave their houses.

The Mediterranean field-work of Cohen and others confirms the familiar picture of separate male and female social spheres, public space which belongs to men, and houses which must not be violated by intruders. Ideological statements reinforce these principles. But, provided the principles can—in principle—be maintained, women have, in practice, considerable scope. They do not leave their houses—except to fetch water, or to make inconspicuous visits to friends and neighbours, or with some other socially acceptable reason. They are not, in fact, isolated. As Cohen warns, we cannot assume that past societies worked in the same way, but the anthropological work allows the possibility of reading ancient sources in a new light. If (for instance) a speaker in an Athenian lawcourt says (Lysias 3. 6) that the women of his family are embarrassed to be seen even by their own male relatives, we should not conclude that it must be true of Athenian society, if not of his own family, because he expects the jury to believe it; we may even suspect that the women of his family goaded him into bringing this lawsuit, and though nobody will say it, everybody knows it.

Jane Gardner's paper on 'Aristophanes and Male Anxiety: The Defence of the *Oikos*', in the same April 1989 issue, shows Aristophanes exploiting the contrast between ideal behaviour and what men thought women did when they had the chance. She does not treat Aristophanes' plays as an accurate social record, but she does suggest that they had to 'strike a chord' in their male audience, and that one of the things comedy does is to express, and thereby relieve, the 'mild, underlying paranoia' of a given society. If that is right, Athenian men were mildly paranoid about the security of their households. They feared that marriage allowed women to infiltrate and exploit the household, leaching away its supplies, smuggling in lovers and other people's babies, and allowing the suspicion that their children were neither heirs nor citizens. They also feared the divided loyalties of resident foreigners and the impact of rebellious sons. Overall, Gardner suggests, it was the *oikos*, the household, which was of central importance in the lives of men. This, again, undermines any distinction between the public (male) and private (female) sphere.

Lorna Hardwick's 'Ancient Amazons: Heroes, Outsiders, or Women?' (1990) argues that Amazons both were and are interpreted in terms of current social concerns, whether as threat or as glorious potential. The paper covers an impressive range of material, and its style, especially in the introductory section, may sometimes need further explanation for school (and even university) students. Hardwick, like almost all present-day scholars, thinks that we have no historical evidence for Amazons, a race of warrior women who lived independently of men. What we have is Greek (written and visual) texts which look much more like a 'reversal myth' than like a careful historical record. 'Structuralist' analysis of myth is an important influence here: that is, analysis which focuses on the overall structure of the story and especially on any pairs of opposites within it, rather than on variants over time and in different contexts. Greek representations of Amazons, and indeed of other non-Greek cultures, emphasize contrasts with Greek culture. This is always a hazard for anthropologists, who will naturally notice what seems to them unusual, but Greek patterns of thought appear to show a special liking for antithesis and for 'polar' opposites. Thus women who are warriors and not wives, who live at the ends of the known world, who are wanderers without settlements, are the opposite of proper Greek women, and the stories about Amazons tell us more about the concerns of Greek society than about a different culture. But Hardwick resists (or, as she puts it in her addendum, the Amazons resist) any one dominant interpretation. The stories vary over time, different authors have their own concerns, and artists may be interested in the decorative qualities of women warriors quite as much as in any message about male triumph over resistant women.

Andrew Fear's 'The Dancing Girls of Cadiz' (1991) takes us from the fantasy warrior to the women who satisfied other kinds of male fantasy. This is the only paper on 'entertainers', and it is a reminder of the diversity of women's lives and of the continuing diversity of scholarship concerned with women. Fear collects evidence for the activities of Gaditane dancers with evident enjoyment and learning, and leaves the reader to deduce what he thinks about the questions of exploitation or voyeurism (ancient and modern). This is, no doubt, a conscious choice: no comment. Readers may choose to consult *Pornography and Representation in Greece and Rome*,[17] edited by Amy Richlin, and may be cheered by the thought that belly-dancing has lately been reclaimed as a healthful female activity.

Finally, and appropriately, H. S. Versnel in 'The Festival for Bona Dea and the Thesmophoria' (1992) restores both Athenian and Roman women to the centre of the city, and evokes many concerns of other papers in this collection. Athenian public business stopped for the second day of the Thesmophoria; the Bona Dea festival took over the house of a Roman magistrate, which was not an inviolable private space but a political and economic centre of operations. For both festivals, women had their own civic organization. The festivals are difficult to interpret because men were excluded, and all we have is speculation and fragments of information about ritual. Versnel tries out some of the most favoured theories of ritual as evidence for social concerns and for structures of thought, deliberately linking approaches which derive from different national traditions.

It seems obvious that the central concern of both rituals is fertility, of the land and of women. The 'functionalist' approach asks what is the function of a ritual in the workings of a particular society, and here the answer appears to be that it suspends or reverses normal, civilized, domestic life. The 'semiotic' approach asks what symbols the ritual uses and what messages it sends. Versnel notes the paradoxes of these rituals. They are concerned with fertility, using overtly sexual symbols as well as wine, which was assumed to stimulate sexual desire, but they exclude men and affirm female chastity. They are rituals for women, but women take over some male functions in that they occupy public space and perform sacrifice. Versnel's tentative explanation invokes another favoured theory about structures of thought and another piece of 'gendering': the antithesis between nature and culture, the wild and the tamed, as expressed in the unmarried girl and the married woman. Women in these festivals do not behave like proper married women, so they must temporarily be associated with wildness, primitive lifestyle, and virginity.

This explanation suggests that women accepted these categories of thought, or that men were able to impose the categories on a women's ritual. Another possibility is that the Thesmophoria and the Bona Dea are rituals of female solidarity, reaffirming the kinship networks of women who have married into other households, and perhaps also reaffirming women's control of their bodies. The *agnus castus* or 'chaste tree', the shrub which (like bracken or heather) provided temporary beds at the Thesmophoria, is usually assumed to symbolize temporary sexual abstinence. But it was also used to regulate menstruation and to stimulate lactation, and both of these can be obstacles to fertility. (*Agnus castus* is still prescribed by herbalists for a range of menstrual problems, and is thought to affect the oestrogen–progesterone balance.) We do not know how women interpreted these festivals, but we need not assume that they thought fertility rituals were all about the lawful procreation of citizen children.

The papers in this collection are concerned with what women did, what women may have felt, and what men thought about the women they knew, and about what it was to be a woman. The subject has moved on because of constant questioning of assumptions: do we know, or is it obvious, what it is to be a woman, or to be in love, or to read a text? I remarked earlier that these papers share a certain confidence that we do know something about the experience of women, and a certain optimism about the lives of women. The reasons for it have gradually shifted from 'yes, the status of women was shocking, but never mind, we can see that men loved their wives' to 'yes, the status of women was shocking, but never mind, social reality does not correspond to ideological claims'. Social change, comparative anthropology, and feminist readings have combined to produce new ways of seeing women's lives in classical Greece and Rome, rather like the ethological shift from seeing the male lion with his harem to seeing the lioness collective with a tolerated male on the outskirts. It is possible to argue that women were not excluded, secluded, and oppressed, but that there was a women's community which had its own society and politics. In Rome, the great houses were themselves a centre of politics and patronage, and women from leading families had contacts and finance at their disposal far more openly than Athenian women did. But the Athenian house too could be taken as central: instead of thinking that Athenian women were excluded from political life, we could think that Athenian men were sent off to pursue the concerns of the household in the outside world.

Whether we can write the history of households, or integrate the women's concerns with the political and cultural history of Greece and Rome, is a question for the future. We can at least keep on reminding ourselves that the history of war and public debate is simply inadequate as a human record, and that maleness, so far from being the norm of humanity, imposed constraints and conventions just as femaleness did. And to have got that far is quite an achievement.[18]

## NOTES

1. Ed. Pauline Schmitt Pantel (Cambridge, Mass., 1992).
2. Edd. Averil Cameron and Amélie Kuhrt (London, 1983, rev. edn. 1993).
3. Edd. Léonie J. Archer, Susan Fischler, and Maria Wyke (Basingstoke, 1994).
4. Ed. Helene Foley (New York, 1981).
5. See n. 2 above.
6. Brussels, 1964.
7. Edd. John Peradotto and J. P. Sullivan (New York, 1984).
8. New York, 1975.
9. New York, 1974.
10. Toronto, 1977.
11. Edd. Elaine Fantham, Helene Foley, Natalie Kampen, Sarah Pomeroy, and Alan Shapiro (Oxford, 1994).
12. Oxford, 1993.
13. New York, 1978, 1985, 1986.
14. See, e.g., David Konstan, *Sexual Symmetry* (Princeton, 1994).
15. See Nancy Rabinowitz and Amy Richlin (edd.), *Feminist Theory and the Classics* (New York, 1993).
16. London, 1990.
17. Oxford, 1992.
18. For a fuller bibliography, see my *Women in the Ancient World: Greece & Rome New Surveys in the Classics* 21 (1989, reissued with addendum 1993).

# TACITUS AND THE GOVERNOR'S LADY: A NOTE ON *ANNALS* 3. 33–4

*By* ANTHONY J. MARSHALL

Until the last years of the Republic, Roman governors might officially see their wives present in their provinces only in the form of honorific statues. The chaos of civil war was to bring to a number of senatorial husbands, as they mounted their campaigns in the eastern provinces, the solace of their wives' companionship in the flesh. First in time amongst these refugee wives was Caecilia Metella, who was present with Sulla at Athens in 86 B.C. Later, and in less auspicious circumstances, Cornelia was to travel to Lesbos and then to Egypt to be with the doomed Pompeius in 49–48 B.C.[1] Occasionally, such loyal wives joined their husbands over the latters' objections. They might, it seems, be expected to remain in Italy in order to avoid danger or even proscription, and not least to defend the family interests so far as this was possible.[2]

It is presumably out of the innovation of those troubled times that the custom arose by which wives of the second Triumvirs accompanied their husbands on their protracted tours of duty in the provinces.[3] From this custom there arose in turn the regular practice of the men of the Julio-Claudian house of taking their wives out on official travels. As a result of this practice, provincial cities were able to claim the prestige accruing to the birthplace of a member of the imperial family.[4] The lavish honours decreed by provincial cities to ladies of the imperial house show that they were seen as fulfilling a public duty in consort with their husbands; to please Augustus even Julia maintained in the provinces the role of dutiful helpmeet to Agrippa. The title 'New Aphrodite' was among the official tributes which she received.[5]

By the first decade of the principate of Tiberius, this dispensation is found to have extended to the governors of both senatorial and imperial provinces, whose wives are now seen to accompany them regularly on their provincial duties. It has recently been argued that this development may also be attributed to the relaxation of the traditional rule during the civil wars, since it represents a trend which Augustus was unwilling or unable to reverse by reaffirmation of the old restriction.[6] However, the evidence for the attitude of Augustus towards this practice on the part of his own *legati* implies, on the contrary, that he not only disapproved of it but attempted to curb it. Suetonius records that the princeps gave a very reluctant permission for occasional visits by wives during the winter months only, and adduces this regulation, which itself suggests that it was not customary for the wives of *legati* to live with them all the year round, to illustrate the efforts of Augustus to restore strict discipline and 'antiquus mos' in military conduct. His words further imply that there was no blanket permission for such visits and that each *legatus* had to apply for individual permission for these marital reunions.[7]

The rule was relaxed under Augustus for members of the imperial family because they had to undertake longer and more frequent tours of duty than regular governors; but we have no evidence that the practice became common and unremarkable for ordinary governors before the reign of Tiberius.[8] If an explanation for the general relaxation is to be sought, it may be found more plausibly in Tiberian policy. For it was Tiberius who made the considerable innovation of greatly extending the service period of governors of both senatorial and imperial provinces. This policy change would surely have created much personal hardship, and with it opposition, in senatorial families, had not the old rule also been fully abandoned. We may assume that this was done with the emperor's approval.[9]

Not everyone, however, approved of the new dispensation, and some governors even preferred to continue voluntary observation of the Republican rule of separation. Such were the feelings of A. Caecina Severus, who in A.D. 21 moved before the senate the famous resolution 'ne quem magistratum cui provincia obvenisset uxor comitaretur', and tried to reverse the trend in a supporting speech which itself shows how established the new custom had become.[10] His vigorous speech and its rebuttal by Valerius Messalinus have been variously cited, though always without regard to the context, to illustrate supposed trends in Roman social attitudes. The debate is a special favourite of historians who seek to plot the course of male conversion to the cause of woman's emancipation. J. Donaldson, during the course of a vigorous defence of the good sense and kindliness of Roman women, presents the defeat of Caecina's resolution as proof that the active help of their wives was beneficial to governors.[11] By contrast, L. Friedländer cites Caecina's strictures upon wifely interference with emphatic approval, as support for the process of the degeneration of women's morals which he claims to discern in Roman history.[12] For Claudine Herrmann, Caecina's speech is evidence for anti-feminism, and her discussion sets it in an anachronistic perspective which views Roman women as operating throughout their history as a single, coherent group struggling for 'emancipation', and strains to see all actions detrimental to women's interests as instances of deliberate anti-feminism.[13] To Ronald Syme, it is apparent that Tacitus shows no sympathy with Caecina but approves the counter-arguments of Messalinus; the latter's 'graceful plea that the times change, and not always for the worse' is adduced by this distinguished scholar to show that Tacitus was neither blindly romantic about the past nor convinced of a decline in moral standards.[14] J. P. V. D. Balsdon roundly describes Caecina's speech as 'reactionary', and sees his whole proposal as a mere piece of amusing Victorianism.[15]

However, Caecina's speech does have an important frame of reference within contemporary history. Although he does not cite specific cases of meddlesome wives, the phrase used in the speech to describe interference with military drill so closely echoes the phrase earlier used to describe the activities of Munatia Plancina during Piso's Syrian command, that Caecina's proposal seems to have been prompted, at least in part, by Plancina's involvement in her husband's disgrace in the previous year.[16] If this is so, Tacitus himself, although he took his own wife to his province as Agricola had done, is likely to have seen Caecina's criticisms as well-grounded.[17] It has been suggested that Caecina's speech even contains a veiled attack upon Agrippina the Elder for her activities in Germany and Syria, thus prompting the diplomatic intervention of Drusus, who closed the debate with a defence of the conduct of imperial wives.[18] This seems less plausible since Drusus was quite in order, as consul of the year, to speak at that juncture, while the misbehaviour of Plancina seems to be deliberately employed by Tacitus as a foil for the heroic conduct of Agrippina in the provinces.[19]

There is another indication that Caecina's proposal should not be seen as the isolated outburst of a reactionary opposed to social progress. Only three years later a *senatus consultum* was passed which made governors fully accountable for their wives' misdemeanours in their provinces even if they were ignorant of them.[20] Tacitus relates this decree to the case of Sosia Galla, who was exiled in A.D. 24 after being tried as co-defendant with her husband C. Silius, ex-legate of Upper Germany, on a charge of *maiestas*; it is significant that by this time wives are found suffering trial and exile through involvement in charges brought against their husbands of *maiestas* in the provinces.[21] There had been just long enough in the period since A.D. 14 for irregularities consequent upon the Tiberian innovation to come to light, and to suggest that regulation would be advisable.

However, the significance of Caecina's proposal cannot be fully grasped if we relate it simply to its historical context of misbehaviour by certain prominent wives. A more immediate context is provided by the actual setting of the debate within the *Annals*, and a full consideration of this suggests that Tacitus intends the episode to carry a far wider, thematic importance for his overall plan of portraying the decline of senatorial integrity. Previous interpretations of Caecina's motion have not allowed for the fact that it is presented during the course of a debate on the African command, and that his speech and its rebuttal are set between two significant termini. Immediately beforehand we have a description of the senate's irresolute and petty factionalism over the appointments to governorships in Asia and Africa, while immediately after the debate we are given Tiberius' letter to the senate in which he responds to the senators' reference of the African appointment back to him and complains of their lack of initiative. It is significant that even then M'. Lepidus, one of the emperor's nominees, seeks to excuse himself, partly on the grounds of family ties.[22] Surely, Tacitus is here concerned to demonstrate how the rebellion of the petty chieftain Tacfarinas was showing up the senate's incompetence and irresolution over the sole military responsibility which was left to it as a body. Africa, as Tiberius crisply pointed out, required prompt military attention, but the Tiberian senate appears too enervated and servile to cope even with this petty war. The senate's generals abused the African command by claiming idle insignia which merely flattered their vanity, and the senate itself, through its irresolution, let effective control slip into the emperor's hands.[23]

I would further contend that the debate on Caecina's proposal receives such full attention within this context in order to allow him, in recalling the strictness of the Republican provincial regime and the self-denial of its governors, to speak as the embodiment of a military integrity which he feels to be all but lost. Such a picture of Republican practice may well have been distorted by nostalgia, since the wifeless governors of those days had been attacked for seduction of provincials' wives and dalliance with courtesans. One need only recall the delicious malice with which Cicero accused Verres of so neglecting his official duties for such diversions that the din of music and female voices contrasted with the silence of the forum. Love-bites were the scars brought back to Rome from the inglorious campaigns of this warrior.[24] Earlier, L. Quinctius Flamininus, seen off at the city gate by his dutiful wife, staged an execution at dinner in his province in order to gratify a courtesan's morbid curiosity.[25] But the ideal of the lost Republic remained a potent one. Caecina's unsuccessful bid to recall the senate to the supposed discipline and austerity of Republican practice, coming at a point in the narrative where the senators are shirking their responsibilities and letting slip their last powers of appointment to military proconsulships, serves to underline the decay of the Republican ideal and their loss of effective control to Tiberius. It was this same Tiberius who had introduced the general dispensation allowing the presence of wives in provinces which Caecina attacks, and Caecina, himself an experienced general who is favourably presented in the *Annals* for the soldierly ability and courage which he displayed in Germany, openly declares his disapproval of the new custom.[26]

It has also escaped notice that Caecina's arguments for a return to Republican practice are presented in a significant order. He first stresses the adverse effect of wives on military planning and actual manœuvres in the field, proceeds to their interference in the management of the camp and garrison, and only then, in closing, deals with their effect on general civil administration. His concern is primarily with military efficiency, not general administration, and it is clear that he is mainly thinking of the militarily 'forward' provinces. The thought-connection with the continuing crisis of the African command is here discernible. It is equally significant that when Caecina, at the very end of his speech, plots the progress of the decay as he sees it, he represents woman's improper influence as extending from the initial domination of Roman *domi* to subsequent control of civil *fora*, and now as presenting the culminating challenge to proper management of the *exercitus*. The overall concern of his remarks is with the decay of army morale and efficiency and this concern must be related by its context to the decay of the senate's own morale, as evidenced by its vacillation when called upon to select a general to face Tacfarinas.[27]

The rebuttal of Messalinus sustains this impression. His speech is preceded by a careful indication from Tacitus that the attack on Caecina was largely motivated by sycophancy to Tiberius, an indication contained in the senators' complaint that he was usurping censorial prerogatives which were proper to the emperor alone.[28] Moreover, the tone of his speech is in marked contrast to the robustly moral and forthright oration of Caecina. Messalinus employs *facundia* rather than moral force or historical precedent, and his speech is replete with bland generalities, abstract debating points, and rhetorical questions. His argument remains at the theoretical level, and he does not attempt to meet the blunt particularity of Caecina's charges.[29] In strong contrast with the focus of Caecina's concern, Messalinus briefly dismisses military considerations with the observation that the hard times and dangers of the Republic are eased. Before moving on to his generalities, he complacently declares that the provinces are no longer a battlefield, a declaration which may be seen as a wilful delusion in view of the African situation which had given rise to the debate.[30] Drusus, son of Tiberius, speaks briefly after Messalinus and effectively kills the proposal by *auctoritas* and precedent arising from the practice of the imperial family.

Tacitus describes the defeat of Caecina's motion in the telling phrase 'sic Caecinae sententia elusa est', employing a verb which conveys the suggestion that this problem, too, was sidestepped rather than squarely faced by the senate.[31] He proceeds directly to a description of the emperor's contemptuous, if covert, reprimand of the senators' dilatory conduct over the African war, a reprimand which is the more galling if we view Tiberius through Tacitean eyes as the insidious tyrant who eroded Roman military prestige from timidity and jealousy. Indeed, for all his insistence on efficiency, he even, according to Tacitus, regarded with jealousy any real military distinction won by a senator in Africa.[32]

Caecina's proposal met defeat, but his speech deserves better than random citation to illustrate romantic 'conservatism' or 'anti-feminism'. It plays a significant part in Tacitus' demonstration of the stages of the decline of Roman *virtus*.

## NOTES

1. For the Republican rule of separation, see Cic. *Att.* 7. 2. 2, *Fam.* 14. 5; Sen. *Controv.* 9. 25. 1; Tac. *Ann.* 3. 33. 2. For statues, see Pliny, *N.H.* 34. 14. For an example, see O. Kern, *Die Inschriften von Magnesia am Maeander* (Berlin, 1900), no. 145. For Metella and Cornelia, see Plut. *Sulla* 6. 12; Sen. *De Matr.* 63; Plut. *Pomp.* 74. H. G. Pflaum, *Les Procurateurs équestres sous le Haut-Empire romain* (Paris, 1950), p. 297, is mistaken in claiming Octavia as the first wife to accompany her husband to the East.

2. See, e.g., Val. Max. 6. 7. 3; App. *Bell. Civ.* 4. 39–40, 48; Dio 54. 7. 1. For the services of wives who stayed home, see Cic. *Fam.* 14. 7. 2, with B. Förtsch, *Die politische Rolle der Frau in der römischen Republik* (Stuttgart, 1935), pp. 79ff. See also the loyalty praised in the so-called 'Laudatio Turiae', in S. Riccobono, *Fontes Iuris Romani Antejustiniani*, vol. iii (Florence, 1940–3), no. 69, with M. Durry, *Éloge funèbre d'une matrone romaine* (Paris, 1950).

3. See, e.g., Plut. *Ant.* 33. 3; App. *Bell. Civ.* 5. 76.

4. See Tac. *Ann.* 3. 34. 6; D. Magie, *Roman Rule in Asia Minor* (Princeton, 1950), pp. 476ff.; *IG* xii. 2. 258. For imperial child-bearing abroad, see Suet. *Calig.* 8, *Claud.* 2. 1; Tac. *Ann.* 1. 40. 3, etc. Cf. J. P. V. D. Balsdon, *Life and Leisure in Ancient Rome* (London, 1969), p. 238.

5. See Magie, loc. cit.

6. See Balsdon, op. cit., p. 237; also his *Roman Women, their History and Habits* (London, 1962), pp. 59ff.

7. Suet. *Aug.* 24. 1: 'ne legatorum quidem cuiquam, nisi *gravate* hibernisque demum mensibus, permisit uxorem *intervisere*.' Military duties would, of course, be more pressing for imperial than for senatorial governors.

8. Cf. Tac. *Ann.* 3. 34. 6, 'nam principibus adeunda saepius longinqua imperii'.

9. For extension of governors' terms, beginning early in the reign of Tiberius, see Tac. *Ann.* 1. 80, with F. B. Marsh, *The Reign of Tiberius* (Oxford, 1931), pp. 157ff.; M. P. Charlesworth, *Cambridge Ancient History* vol. x (1934), pp. 648 ff.; R. Syme, *Tacitus* vol. i (Oxford, 1958), pp. 441ff. Pflaum, op. cit., p. 302, oddly suggests that it was the presence of their wives which caused governors, once settled *en famille*, to be unwilling to move sooner to new posts.

10. Tac. *Ann.* 3. 33. The wording of the motion suggests that it referred primarily to the senate's governors rather than to the *legati pro praetore* appointed by the emperor.

11. J. Donaldson, *Woman: Her Position and Influence in Ancient Greece and Rome, and among the Early Christians* (London, 1907), p. 122. Donaldson does not seem bothered by the cynical argument of Messalinus that women were morally too frail to withstand the temptations of 'grass-widowhood' in Rome, or by his declaration that husbands are set as moral watchdogs over wives.

12. L. Friedländer, *Roman Life and Manners under the Early Empire*[7] vol. i (Eng. trans. London, 1907), p. 251. He begins a belated corrective at pp. 261ff., after noting too late that 'literature prefers dwelling on the frailties and vices of women, as being better copy, than on the inconspicuous virtues'.

13. Cl. Herrmann, *Le Rôle judiciaire et politique des femmes sous la République romaine*, Coll. Latomus 67 (Brussels, 1964), p. 55. This work explains the cults of Bacchus and Cybele as being instruments of the feminist cause (pp. 58ff., 68ff.), sees cases of poisoning as feminist activism (pp. 78ff., 85), and explains an ex-censor's exile as feminist revenge for his dour views on marriage (p. 94). Not one gleam of humour appears to lighten this fanciful exegesis.

14. Op. cit. i. pp. 444, 535; ii. p. 564.

15. *Roman Women*, pp. 60ff.

16. See *Ann.* 3. 33. 3, 'praesedisse nuper feminam exercitio cohortium, decursu legionum'. Cf. *Ann.* 2. 55. 6, 'nec Plancina se intra decora feminis tenebat sed exercitio equitum, decursibus cohortium interesse'. For Caecina's hostility to Piso, see *Ann.* 3. 18. 2. For Plancina's involve-

ment in Piso's disgrace, see *Ann.* 3. 15ff., with R. S. Rogers, *Criminal Trials and Criminal Legislation under Tiberius* (Middletown, 1935), pp. 42ff. Plancina was saved by Livia's intervention (*Ann.* 3. 15. 1).

17. See Tac. *Agr.* 6. 3, etc.

18. *Ann.* 3. 34. 6. See Balsdon, *Life and Leisure in Ancient Rome*, p. 238; E. Koestermann, *Cornelius Tacitus, Annalen*, Band i (Heidelberg, 1963), p. 483. Pflaum, op. cit., pp. 299ff. sees the criticism as extending to Livia.

19. *Ann.* 3. 31. 1. H. Königer, *Gestalt und Welt der Frau bei Tacitus* (Erlangen, 1966), pp. 24ff., sees the meddlesome Plancina as providing 'eine Kontrastfigur' to the entirely constructive participation of Agrippina in the military duties of Germanicus (*Ann.* 1. 69. 1ff.). Agrippina does remain artistically subordinated to the depiction of Germanicus as a hero.

20. See *Ann.* 4. 20. 4 (A.D. 24). Ulpian, *Digest* i. 16. 4. 2, dates what seems to be the same decree to A.D. 20. Rogers, op. cit., pp. 51, 79, upholds Ulpian's dating and contends that the decree was prompted by Plancina's case. But it seems more probable that Ulpian was misled by the name of Messalinus Cotta, mover of the decree, into dating it by a natural assumption to the latter's consulship in A.D. 20.

21. For Sosia Galla, possibly indicted for complicity in extortion as well as *maiestas*, see *Ann.* 4. 19. 4ff., with Rogers, op. cit., pp. 75ff. Plancina was indicted for complicity in *maiestas* (above n. 16). Juv. *Sat.* 8. 127ff. lists an upright wife as being as important for a governor's good reputation as an incorruptible *cohors* and *viator*. Pliny, *Ep.* 10. 120–1, carefully consults Trajan before allowing his wife to use public transportation for personal reasons.

22. *Ann.* 3. 32. 2, 35. 1–2.

23. For the directive of Tiberius, see *Ann.* 3. 32. 1. Cf. *Ann.* 4. 23. 1, 'nam priores duces, ubi impetrando triumphalium insigni sufficere res suas crediderant, hostem omittebant; iamque tres laureatae in urbe statuae, et adhuc raptabat Africam Tacfarinas . . '. This recalls the bitter irony of the description in *Germ.* 37. 6 of the Germans as 'triumphati magis quam victi'. For Tacfarinas, see Marsh, op. cit., pp. 148ff.; Charlesworth, op. cit., pp. 643ff.; R. Syme, in P. R. Coleman-Norton (ed.), *Studies in Roman Economic and Social History in Honor of Allan Chester Johnson* (Princeton, 1951), pp. 113ff.

24. For the charge that Verres seduced provincials' wives, see Cic. *Verr.* 2. 2. 14. 36. For Verres' dalliance with Tertia, see *Verr.* 2. 3. 34. 78, etc.

25. See Sen. *Contr.* 9. 25. Cf. Cic. *De Sen.* 12. 42. Livy 39. 42. 8ff. and Plut. *Flamin.* 18 present a variant version featuring a male lover.

26. For Caecina's military record, see *Ann.* 1. 31. 2, 3. 33. 1; Vell. Pat. 2. 112. 4; Dio 55. 29–32; *PIR*² ii, no. 106. Cf. Marsh, op. cit., pp. 53ff., 70ff. For Tacitus' own approval of old-fashioned discipline in Africa, see *Ann.* 3. 21. 1. For his disapproval of the presence of wives in the camp, see *Ann.* 15. 10. 3–4. Cf. *Ann.* 12. 37. 4 (of Agrippina the Younger), 'novum sane et moribus veterum insolitum, feminam signis Romanis praesidere'.

27. *Ann.* 3. 33. 4, '. . . nunc vinclis exsolutis domos fora, iam et exercitus regerent'. Pflaum, op. cit., p. 298, implausibly assumes that Caecina's motion raised a question quite unrelated to the debate over the African command.

28. *Ann.* 3. 34. 1, 'plures obturbabant . . . neque Caecinam dignum tantae rei censorem'.

29. B. Walker, *The Annals of Tacitus*² (Manchester, 1960), p. 260, describes this speech as 'a typical example of argumentative rhetoric, full of rhetorical questions'.

30. *Ann.* 3. 34. 2, 'multa duritiae veterum in melius et laetius mutata; neque enim, ut olim, obsideri urbem bellis aut provincias hostilis esse'.

31. *Ann.* 3. 34. 6.

32. Cf. *Ann.* 2. 26. 4, 3. 21. 3. For a more positive view of the military caution of Tiberius, see Vell. Pat. 2. 113ff.

## ADDENDUM

The following studies, which have appeared since this article was written, may also be consulted with profit: L. Fanizza, 'Il senato e la prevenzione del "crimen repetundarum" in età Tiberiana', *Labeo* 23 (1977), 199–214; B. M. Levick,

*Tiberius the Politician* (London, 1976), ch. IX, 'Provincial and Foreign Policy'; R. MacMullen, 'Women in Public in the Roman Empire', *Historia* 29 (1980), 208–18; A. J. Marshall, 'Roman Women and the Provinces', *Ancient Society* 6 (1975), 109–27; id., 'Ladies in Waiting: the Role of Women in Tacitus' *Histories*', *Ancient Society* 15–17 (1984–86), 167–84; id., 'Women on Trial before the Roman Senate', *Echos du Monde Classique/Classical Views* 34, n.s. 9 (1990), 333–66; M. -Th. Raepsaet-Charlier, 'Épouses et familles de magistrats dans les provinces romaines aux deux premiers siècles de l'Empire', *Historia* 31 (1982), 56–69; *Prosopographie des femmes de l'ordre sénatorial (Ier–IIe siècles)* (Louvain, 1987), i. 692–5, 'Femmes en province'; R. P. Saller, *Personal Patronage under the Early Empire* (Cambridge, 1982), pp. 161–2.

# 'NEITHER MALE NOR FEMALE'

*By* AVERIL CAMERON

The prominence of women in the spread of Christianity in the earliest period has long been a commonplace.[1] It was recognized as such by the early Christians themselves.[2] On the other hand, St. Paul's willingness to use women in setting up the organization of the early Church seems to conflict with his opinion that they should stay in their subordinate place.[3] Now Christian women of the Early Empire do not usually fall into the scope of books on women in antiquity.[4] But there is no obvious reason for this exclusion, especially when the role of women in the early Church figures prominently in the work of New Testament scholars. A closer look suggests that each side has something to learn from the other, and this paper sets out to examine from the point of view of classicists some of the large claims made in recent New Testament scholarship,[5] which are indeed being brought into sharp focus by the current debate on the ordination of women. In particular, a recent book by John Gager[6] has stressed Christianity's appeal to women as an important factor in its success, while an interesting article by W. Meeks[7] relates the well-known prominence of women in the Acts of the Apostles to a supposed rising status of women in the contemporary Greek world and to a general questioning of male/female roles which is said to have been taking place in the Early Empire. It is obviously vital for anyone interested in the position of women in antiquity to consider these claims seriously.

St. Paul's 'patronesses' are famous. Priscilla, Lydia, Phoebe, Mary, to name only some among others.[8] Some of these women have positions of leadership in their Christian communities, for instance the two women at Philippi, Phoebe 'our sister, a servant of the church', perhaps also 'our beloved Apphia'.[9] Women are frequently mentioned by name—in Romans fifteen women as against eighteen men. We encounter, for example, Mary at Jerusalem (Acts 12:12: cf. 5:14), Tabitha at Joppa (9:36 f.), Lydia at Philippi (16:14), Damaris at Athens (17:34). And upper-class women are specifically mentioned as a group at Pisidian Antioch (13:50), Thessalonika (17:4), and Beroea (17:12).

These women, then, seem to be people of some position—cf. 'chief women' (17:4, Thessalonika), 'honourable women' (17:12, Beroea). Some of them have 'households' which they are able to influence, e.g., Lydia, baptized with her household (16:15). If the Christian community can be said to be 'in' someone's house, a personage of some substance must be indicated: so with Priscilla (Rom. 16:5) and Mary (Acts 12:12). Another recent work has described these and others of Paul's 'sponsors' as a 'cultivated social élite', through whom Paul was able to reach their social dependents by a sort of *clientela* system.[10] Paul's appeal, then, is seen as operating through the 'educated classes', his methods as 'intellectual'. Enough to say that this observation, even if right, does not explain why *women* feature so markedly among these early converts. How then to explain it? The study already cited maintains that Paul's female converts demonstrate a 'freer participation of women in the economic life of Greco-Roman society'.[11] Priscilla, described as a tentmaker like her husband (Acts 18:3) and expelled with him from Rome when Claudius expelled Jews, moved to Corinth, where the couple started a 'church' in their house like the one they had had in Rome (1 Cor. 16:19; Rom. 16.3). Their story is said to amount to a 'functional equality in leadership roles that would have been unusual in Greco-Roman society as a whole'. I wonder whether this is true, and if so, what it tells us about women or about the early Church. One must ask, 'freer than what?' Was the relationship of this 'functional equality' to the Christian church one of cause or effect? That is, did the Church offer a better chance to women as something new and distinctively Christian, or was it itself profiting from an existing trend in the Late Hellenistic world?

It is obviously crucial to know whether most of these women were Jewish or not. Probably most of them were.[12] Yet Meeks's argument at least proceeds on the assumption that women in the Late Hellenistic East were a homogeneous group. An index of the extent of the problem is, however, the desperately inadequate evidence on which not merely the above generalizations but also more sober analyses have to be based.[13] Neither Hellenistic queens nor Egyptian papyri will necessarily tell us about the women of the cities of Asia Minor, especially when one city differs so widely from another. And the apparently freer pattern of upper-class marriage in Late Republican Rome also cited as a sign of the rising status of women generally may have an explanation in terms far more practical than female emancipation.[14] Those who advocate that such varied and patchy evidence indicates either a 'heightened awareness of the differentiation of male and female' in Hellenistic society in the Roman Empire, or a 'vastly improved' social status of women[15] do so, I suspect, because of an over-rigid conception of male dominance to date, as well as a regrettable tendency to lump together all women of all classes, whether Jewish, Greek, or Roman. Already, in fact, in Late Republican and Early Imperial Rome large numbers of women of lower- and middle-class status must have lived relatively active lives. As peasant women no doubt worked in the fields alongside their husbands, so middle-class women will surely have been associated with their husband's profession, like St. Paul's Priscilla. We must assume that the same held for the Greek East. As in many societies, the legal inferiority of women did not prevent them from leading active lives, while seclusion was normally for good reason the privilege of the upper class. There is no good reason, then, to see a basic innovation in the prominence of women among Paul's early converts; they would have been there naturally in the urban demi-monde in which Paul moved.

What then of the view that these women were upper-class?[16] We must be clear what we mean. There is no clear evidence that the 'patronesses' of Paul were truly wealthy. Rather, they belonged, like Priscilla and Aquila, to the middling level of people largely engaged in trade (Lydia was a seller of purple dye, Acts 16:14), well enough off to own slaves, but hardly aristocratic. Naturally their status is emphasized (e.g., the 'honourable' women of Beroea, Acts 17:12), but the concept of *clientela* is hardly applicable, even if there are Roman citizens among them. Roman citizens, it is clear, might be as sharply differentiated in wealth and social standing as non-citizens. It seems more striking, in fact, to note the high proportion of *non*-Roman names even among the community at Rome (Rom. 16:1–15). 'Cultivated social élite' is as vague and misleading as 'upper-class'. It hardly seems plausible to regard the members of this commercially orientated group as in any sense intellectuals, and the notion that they had mostly received a Greek education seems quite unproven. It is surely also a mistake to put too much emphasis on the famous speech to the Athenians (Acts 17:18 f.), or to generalize from it, for the speech is deliberately adapted in style in response to a direct challenge from pagan philosophers; we must not make the assumption that such was Paul's usual approach. Paul's patronesses and their male friends and relatives are in fact distinguished as a group not by their education but by their position in the interaction of economic life at daily level, where Jews and Gentiles actually met, and where women far removed from the Roman aristocracy very probably did already commonly share in the business pre-occupations of their husbands. When therefore we are told that their leadership roles in the early Church would have been 'unusual in Greco-Roman society as a whole and quite astonishing in comparison with contemporary Judaism',[17] both parts of the proposition are vulnerable, for it is doubtful whether one can legitimately speak of 'Greco-Roman society as a whole' in relation to women, while the position of these particular women in relation to Judaism remains an uncertain factor.

If it was not either a generally improving status for women or the offer of one that is reflected in their position in the early Church, how do we explain the numbers of female converts, especially as they do seem often to be, if not upper-class, certainly of substantial means? For it is beyond doubt that the early Church recruited its members primarily from the lower classes. 'Not many mighty, not many noble are called';[18] that some were[19] does not invalidate the general truth. But women remained marginal in the public life of Rome, at all social levels, even in the Late Republic and Early Empire when a degree of liberation is usually posited for the upper classes.[20] Even at the highest social level the main method open to them for exercising power or influence was intrigue, usually practised from the bedroom. This is not independence. The two Julias, mother and daughter, suffered the same fate after protesting in the only way open to them—through adultery—at their position as matrimonial pawns. Livia, the power behind the throne, remained precisely there—behind the scenes. The major outlet for female activity in the Roman world (aside from the 'salon culture' available only to the few) lay in religion, as Roman men, remembering the Bacchanalian conspiracy, well knew. Perhaps the worship of Isis, which attracted many women,[21] was felt to be safe. We hear several times of Greek women of good status interested in Judaism.[22] Clearly Christianity benefited from this pool of available women converts just as much as rival creeds, and the speed with which converts were won suggests less a rising status for them in their social world, or a real new role now offered to them, than their own lack of public position, which took them to the mysteries, to Isis, and to Judaism as well as to Christianity. But once converted to Christianity, they brought to it the same energy and organizational skill that many of them employed in their commercial lives.

The paradox was, of course, that women, like slaves, those other underprivileged early Christians, were joining a sect which on any interpretation of Pauline teaching, officially urged them to stay in their subordinate role, and indeed added a new justification for their subordination. Slaves and women were to stay in their places, and no amount of special pleading will make Paul into an advocate of social reform.[23] Paul's arguments about women in the church of Corinth (1 Cor., especially chapter 11), can seem indicative of the unusual freedom which they enjoyed (cf. 11:5, 'every women that prayeth or prophesieth . . .'); but in the same chapter Paul justifies his own repressive attitude—'For a man indeed ought not to cover his head, forasmuch as he is the image and glory of God; but the woman is the glory of the man. For the man is not of the woman; but the woman of the man. Neither was the man created for the woman; but the woman for the man' (11:7–9). The fact remains that Pauline Christianity offered little direct encouragement to women to think that they were or could be really equal to men. The famous pronouncement, 'There is neither Jew nor Greek, there is neither bond nor free, there is neither male nor female; for ye are all one in Christ Jesus' (Gal. 3:28; cf. 1 Cor. 12:13, and Coloss. 3:11), offers spiritual equality and the destruction of barriers, including sex barriers, through Christian baptism, but not worldly betterment. The patriarchal order of marriage was to be preserved, and ultimately women were to realize new potential only through *denying* their sex in the Christian idealization of virginity.[24] The position of women at Corinth is puzzling, but Paul's words at 1 Cor. 14:34–5 make it very clear that what he offered to women did not consist in a leadership role in the Church proper—'if they will ask anything, let them ask it of their husbands at home; for it is a shame for women to speak in the church.'

What Paul was prepared to allow to women in the Church itself, and how they participated in the quasi-domestic organization of Christian communities are two quite different questions. In the 'baptismal formula', as in Gal. 3:28, Paul was offering spiritual equality, while at the same time refraining from a real assessment of male and female roles.[25] But what is still very much open to doubt is whether the promise of the abolition of sex differences in the formula is a response to any real degree of contemporary controversy about sex roles. The Pauline message is less an answer to current dispute than an understandable attempt to deal with the application of Christian faith to family life, all the more necessary for a community whose members had very widely differing cultural origins.

The assumption, then, that Christianity would have a special attraction for women (and slaves) as representing the underprivileged is not subtle enough. But we find much the same thinking, if in a more acceptable form, in the theory of 'relative deprivation' used to explain the spread of Christianity among groups on the edge of Roman society.[26] This thinking conceals two false assumptions, (*a*) that Christianity had something extra for the underdog, over and above other cults, and (*b*) that both women and slaves can be lumped together as a homogeneous disadvantaged group, when in fact some slaves, like some women, enjoyed considerable status and indeed freedom of action. The evidence of other cults suggests that it was not unusual to admit slaves.[27] Tacitus, for example, records the expulsion of 4,000 slaves and freedmen from Rome under Tiberius for being tainted with Egyptian and Jewish superstition.[28] Now this spread of slave membership in religious cults suggests that slaves were as eclectic in their religious choice as free people, and might have as many different motivations. The same must follow for women. We have met women in the cult of Isis, and seen that it is tempting to explain their prominence in terms of the special appeal of the cult for them as a group. But a vertical analysis by social class might be more useful, showing here as in Christianity that many devotees were neither particularly secluded nor noticeably deprived.

The real role of women in the early spread of Christianity was perhaps more fortuitous, and therefore less significant, than scholars have been prepared to admit. Beginning, as it did, in the *chora*, among uneducated peasants, and, moreover, in an area which many Romans must have regarded with suspicion and dislike, Christianity could not hope to attract the Roman upper classes or to make headway among Romans at large.[29] It belonged naturally to a milieu which by official Roman standards was indeed 'marginal', to say the least. And even when the message was carried beyond the Jewish community proper, its audience was still likely to be found in the lower-middle or middle classes rather than the upper, and among provincials rather than Romans. Such were the cultural barriers which separated the Roman élite from their subjects that penetration of the upper classes was bound to be extremely restricted, especially among the men, who were more deeply indoctrinated, and more committed in terms of their own advancement, to traditional Roman values. When Christianity did reach the Roman aristocracy it was the women it usually touched first. But in the urban and largely eastern Mediterranean milieu of the early days of Christianity the classes most likely to be reached by Christian preaching were socially and culturally ambiguous; the notable number of women mentioned in this early phase is more likely to reflect their real and unsurprising status in these classes than to indicate a new or special role being offered to them.

Paul's reactionary attitude did not prevent women from continuing to take an active role in the first two centuries as Christian teachers and deaconesses.[30] But as orthodox Christianity came more and more to embrace the ideal of celibacy and to clamp down on the heresies where women were most involved,[31] it excluded women more completely from the organization of the Church. A different role was offered instead. The consecrated virgin, the chaste widow, and later, the wife choosing to live henceforth in celibacy, could now gain social status and spiritual value. The female virgin could even be surpassed by the female martyr, best of all the virgin martyr. Ultimately, though only slowly, the cult of the Virgin Mother gave an overwhelmingly complete validation for the Christian woman in terms of the 'female' virtues of purity, gentleness, and motherhood.[32] The repressive side of Paul's attitude to women was thus to triumph. But these developments for women emerged only slowly, with the social and historical development of the Church itself. Paul's 'patronesses' are light years away from the bands of virgins extolled by the Christian poets, or the aristocratic ladies who dressed in sackcloth and ran after St. Jerome. The frequency with which they are named in Acts and elsewhere is indeed striking, and invites comparison with the numbers of Roman women named in Tacitus' *Annals* for a very different purpose, in connection with treason trials. The comparison is not without its use if it causes us to pull up short before too hastily assuming that either text, or set of texts, is evidence for a real change in the position of women in society as a whole. The salon culture of the Roman aristocracy exposed its women as much to political danger as its men, while the spiritual bonds of Christianity joined men and women together in a new society. But in neither case can one safely argue that there had been a significant change or improvement for women in general, still less a realistic debate about sex-roles.

## NOTES

1. See, e.g., A. Harnack, *The Mission and Expansion of Christianity during the First Three Centuries*, i-ii (2nd edn., Eng. trans., London, 1908), ii. 64–84.

2. Clement, *Strom.* 3. 6. 53. And by their opponents - e.g., Celsus, ap. Origen, *c. Cels.* 3. 44.

3. The positive view of Paul's attitude to women is well put by Constance F. Parvey, 'The Theology and Leadership of Women in the New Testament', in R. Ruether (ed.), *Religion and Sexism* (New York, 1974), pp. 117–49. But already in the early eighteenth century Mary Astell was arguing that Paul was writing allegorically - *Reflections upon Marriage* (1700), cited by Juliet Mitchell in Juliet Mitchell and Ann Oakley (edd.), *The Rights and Wrongs of Women* (Penguin, 1976), pp. 387–8.

4. E.g., they are omitted from Sarah B. Pomeroy's standard book, *Goddesses, Whores, Wives, and Slaves: Women in Classical Antiquity* (New York, 1975), as well as J. P. V. D. Balsdon's *Roman Women* (London, 1962). An honourable exception however is the entry by K. Thraede, s.v. 'Frau', in *RAC*, and there is a useful bibliography on 'Women under Christianity' by M. Southall, *Arethusa* 6 (1973), 149–52.

5. It originated as a contribution to the seminar on Acts organized by the Revd. Professor C. F. Evans in the Theology Faculty at King's College in 1976, and I am grateful for comments from colleagues on that occasion.

6. *Kingdom and Community: the Social World of Early Christianity* (New York, 1975), described by a reviewer as an 'exciting initial [*sic*] exploration of the application of sociological concepts to early Christian history' (*JTS* 27 [1976], 209).

7. 'The Image of the Androgyne: Some Uses of a Symbol in Earliest Christianity', *History of Religions* 13 (1974), 165–208.

8. Acts 16:14; Rom. 16:1–3, 6; See Meeks, art. cit., 197 f.; Harnack, op. cit., ii. 66.

9. Philipp. 4:2; Rom. 16:2; Philemon 2.

10. E. A. Judge, *Journal of Religious History* 1 (1960/1), 125 ff.

11. Meeks, art. cit., 198.

12. Parvey, art. cit. (n. 3), p.144.

13. Meeks, art cit., 168 f. Significant also is the brevity of the section on Hellenistic women in Sarah Pomeroy's useful general bibliography on women, *Arethusa* 6 (1973), 127 ff. Parvey, art. cit., pp. 118 ff., tackles the problem of the 'Hellenistic and Jewish background', but her remarks are almost entirely confined to Jewish women and Roman women. Interesting new evidence is however presented by Pomeroy in 'Technikai kai Mousikai. The Education of Women in the Fourth Century and in the Hellenistic Period', *Am. Journ. Anc. Hist.* 2 (1977), 51–68.

14. See Pomeroy, *Ancient Society* 7 (1976), 215–27.

15. Meeks, art. cit., 179; cf. 207. Meeks is on stronger ground when he relates Paul's pronouncements on women to the philosophical and religious background (pp. 169 f.), but how far any of this related to or reflected real social conditions remains very uncertain.

16. Judge, *The Social Pattern of Christian Groups in the First Century* (London, 1960), pp. 49 ff.

17. Meeks, art. cit., 198.

18. 1 Cor. 1:26.

19. E.g., the proconsul of Cyprus (Acts 13:7f.). See M. Hengel, *Property and Riches in the Early Church* (Eng. trans., 1974), p. 38.

20. Balsdon, op. cit., pp. 45–62; Pomeroy, op. cit., pp. 150–89; cf. Keith Hopkins's notion of a 'salon culture', 'Contraception in the Roman Empire', *Comparative Studies in Society and History* 8 (1965/6), 124–51.

21. See S. K. Heyob, *The Cult of Isis among Women in the Greco-Roman World* (Leiden, 1975).

22. Acts 16:13f., 17:12. Women in a traditional society are always likely to find in religion an outlet denied them in other spheres; cf. Mary Douglas, *Natural Symbols* (Penguin, 1973),

pp. 117f., and see I. M. Lewis, *Ecstatic Religion* (Penguin, 1971). The question is whether this influences their social condition at all.

23. E.g., S. Scott Bartchy, *First-Century Slavery and I Corinthians 7.21* (SBL Diss. Series 11, Montana, 1973), which is vitiated by false assumptions about ancient slavery. Contra, G. E. M. de Ste Croix, 'Early Christian Attitudes to Property and Slavery', *Studies in Church History* 12 (1975), 1–38, especially p. 19, and see 1 Cor. 7:20, 'Let every man abide in the same calling wherein he was called'.

24. For the latter see Mary Douglas, *Purity and Danger* (London, 1966), pp. 186–7 (but perhaps overemphasizing the extent to which Paul's offer was directed at Jews, and thus reflects the Jewish background, and implying that the Christian idea of virginity was free of the association of women and sin with sex pollution: contrast Tertullian, *de Cultu Feminarum* 1. 1. 2, 'tu es diaboli ianua', and the like).

25. Meeks, art. cit., 206. See too R. Scroggs, *Journal of the American Academy of Religion* 40 (1972), 283ff. For Corinth, S. Lösch, *Theologische Quartalschrift* 127 (1947), 216ff., and Parvey, art. cit., pp. 123ff.

26. Gager, op. cit., e.g., pp. 27f., 33 ('liminal groups or persons'). Against such 'compensation-theory', F. C. Grant, *Roman Hellenism and the New Testament* (Edinburgh and London, 1962), p. 90.

27. Meeks, art. cit., 169.

28. *Ann.* 2. 85.

29. See de Ste Croix, art. cit. (n. 23). It spread in urban centres, but not in the circles of Roman élite culture (if any). De Ste Croix rightly emphasizes the enormous social variety among the towns described as having Christian communities: Corinth was hardly on the same footing as, say, Beroea or Joppa.

30. See Harnack, op. cit., ii. 73f.

31. For Gnosticism see the interesting paper by Elaine Pagels, *Signs* 2 (1976), 293–303.

32. See Averil Cameron, *JTS* 29 (1978), 79–108.

## ADDENDUM

This short article was written with a specific point in mind: to argue against what seemed like an unjustified assumption in some New Testament scholarship at the time about the general role and status of women in the Roman Empire in the first century A.D., and to warn against a too-literal reading of Paul's famous formula at Gal. 3:28. Taken on those terms, my argument still seems to me to hold up. That does not mean, however, that I would write the same article today. In 1976 (see n. 5) publications on women in antiquity inspired in whatever form by the Women's Movement were only just beginning to appear, as can be seen from the fact that J. P. V. D. Balsdon's *Roman Women* is still cited here as the standard work (n. 4). The article appeared three years before the first edition of *Images of Women in Antiquity*, edited by Averil Cameron and Amélie Kuhrt (London, 1983, rev. ed. 1993); a similar interval also elapsed before the publication of E. Schussler Fiorenza's book, *In Memory of Her. A Feminist Theological Reconstruction of Christian Origins* (New York, 1983), a work which marked something of a landmark in the application of feminist historical methodology to early Christian material, including the New Testament evidence discussed here. Since then there has been a deluge of writing on women in early Christianity, both within the context of the general study of women in antiquity and under the influence of feminist theology, devoted to 'recovering' a lost tradition of early Christian women. It is also fair to say that both early Christianity and the process of Christianization have been increasingly recognized as belonging to the proper field of the ancient historian. For these reasons I have chosen not to attempt to revise the text of the original article, but merely to add additional notes, indicating briefly where there have been significant developments in the field. It was interesting and illuminating to me to see how far and in what directions things had progressed in the relatively short interval since it was first published: I hope that readers might find the additional notes interesting for that reason too.

## ADDITIONAL NOTES

p. 26, lines 13–14: in November 1992 the General Synod of the Church of England voted to allow the ordination of women as priests. Much discussion focused in the debate on the interpretation of 'headship' in, e.g., I Cor. 11:3 and on the applicability of Paul's injunctions about women in that chapter and at I Cor. 14:34–5: 'Let your women keep silence in the churches for it is not permitted unto them to speak, but they are commanded to be under obedience, as also saith the law. And if they will learn anything, let them ask their husbands at home, for it is a shame for women to speak in the church.'

pp. 27–8:the women given such prominence (despite the note above) in Acts and Romans have been much discussed elsewhere; see, e.g., Fiorenza, *In Memory of Her* and 'Word, Spirit and Power: Women in Early Christian Communities', in Rosemary R. Ruether and E. McLaughlin (edd.), *Women of Spirit: Female Leadership in the Jewish and Christian Traditions* (New York, 1979), pp. 29–70; Bernadette J. Brooten, 'Early Christian Women and the Cultural Context: Issues of Method in Historical Reconstruction', in Adela Yarbro Collins (ed.), *Feminist Perspectives on Biblical Scholarship* (Chico, Ca., 1985), pp. 65–91; Ben Witherington III, *Women in the Earliest Churches* (Cambridge, 1988); Ross Shepard Kramer, *Her Share of the Blessings. Women's Religions among Pagans, Jews and Christians in the Greco-Roman World* (Oxford, 1992), Chap. 10, with full bibliography. For the interpretation of Gal. 3:28 and in general see also Raoul Mortley, *Womanhood. The Feminine in Ancient Hellenism, Gnosticism, Christianity and Islam* (Sydney, 1981).

p. 27: since 1980 the re-examination of Jewish groups outside Palestine in the Early Roman Empire has become the focus of lively interest, with an emphasis on social integration and on the general religious openness of this period. See, e.g., Judith Lieu, John North, and Tessa Rajak (edd.), *The Jews among Pagans and Christians in the Roman Empire* (London, 1992), especially John North, 'The Development of Religious Pluralism', pp. 174–93. Like 'paganism', and indeed 'Christianity' (for the early pluralism of the latter, see Rowan Williams, 'Does it make Sense to Speak of Pre-Nicene Orthodoxy?', in Rowan Williams [ed.], *The Making of Orthodoxy, Essays in Honour of Henry Chadwick* [Cambridge, 1989], pp. 1–23), 'Judaism' too has of late become something of an umbrella term for many and shifting allegiances rather than the name of a readily definable single religion.

p. 28: the theory of the development of a more companionate marriage among the Roman upper class in the late first and early second centuries A.D., put forward by P. Veyne in an article of 1978 and taken up by several other scholars (see my review article 'Redrawing the Map: Early Christian Territory after Foucault', *JRS* 76 [1986], 265–71) has recently received a more mixed reception. This discussion does, however, draw attention to the similarity between Plutarch's precepts on marriage and the so-called 'household codes' in the later, or 'Deutero-Pauline', strata of the New Testament (e.g., I Tim 2:9–15); and gives support to the idea that whatever contradictions there may have been in Paul's own approach an early and more positive acceptance of women within some Christian groups soon gave way to a more prescriptive stance as the institutional church developed (see p. 31 above).

p. 29, line 2: 'liberation' no longer seems a suitable term in relation to women in classical antiquity, though it has often been argued in recent years, especially by feminist writers, that Christianity itself brought a degree of 'liberation' to women who would not have been allowed independent action otherwise. This line of argument relates more, however, to the active upper-class Christian ladies of the late fourth century and later than to the early period. Just how independent and influential the former could be is now well brought out by Elizabeth A. Clark, *The Origenist Controversy: the Cultural Construction of an Early Christian Debate* (Princeton, 1982), ch. 1.

p. 29: for the move towards subordination see also Peter Brown; *The Body and Society: Men, Women and Sexual Renunciation in Early Christianity* (New York, 1987), pp. 57f.

p. 30, line 1: much has been written also on asceticism, celibacy, and the ideal of virginity in the early Church; see, e.g., Brown, op. cit.; Aline Rousselle, *Porneia* (Paris, 1983); Averil Cameron, 'Virginity as Metaphor', in Averil Cameron (ed.), *History as Text* (London, 1989), pp. 184–205 and 'Early Christianity and the Discourse of Desire', in Léonie Archer, Susan Fischler, and Maria Wyke (edd.), *An Illusion of the Night: Women in Ancient Societies* (London, 1993); for the related question of early Christian misogyny see Elaine Pagels, *Adam, Eve and the Serpent* (London, 1987).

p. 30: I would like to think (though one still finds the old view lingering) that the stubborn idea of Christianity as filling an alleged spiritual gap left by the supposed decline of late Hellenistic paganism has now given way before that of early Christian groups as offering one or more options out of many religious possibilities.

pp. 30-1: Edwin Judge and others have also questioned the equally persistent assumption that Christianity spread chiefly among the lower classes (a view which itself rests on a hidden agenda); for discussion see Averil Cameron, *Christianity and the Rhetoric of Empire* (Berkeley and Los Angeles, 1991), ch. 1, and in general, Dimitris J. Kyrtatas, *The Social Structure of Early Christian Communities* (London, 1987).

p. 31–2: the development within Christianity over the period from the Early Roman Empire to late antiquity towards a systematized and rule-based religious scheme, with broad social implications as the Empire became more Christianized, is a theme of Cameron, *Christianity and the Rhetoric of Empire* (later developments relating to women, including the Apocryphal Acts, the growth of asceticism, and the development of the cult of the Virgin, are also discussed there).

# ROMAN WOMEN

*By* GILLIAN CLARK

## I

Times have changed for Roman women. To an undergraduate—even a woman undergraduate—reading Greats some fifteen years ago, they were obviously a fringe topic, worth at most a question on the General Paper. There were pictures of dresses and hairstyles, in most of which it looked impossible to move. There were snippets of anthropology from Plutarch, as that a bride had her hair parted with a spear (*Moralia* 285b): entertaining, but about as relevant to the views of a bride in the Late Republic as are wearing a veil (to symbolize being under authority) and being pelted with confetti (in hopes of many children) to a bride in the 1980s. There was an account of forms of marriage, with, usually, a panegyric of a Roman matron and a denunciation of the laxity of the Late Republic and immorality of the Early Empire; and a handful of brief biographies: Cornelia, Sempronia, Arria. This information would be found somewhere around chapter 15 of a general handbook, once the author had dealt with the serious business of life, like the constitution and the courts and education and the army and the provinces. J. P. V. D. Balsdon's book made a difference, since he never forgot that he was writing about human beings, who worried about their children and ran their households and had long days to fill. But the real change came in the 70s, as the Women's Movement—a decade late—got through to the classics. First there was the new perspective offered by general feminist histories, though their scholarship was second-hand and often wild; then articles and books, though still only a few, trying to answer the sort of questions it now seems so odd we did not ask.[1] What did Roman women do all day, besides getting dressed? How did they feel about it? What else could they have done? Were they oppressed, and did they notice? Why do we know so little about half the human race?

The perspective has shifted, and that may bring different pieces of evidence into focus; some of the questions are different too. But it is still not easy to answer them. We are still working with evidence strongly biassed towards the upper classes and the city of Rome. The lives of women not in, or in contact with, the senatorial class, can only be guessed at from inscriptions, if someone troubled to put one up. And even within the senatorial class, it was not the women who wrote. They wrote, as always, letters, their conversation might be admirable and their language reflect the purer Latin of a bygone age.[2] There survive two letters of Cornelia to her sons, if they are genuine, and an item from Agrippina's memoirs, which Tacitus consulted (*Ann.* 4.53); but the only extended work of literature to survive from the period I shall concentrate on, that of the Late Republic and Early Empire, is the elegies of Sulpicia, and they are not so much a revelation of the inner experience of womankind as a demonstration that women can write conventional elegiacs too.[3] Moreover, there is little Roman literature which is concerned with the daily life and experience of particular people: the lives of women tend to be incidental to oratory or history or philosophy or agriculture, or to the emotions of an elegiac poet.

## II

What then can be said? There is an obvious temptation to generalize, and to apply pieces of information regardless of time, class, or place. But sometimes the generalizations hold for a wide range of society, and sometimes they can be made more precise. To begin at the beginning: a girl's chances of being reared were less than her brother's. *Patria Potestas*, as the jurist Gaius observed (*Institutes* 1.55), was uniquely strong in Rome, and if a father decided that his new-born child was not to be reared there was no law (before the time of the Severi) to prevent him.[4] The foundling girls of Plautus' (*Casina* 39 ff., *Cist.* 124) and Terence's (*Heaut.* 627 ff.) standard plots may not be evidence for Roman practice, for they may have been taken over from Greek models which had to find some way of getting well-born girls out of their seclusion to meet well-born boys. But Cicero (*de Legibus* 3.19) and Seneca (*de Ira* 1.15.2) reveal that deformed babies were exposed (as they still are, though less obtrusively, if the handicap is bad enough), and it was part of a midwife's training to decide which babies were worth rearing.[5] Healthy but inconvenient babies might also be left to die. Musonius Rufus (p. 80 ff. Hense) in the mid-first century A.D. devoted one of his lectures on ethics to the question whether one should rear all one's children. The rich do not, he says, so that there shall be fewer children to share the family property; Petronius (*Sat.* 116) and Tacitus (*Ger.* 19, *Hist.* 5.5) echo the complaint. Since the law required property to be shared among *sui heredes*, it must have been a temptation. Among the poor, there was no question of splitting up an estate. Pliny (*Pan.* 26.5) praises Trajan's extension of the grain-dole to children:

> There are great rewards to encourage the rich to rear their children, and great penalties if they do not. The only way the poor *can* rear their children is through the goodness of the princeps.

If a family did, from greed or necessity, expose a child, it would probably be a girl. Dionysius of Halicarnassus, writing his *Antiquities of Rome* (2.15) under Augustus, included a 'constitution of Romulus' which has strong links with first-century thought.[6] It provides that citizens must rear all male children (except those who are acknowledged by five neighbours to be deformed)—and the first girl. Apuleius (*Met.* 10.23) has a prospective father instruct his wife: 'si sexus sequioris edidisset fetum, protinus quod esset editum necaretur.' (This father, like those who speak now of 'the product of conception', is not prepared to acknowledge the child's humanity.) Some odd facts about sex-ratios make it likely that Dionysius and Apuleius reflect a general tendency. We simply do not hear of spinsters, except the Vestals—and Augustus found it difficult enough to recruit them. (Even they could marry at the end of their term of office, aged 36–40, though they tended not to.)[7] There is not even a normal word for a spinster. Livy (1.46.7) once used *vidua* as a female equivalent of *caelebs*, and the jurist Labeo (*Digest* 1.16.242.3) claimed that *vidua* can mean 'unmarried woman' as well as 'widow', but it is evidently a forced usage. Unmarried women were young *virgines*—and there were no nunneries for the women who did not marry.

Some families did, of course, raise more than one daughter. The daughter of L. Aemilius Paullus Macedonicus had three daughters and three sons; Appius Claudius Pulcher, cos. 79 B.C., also had three daughters. There is even a Septuma on a tombstone (but it may be a *nomen*, not an indication that she was the seventh daughter). But tombstones in general record many more men than women, and this again suggests that either more males were reared or they mattered more to their families.[8] Sometimes there is information about a specific group. A list of aqueduct maintenance men and their families (*CIL* 14.3649), found at Tibur, includes two families with two daughters each, but shows a very low proportion of daughters to sons overall. Trajan's alimentary scheme at Veleia supported only 36 girls out of 300 places: this cannot be used straightforwardly as evidence for sex-ratios, since girls got a smaller food-allowance and a family would obviously claim for a boy if it could, but does suggest that there were few families satisfied with daughters alone.[9] Most impressive, if Dio interpreted it correctly, is Augustus' concession that 'well-born' men, other than senators and senators' sons, might marry *libertinae*. Dio (54.16.2) says there were just not enough women of good family to go round—and if this is true, after several decades of bloody civil war, then people must have been choosing not to rear daughters. But is Dio guessing? The senate, according to him, said that young men were not marrying because of their *akosmia*, their failure to settle down, not because they could not find wives.

There are, of course, other causes than selective infanticide for a relative shortage of women. Many must have died in childbirth, from infection or difficult births, or because they were just too young. Soranus (1.9.34), the second-century A.D. physician whose work was the basis of gynaecology until well on in the nineteenth century, thought fifteen was the earliest suitable age for conception: most gynaecologists now would add three years to that. Child mortality too was alarmingly high, as it has been at all times and places except for some privileged Western countries in the twentieth century. The Augustan laws of inheritance (Ulpian 16) allowed spouses to inherit from each other if they had a child living, or had lost one after puberty, two after age three or three after naming. Girls are usually tougher than boys, but some societies undernourish them, either because they value girls less or because they think (wrongly) that girls need less. Roman governmental schemes like that at Veleia, and several private schemes, gave girls a smaller food-allowance.[10] But these factors have affected other societies which do not show the same apparent shortage of women: so perhaps we do have to come back to parents not rearing girls.

How could they bear it? Even abortion, in this society, is tolerable only so far as we can avoid seeing the foetus as a baby: once the child is born, even for some time before birth, her rights are protected. But the father's right to decide the fate of his own infant probably seemed as obvious as, now, a woman's right to decide about her own body: so infanticide was not made criminal, even though low birth-rate was a persistent anxiety. Besides, Roman parents could not plan their families with much success. Contraceptives varied from quite effective spermicides and pessaries (some are still recommended, *faute de mieux*) to decoctions of herbs (and worse), faith in douches and wriggling, and entirely magical beliefs. The ovum was undiscovered and the relation between menstruation and fertile periods was misunderstood; this is less surprising in that conception can occur before the first menstruation if a girl marries before she reaches puberty. Observers may also have been confused by amenorrhea (failure to menstruate), which is a common reaction to stress and poor diet and which gets a lot of space in ancient medical text-books. Soranus (1.10, 1.19.61) held that the best time for conception was at the end of a menstrual period, when (he says) a women's desire is strongest, and suggested a rhythm method based on this belief.[11] No wonder Augustus' daughter played safe, and never took a lover unless she was legitimately pregnant (Macrobius, *Sat.* 3.5). And no wonder abortion was also practised. Doctors used herbal baths, suppositories, and potions first; then purges, diuretics, massage, violent exercise, and hot baths after drinking wine. If these ancient equivalents of gin, hot baths, and jumping off the kitchen table failed, there seem to have been back-street abortionists using the knitting-needle technique.[12]

Abortion, like infanticide, was not a crime before the time of the Severi, and then the crime was not against the foetus, who was not a person in law, but against the defrauded husband.[13] Why was it not made illegal before? There was strong feeling against abortion, which was taken to be proof of vanity (Seneca, *ad Helviam* 16.1) or, worse, of adultery (Juvenal 6.592 ff.) on the part of the mother. Perhaps it was simply too difficult to prove deliberate as against spontaneous abortion: Soranus' (1.14) list of causes for the latter make one wonder how anyone ever managed to have a baby.[14]

An unwanted pregnancy may yet produce a wanted child, but there were some practices which may have prevented, at least among the upper classes, the emotional bonding of mother and baby. Many mothers did not breast-feed, because it is tiring, but expected to use a wet-nurse.[15] The wet-nurse's own baby had perhaps died, or been exposed, or was expected to manage on some substitute for breast-milk—which last was a major cause of child mortality in the nineteenth century. If Soranus' instructions (2.11.17, 2.12.19 ff.) reflect general practice, the new-born was washed, swaddled, and then put somewhere to be quiet, and to be fed, if at all, the equivalent of glucose (boiled honey and water): Soranus advocated breast-feeding but thought colostrum was bad for babies. So the mother might scarcely have seen the child before the decision to expose it. Poorer people could not afford luxuries of feeling. It may have seemed better to expose the child and hope for the fairy-story to come true and the child to be rescued by some wealthy childless couple. Just occasionally it did. Slavery or a brothel (Plautus, *Cist.* 124) were more likely fates, but even that may have seemed more like putting a child to be raised 'in service', where the chances were better and at least there was food.[16]

## III

If, then, a Roman girl survived her parents' possible indifference, or resignation, to her death, and if she did not despite their best efforts die anyway, what would her life be like?

If she were a slave, she might have little time with her parents: she, or they, could be sold at any time, and there are epitaphs of very young children who had been freed by someone other than the master who freed either parent. But it may have been a relative who bought out the child, since at least the family was united enough for the epitaph to be made. Some slave families did manage gradually to buy the freedom of spouses and children.[17] What a slave girl did depended on the size and type of household to which she belonged. She was most likely to be an *ancilla*, which may mean anything from a maid-of-all-work to a lady's maid—

obviously the second was a better chance, since she could collect tips and win her mistress' (or master's) favour. She might have special skills: some slave-girls were dressers, hairdressers, dressmakers, woolworkers, and some perhaps worked in small factories rather than for the household stores.[18] Some were childminders (Tacitus, *Dialogus* 29.1), which was a job not regarded as needing skill, or, if they were lactating, wet-nurses.

Some households were brothels, and so in effect were some eating- and drinking-places (*Digest* 23.2.43). A few slave-girls, who had other abilities for entertaining, were trained to dance, sing, and act: there is an epitaph of one, Eucharis, 'docta erodita omnes artes virgo' (*CIL* 1.1214). The most famous was Cytheris, who rose to be Antonius' mistress and to dine with Cicero (*Fam.* 9.26; *Phil.* 2.69), who was pleasantly shocked.

If a slave-girl were freed, it did not much enlarge the possibilities: she might be a prostitute, a *mima*, or, if she were lucky, a housewife, doing much the same work as an *ancilla* did but in her own home.[19] If she had caught the fancy of someone of high social status, she would be his *concubina* not his wife: it was not respectable to marry a *libertina*, though it had been known to happen even before Augustus allowed it for non-senators.[20] Housework was hard: there was spinning and weaving and sewing and mending, cooking and cleaning, and water-carrying and baby-minding. Doubtless one reason for child mortality was the impossibility of keeping a swaddled baby clean on the fourth floor of a tenement with the water-supply at the end of the street. Soranus (2.9.14) said babies should be bathed and massaged once a day; the undersheets should often be aired and changed and one should watch for insect bites and ulceration. It sounds optimistic. If the housewife had learnt a trade before she married—baking, brickmaking, selling vegetables—she would probably go on with it, often working with her husband. The nearest approach to a professional woman would be a woman doctor, or the midwife who was called in for female complaints, though their social status was not high.[21]

Rich girls had to learn to run a household rather than doing its work, but they too had spinning and weaving. By the first century B.C. there were ready-made fabrics for those who could afford them (Columella, 12 pr. 9), but *lanificium* was part of traditional devotion to the home and was still, for most women, an essential part of household economy. A bride carried a spindle and distaff (Plutarch, *Moralia* 271f): this is one marriage custom with an obvious relevance. Whether *lanificium* was an enjoyable craft skill or an exhausting chore depended on how much one had to do. Livy's picture (1.57.9) of the virtuous Lucretia, sitting up with her maids doing wool-work by lamplight, needs to be supplemented by Tibullus' (1.3.83 ff., 1.6.77) of the weary slave falling asleep over her work, and the neglected old woman who has no other resource. Too much woolwork, despite the lanolin in the wool, hardened the hands—a point to bear in mind when choosing a midwife (Soranus 1.2.4). But the custom was kept up by ladies of old-fashioned virtue. There were looms in the *atrium* of M. Aemilius Lepidus when thugs broke in on his admirable wife; Augustus' womenfolk kept him in homespun, though Livia had a large staff of skilled workers.[22] *Lanificium*, for ladies, perhaps took the place of the 'accomplishments'—music, drawing, fine sewing—which young ladies of the nineteenth century learnt before marriage and used to fill idle hours after. There were refinements of skill. Cynthia, waiting up for Propertius (1.3.41–2), tried first her 'purple thread' and then her music; Varro (ap. Nonius 239L) said that girls should learn embroidery so as to be better judges of home furnishings. Not everyone had these resources. Ummidia Quadratilla, a formidable old lady, told the Younger Pliny (*Ep.* 7.24.5) that, *ut femina in illo otio sexus*, she passed the time playing draughts or watching her mime-troupe.

Little is heard of more intellectual pursuits. There was a chance of picking up some education from parents, brothers, even a sympathetic husband. The Younger Pliny and his friend Pompeius Saturninus, who were civilized people, both continued the literary education of their wives (*Ep.* 1.6, 4.19). Pompeius' wife wrote letters which sounded like prose Plautus or Terence, so pure was their Latin (Pliny was inclined to give Pompeius the credit). Pliny's wife set his verses to music with no tutor but Love, which sounds less promising. Atticus' daughter was still being tutored, by his freedman Caecilius Epirota, when she was a married woman (Suet. *de Gramm.* 16). An unsympathetic husband, on the other hand, could make difficulties. Seneca's father (*ad Helviam* 17.3) refused to allow his intelligent wife any more than a superficial study of philosophy—but this, Seneca says, was *antiquus rigor*.

Some girls may have gone to school, at least for primary schooling, and some had private tutors. Pompeius' wife Cornelia had been taught literature, music, and geometry, and had 'listened with profit' to lectures on philosophy—which may mean ethics or physics. She was, Plutarch (*Pomp.* 55.1) reassures the reader, 'free from the distasteful pedantry which such studies confer on young women'. Pompeius' daughter had a tutor for Greek (Plutarch, *Moralia* 737b). Pliny's friend Fundanius had *praeceptores* for his daughter, but he was a progressive: a philosopher, a friend of Plutarch who wrote on the education of women, a pupil of Musonius who argued for equal education for girls.[24] These people may be exceptions. Ovid (*Ars Am.* 2.281–2) reckoned that there were some women who could appreciate poetry, but very few (far fewer than would like to).

Some girls learnt music and singing, and the dramatic recitations which rose to a form of ballet and could be very strenuous, but it was not proper for them to aim at a professional standard. Scipio Aemilianus had been shocked, as early as 129 B.C., to find well-born boys and girls at a dancing class; Sallust's Sempronia was far better than she should be; and Horace thought it was part of the rot that grown girls should learn *Ionicos motus*.[25]

Some women, then, were reasonably well-educated: Quintilian (1.1.6) cites as shining examples Cornelia (mother of the Gracchi), and Hortensia and Laelia who were daughters of orators. Much of the evidence, unfortunately, comes in the complaints of Juvenal (6.434 ff.) and the admiration of Catullus (35) and Propertius (2.13.11), none of whom was chiefly concerned with accurate reporting. But at the age when a boy was going on to the secondary education which trained him in the use of language and prepared him for public life, a girl was entering her first marriage. Fundanius' daughter, so carefully taught, died when she was not yet fourteen: the wedding invitations had already been sent out.[26]

## IV

Fourteen was evidently a proper age for marriage. It was assumed to be the age of menarche, though if a girl had not reached puberty the marriage might well be arranged anyway, and menstruation encouraged by massage, gentle exercise, good food, and diversion.[27] The legal minimum age of marriage, as fixed by Augustan legislation which followed Republican precedent, was 12: earlier marriage was not penalized, but was not valid until the girl reached 12. (It followed that she could not be prosecuted for adultery.)[28] Some marriages were certainly pre-pubertal. Augustus' own first wife was *vixdum nubilis*, and Suetonius (*Divus Aug.* 62.1) found it worth recording that he sent her back *intacta*. One girl (*ILLRP* 793) was 'taken to her husband's bosom' at 7: perhaps the marriage was not consummated, though Petronius (*Sat.* 25–6) relates (in order to shock?) the defloration of a seven-year-old. By contrast, the daughters of Germanicus were almost on the shelf—*instabat virginum aetas*—when they married. They were 15 and 17 (Tacitus, *Ann.* 6.15).[29]

Plutarch, not surprisingly, thought that Roman girls married too young, and that Lycurgus was right in ensuring that brides should be ready for childbearing. Romans, he says, were more concerned to ensure an undefiled body and mind (*Moralia* 138e). Evidently they thought they had to catch the girls young to be sure. Doctors supposed that sexual desires began at puberty, especially in girls who ate a lot and did not have to work;[30] society made provision for such desires instead of trying to sublimate them. Epictetus (*Enchiridion* 40) remarks sadly that when girls are fourteen they begin to be called *kuria*, the address of a grown woman: then they see that there is nothing for it but to go to bed with men, and begin to make themselves pretty in hopes. (His solution is for them to learn that men really admire them for modesty and chastity—and then, one supposes, they may go to bed with philosophers.) So marriage at fourteen was, in one sense, practical. But were girls in any sense ready for it? Physically, no: teenage pregnancies were known to be dangerous, and Soranus (1.7, 1.9.42) stoutly disagrees with the school of thought which held that conception is good for you. Emotionally, Roman girls were better prepared than the innocent bride envisaged by Xenophon in the *Oeconomicus* (3.11 ff., 4.7 ff.) who had spent fifteen years seeing, hearing, and saying as little as possible, and whose mother's advice on marriage was simply *sōphronein*, 'be good'. Nepos (pr. 6) remarks on one striking contrast between Roman and Greek *mores*: the materfamilias was at the centre of the household's social life. Visitors found her in the *atrium* (maybe even doing her woolwork) and conversed with her; she went out shopping, to visit friends, to temples, theatres, and games. Decorum might require her to be suitably dressed and chaperoned, and restrained to the point of discourtesy in returning a greeting, but decorum is not always observed. Probably she had her daughters with her on some of these occasions; she may even have taken them to dinner-parties, though some people thought that girls learnt rather too much when out to dinner.[31] A society which did not segregate women, and which praised wives for being pleasant company, gave married life a far better chance than did the conventions of classical Athens.[32] A fourteen-year-old who had grown up in it, expecting to be grown up at fourteen, might well be reasonably mature. And where the expectation of life was nearer 30+ than 70+, there was no use in delaying recognized adulthood to 16 or 18.

The pressure of mortality was the underlying reason for early marriage. Tullia, Cicero's cherished daughter, was engaged at 12, and married at 16, to an excellent young man. She was widowed at 22, remarried at 23, divorced at 28; married again at 29, divorced at 33—and dead, soon after childbirth, at 34. The evidence of inscriptions shows that she was not untypical.[33] So the fathers who arranged the marriages had good reason to start making alliances, and getting grandchildren, fast.

Fathers arranged marriages: but that was not all there was to it. A father's consent was necessary to the marriage of a daughter in his *potestas*, though he was presumed to have given it unless he explicitly refused. The mother's consent was not relevant. The daughter's consent was necessary, but could be refused only if her father's choice were morally unfit—and, in practice, if she could get relatives and neighbours to back her up (*Digest* 23.2.2.). But, in practice, mothers and daughters might well have a say in the matter. Cicero, admittedly an indulgent father, wondered whether Tullia would accept the suitor suggested by Atticus (*ad Att.* 5.4.1, 6.6.1); Tullia and Terentia presented him with a *fait accompli* and her engagement to Dolabella, though indeed Cicero was out of Italy at the time, and Tullia was a woman entering her third marriage, not a girl of twelve (*ad Fam.* 3.12.2). Anyone who reads Victorian novels will have a picture in mind of the complexities of family feeling and economic necessity which affect the choice of a husband—and of how much can be achieved by helpless young ladies and wives without civil rights. But it seems fair to ask whether the character of a *jeune fille* got much consideration. Pliny (*Ep.* 1.14) was delighted to find the ideal husband for the niece of Junius Mauricus—or rather, as he puts it, a young man worthy to father the grandchildren of Arulenus Rusticus. Minicius, he says, is of a most respectable family, worthy of that into which he will marry. He has already held office, so they will not have the bother of canvassing for him. He is good-looking: Pliny thinks this deserves a mention (other people evidently would not) as a sort of reward for the bride's virginity. He is also rather well off. A very proper display of feeling, which makes no mention of the girl: she had not met her future husband. Another letter (6.26) congratulates a friend on his choice of son-in-law and his future grandchildren, but says nothing about the expected happiness of the friend's daughter. It may be relevant that nowhere in the *Aeneid* are Lavinia's views on her future husband considered: she does, once, blush (12.64 ff.). A suitable connection for the family is what mattered: in the absence of social mobility and Social Security, a family is too much affected by the marriges of its members to leave them to romance.

An arranged marriage, with goodwill and similar expectations on both sides, may have as good a chance of happiness as a romantic marriage (the divorce rate has now reached one in three). Roman marriages were expected to be happy. Musonius (p. 14) rates the mutual affection of husband and wife above all other ties; Epictetus (*Enchir.* 3.14) constantly uses 'wife and child' as an example of what the wise man would hate to lose (though he should not). In the proscription, according to Velleius (2.67), wives showed greater loyalty than sons or slaves. The husband of the lady known as Turia recorded (*ILS* 8393.50 ff.) his acute distress when she offered him a divorce (they were childless), though he said that marriages as happy and long-lasting as theirs, uninterrupted by death or divorce, were a rarity. Augustus and Livia had one (Suet. *Divus Aug.* 99.1). The ideal was long-lived, harmonious, fertile marriage.[34] But the death rate was not the only impediment.

Marriages were in the interest of the family rather than the individual, and Roman naming customs seem to reflect the underlying feeling. A British girl has a personal name (or names) and a family name; when she marries she may take her husband's surname, since a wife belongs with her husband not her father, or retain her maiden name to show that she is not a dependent wife. A Roman woman, in a system apparently unique in

Italy,[35] had only one name, the feminine form of her father's *gentilicium*; she shared it with her sisters and her cousins and her aunts on the father's side, and kept it unchanged through life no matter how many marriages she went through. Of course there had to be devices to stop everyone getting muddled: pet-names (Livilla), public-school systems (Antonia Major and Minor, Claudia Prima, Secunda, and Tertia), sometimes a husband's name (Octavia Marcelli): but we still do not know for certain which of three sisters called Clodia was Catullus' love. We do not know whether it occurred to any such woman to feel more like a token Octavia, a female of the Octavii, than like Octavia who was someone in her own right: but some of the more ruthless divorces, and the general approach to choosing a marriage-partner, do give that impression.

A woman who married *cum manu* did indeed pass out of her father's *potestas* and into her husband's, on a par with his daughter—with two major exceptions. A daughter could not compel her father to anything, but a wife could compel her husband to divorce; and although a husband with *manus* over his wife controlled all that she possessed and inherited, and need surrender only her dowry if they divorced, wives do seem to have kept control over some property (perhaps by sheer force of character or connections).[36] A woman married *sine manu*, as seems to have been the norm by the mid-first century B.C., remained in her father's *potestas*, needed his consent to any major financial transaction, and might have her marriage ended by him even against her wish. Spouses had once been exempted from the ban (in the *lex Cincia* of 204 B.C.) on making gifts of property above a certain limit: they came to be forbidden to give each other property except where the wife's gift would enable her husband to reach a required census. Plutarch (*Moralia* 265e) hopefully says that the point of this was to encourage spouses to think of all property in common, not as his or hers; the *Digest*, with more frankness, that it was *ne mutuo amore invicem spoliarentur*. But who, in a *bene concordans matrimonium*, was being despoiled, except the spouses' families? Marriage *sine manu* allowed a father to keep a close eye on the family money that went with his daughter; and the Augustan adultery laws recognized that his interest in her was stronger than her husband's.[37]

Divorce could in fact end the commitment of wife to husband very easily. There was no need to prove breakdown of marriage; guilty parties needed to be established only in so far as there might be a financial penalty in the divorce settlement (apparently for an adulterous wife or for the spouse who took the initiative in divorcing). There would, of course, be financial tangles over the repayment of dowry and in sorting out the assets which the couple had managed in common, and these might well be enough to ensure that, among poorer people, marriage contracts would be respected: it is difficult to find clear evidence of divorce at that economic level.[38] But legal tangles and massive debts seldom discouraged upper-class Romans, and the financial patterns of marriage *sine manu* suggest that (like some holders of separate bank accounts) they were prepared for a break-up.

It is often suggested that the move from marriage *cum manu* to marriage *sine manu* was prompted by the demands of Late Republican women for greater freedom. 'Women of wealth, birth, charm and talent, unfettered by any moral restraint, hungry for animal pleasure or hungry for power—hungry, perhaps, for both.'[39] (It is not clear who, besides Sempronia, Clodia Metelli, and Fulvia, comes into this category.) The marriage law of the Late Republic is said to have given women exceptional freedom and dignity: 'for the first time in human civilization. . . . a law founded on a purely humanistic idea of marriage, as being a free and freely dissoluble union of two equal partners for life.'[40] Now marriage either *cum manu* or *sine manu* gave women more hope of release, if the marriage was unhappy, than indissoluble marriage, which was believed to have been the rule in the Early Republic. (As always, there were those who thought it was still the best solution to marital problems—especially the problem of how to stop women causing trouble.)[41] And if one's object was to be *sui iuris*, independent but for the nominal control of a guardian,[42] one's father was likely to release one from his *potestas* by dying sooner than one's husband was, so marriage *sine manu* was a better bet. But it does not appear that women were in a position to make a free choice. A *filiafamilias* could not choose her husband unless she could get round her father; could not divorce him without her father's economic support; and could not prevent herself from being divorced at the instigation of her husband, her father, or his father. She was, indeed, almost her husband's equal in this: he too was subject, at least in theory, to his father's financial control, required his consent to marry (but could refuse his own) and perhaps to divorce, and could be made to divorce: but sons had, in practice, more scope.[43] A woman *sui iuris*, like a man, could make independent decisions, allowing for family and financial constraints. But she had one major disadvantage. If she decided for divorce, she would lose her children, for they belonged to the father's family. Women cannot adopt, says the jurist Gaius (*Institutes* 1.104, 1.155), for not even the children of their own bodies are in their *potestas*.

The father presumably decided who actually looked after the children of broken marriages. Scribonia, divorced by Octavian on the day of her daughter's birth, did not rejoin her until her exile 37 years later. Had they seen each other in the meantime? Livia's children by her first marriage did not come to live with her until their father died and left Augustus as guardian, even though one of them had been born after the marriage ended. Octavia, on the other hand, took both her own and Antonius' children when she was expelled from his house; but then he was at the other end of the Mediterranean and had evidently not made arrangements for them.[44] But even the possibility of losing the children must have been hard enough to bear: especially, perhaps, in a culture where women had to rely on their sons for the achievement and status impossible for themselves.

It was one of the standard vices of women (as described by men) to gratify their ambitions through their sons. Seneca (*ad Helviam* 14.2) congratulates his exceptional mother:

> You are an example to those mothers who exercise their influence over their children with all a woman's lack of restraint. Women may not hold office, so they gratify their ambition through their sons; they take over their sons' inheritance, exhaust their sons' eloquence in their own interest. . . .

Livia was perhaps an example of this: indulgent towards her husband, she dominated her sons (Tacitus, *Ann.* 5.1). Admittedly Seneca (*de Prov.* 2.5) also describes the reverse problem, mothers who cannot bear to have their children exposed to the hardships of life, but that too can be put down to a determination to gratify maternal feelings. Augustus' half-sister Octavia, a woman who could justly pride herself on her own conduct and her brother's success, and who had other children dependent on her, collapsed utterly when her firstborn Marcellus died (Seneca, *ad Marciam* 2). That was an extreme case, and not to be emulated, but it was nevertheless one of the standard virtues of women (as described by men) to be devoted to their sons. The classic *exempla* were Cornelia mother of the Gracchi, Aurelia mother of Caesar, and Atia mother of Augustus. All had taken unusual pains over the upbringing of their sons, from breast-feeding and supervised education to (in the case of Atia) fending off lustful older women. The letters of Cornelia reveal just how to put pressure on a son.[45] Roman moralists, praising these women, did not remark that the result of their devotion was sons with a marked sense of their own importance, even at the expense of the Roman commonwealth. But what other outlet could such women find for their talents and energies?

## V

Running a great household might, in fact, be as challenging as many executive jobs, especially if the *materfamilias* concerned herself with investments and *clientes*. The *lex Voconia* of 169 B.C. had tried to prevent women from being left in control of large inheritances, but it applied only where a man entered on the census list for the first class had an only daughter, and even then could be circumvented by leaving the money to a trusted friend who would pass it on.[46] Many women were extremely wealthy, though families of course differed in the extent to which women managed their own wealth. 'Turia' ran the house and left investments to her husband (*ILS* 8393.38 ff.); Terentia, to judge from Cicero's grumbles about her and her agent, managed her own: they included *silvae*, rented *ager publicus*, a *vicus*, and some tenements.[47] Sometimes it is not possible to tell whether a woman—for instance, Eumachia (*CIL* 10.810–2), patroness of the fullers and donor of public buildings at Pompeii—was a manager or just an owner. Women could make wills, though technically they were required to 'change family' (a legal formality) before doing so, but the sources never suggest any difficulty.[48] A widow *sui iuris*, managing her own affairs with only token reference to her guardian and her agnates (or free from *tutela* altogether if she had borne enough children), and old enough (that is, fifty) to escape the obligation to remarry and have more children, was Rome's nearest approach to a legally independent woman.[49] There cannot have been many such; and there were no career women. What career, after all, was open?

Women did not vote, did not serve as *iudices*, were not senators or magistrates or holders of major priesthoods. They did not, as a rule, speak in the courts: Valerius Maximus (8.3) found only three instances, and becomes quite apoplectic about the one who enjoyed herself and did it again. She seems to have provoked a praetorian ruling that no woman should usurp the masculine role of advocate.[50] As a rule, women took no part in public life, except on the rare occasions when they were angry enough to demonstrate, which was startling and shocking. Before the debate on the *lex Oppia*, says Livy (34.1.5), 'the married women could not be kept at home by respect for authority, sense of shame, or the orders of their husbands . . . they even dared to go up to consuls and praetors and other magistrates and ask for their support.' Another demonstration, against the attempt of the Second Triumvirate to confiscate women's property, was a great success (Appian, *Bell. Civ.* 4.33). But in general women worked through private influence. On one famous occasion Servilia, in a family conclave which included her daughter and daughter-in-law, claimed that she could get a corn-commission altered so that Brutus and Cassius did not actually have to supply any corn (Cicero, *ad Att.* 15.11). It is not known whether this claim proved true; but this sort of private influence was expected and feared. Governors' wives, if they went out with their husbands, could 'make another Government House' (Tacitus, *Ann.* 3.33); Seneca's aunt deserved praise for having remained in seclusion while her husband was *praefectus Aegypti* (*ad Helviam* 19.6). Trajan's womenfolk were also laudably restrained (Pliny, *Pan.* 83), but the wife of Pontius Pilatus tried (and failed) to influence a judicial decision

(Matthew 27.19). Livia claimed that she never interfered in Augustus' concerns, but her scope for action was such that the senate honoured her on her death 'because she had saved the lives of many senators, brought up the children of many, and helped many to pay their daughters' dowries' (Dio 58.2.5).

Women might, then, have considerable influence and interests outside their homes and families, but they were acting from within their families to affect a social system managed by men: their influence was not to be publicly acknowledged. Why were women excluded from public life? The division between arms-bearers and child-bearers was doubtless one historical cause, but the reasons publicly given were different. Women were alleged to be fragile and fickle, and therefore in need of protection; if they were not kept in their proper place they would (fragility and fickleness notwithstanding) take over. As the Elder Cato, in a speech expanded, or invented, by Livy (34.1 ff.; *ORF* I. p. 14), said in defence of the *lex Oppia*:

Our ancestors decided that women should not handle anything, even a private matter, without the advice of a guardian; that they should always be in the power of fathers, brothers, husbands. . . . Call to mind all those laws on women by which your ancestors restrained their licence and made them subject to men: you can only just keep them under by using the whole range of laws. If you let them niggle away at one law after another until they have worked it out of your grasp, until at last you let them make themselves equal to men, do you suppose that you'll be able to stand them? If once they get equality, they'll be on top.

This naked appeal to male dominance offended the liberals. Livy composed an answering speech for the tribune Valerius (34.7.7 ff.). Even men, it says, might mind seeing Rome's allies going about better dressed than they are: what then should poor dear little women, *mulierculae*, feel? That is their world, the *mundus muliebris*; they have no magistracies, priesthoods, triumphs, insignia, spoils of war. And there is no danger of their getting out of hand. 'While a woman's relatives are alive, she is never free from slavery, and women themselves detest the freedom conferred by widowhood or bereavement. You should protect them, not enslave them: you should prefer the name of father or husband to that of master.'

Women—touching or menacing—were basically unreliable. They were physically weak and nervous, well-suited for watching over possessions (Columella pr. 12). They were emotional, irrational, and intellectually less capable than men: this *levitas animi* and *infirmitas consilii* made guardians necessary.[51] This argument came to look very silly as more and more women managed their own affairs (Gaius, *Inst.* 1.190), and Stoic philosophers began to challenge its basis. Musonius (p. 8 ff.) declared that women had reason, senses, bodily parts, like men; they too had a natural bent towards virtue; they too would need virtue, and the same virtues as men, to lead decent lives. Women need courage and endurance as much as men do; men should have as high a standard of sexual virtue as women. Musonius makes an interesting comparison here, revealing that the double standard was not just a fear of illegitimate children. A man who goes to bed with a prostitute, he says, need not fear that he is depriving a husband of the hope of offspring—nor was he liable to prosecution—but should consider the horror that is felt when a woman goes to bed with a slave.[52] Seneca (*ad Marciam* 16.1, *ad Helviam* 16.3) agreed in principle about women's natural abilities: and if he regards his mother only as an exception to the vices of her sex (which were, it seems, unchastity, love of riches, shame at pregnancy, and wearing make-up and see-through dresses), it is equally clear that a male philosopher is an exception to the vices of his.[53]

Stoic radicalism went only so far. It followed from Musonius' principles that girls should be educated on the same pattern as boys—but not so as to make them unfeminine or give them undue skill in logic-chopping (which was also undesirable for men). They will philosophize as women: the assumption is that they will exercise their virtues in the home, the men as citizens. Boys should not be taught woolwork, nor girls gymnastics, but each sex should do the job for which it is naturally fitted. In principle Musonius (p. 13ff.) went impressively far:

> Some men, sometimes, might reasonably do the lighter tasks which are thought suitable for women, and women might do the heavier tasks which are thought more appropriate for men: it depends on physical strength, necessity, or the demands of the time. All human tasks, I think, are common to men and women, and nothing is necessarily exclusive to one or the other sex. But some tasks, obviously, are more suited to one nature, and some to the other.

Musonius was perhaps influenced by the prospect of exile, in which the Stoic sage and his wife might have unexpected tasks. But public opinion was not with him. People feared, he says (as perhaps Seneca's father feared), that women who did philosophy would get over-confident, leaving the house to mix with men and talk logic (or worse) when they should be at home getting on with the woolwork. Musonius answered (p. 12) that philosophy would not make women neglect their duties, but ensure that they did them better: though Epictetus (ap. Arrian fr. 15) claimed that some women used Plato's *Republic* to justify their promiscuity. One may doubt whether an exceptional woman who did go outside traditional sex-rôles would have got a better reception than Fulvia, who was reported as a masculinized monster—and subject to female gusts of passion just the same.[54] The answer to Musonius might well be Juvenal's sixth satire.

A social system which restricted women to domestic life, and prevailing attitudes which assumed their inferiority, must seem to us oppressive. I know of no evidence that it seemed so at the time. The legal and social constraints detailed above may have frustrated the abilities of many women and caused much ordinary human unhappiness. But there evidently were, also, many ordinarily happy families where knowledge of real live women took precedence over the theories, and women themselves enjoyed home, children, and friends. There were some women who enjoyed the political game, and who found an emotional life outside their necessary marriages.[55] And there were certainly women who found satisfaction in living up to the standards of the time. They were, as they should be, chaste, dutiful, submissive, and domestic; they took pride in the family of their birth and the family they had produced; and probably their resolution to maintain these standards gave them the support which women in all ages have found in religious faith. But the religious feelings of Roman women, as opposed to the acts of worship in which they might take part, are something of which we know very little. A woman whose child was ill might make, and gladly pay, a vow for his safety: but did she pray for strength and patience while nursing him, and feel that some divine power was sustaining her, or was she supposed to rely on her *virtutes*?[56]

The empress Livia put on a performance of Augustan perfection. Dio (58.2.5ff.) professes to record her explanation of how she kept Augustus' love so long. She never had lovers; she went amiably along with what Augustus wanted; she never interfered; and she pretended not to notice his mistresses. Horace (*Odes* 3.14.5) got as near as he dared (since everyone knew she had left her first husband while pregnant with his child) to calling her *univira*, a one-man woman. The senate gave her the privileges of a mother of three children, though her marriage to Augustus produced only a stillborn son. She made her husband's clothes; she combined traditional chastity with modern charm; and she was, within the limits she herself accepted, a woman of great power.[57] This, presumably, is one picture of the ideal Roman woman: and it might be a woman's ideal as well as a man's. The most moving expression of the ideal is in the elegy for Cornelia written by Propertius (4.11), a poem sometimes (though without evidence) regarded as a recantation, since he portrayed his own love as a subverter of standards. Propertius' Cynthia is independent, probably adulterous,[58] concerned not about house and children but about love-affairs and literature. His Cornelia claims that she has followed the tradition of her family, and her mother (who was Scribonia, Augustus' divorced wife) must approve her. She is *univira*, chaste, and fertile. She is an example to her own children. Her children have survived her, and she has seen her brother consul. She does not say, though it was true, that she has seen her husband consul and censor: perhaps that was not part of her pride in what she was as a representative of her family. But she thinks, though she puts it tentatively, that he will grieve for her and care for their children. It had been a good life.

The son of Murdia, in the age of Augustus, made her a public eulogy. Some of what he said has happened to survive (*ILS* 8394), and, since we should not otherwise know of her existence, may make the best epitaph for the women who did not make the history books.

What is said in praise of all good women is the same, and straightforward. There is no need of elaborate phrases to tell of natural good qualities and of trust maintained. It is enough that all alike have the same reward: a good reputation. It is hard to find new things to praise in a woman, for their lives lack incident. We must look for what they have in common, lest something be left out to spoil the example they offer us. My beloved mother, then, deserves all the more praise, for in modesty, integrity, chastity, submission, woolwork, industry, and trustworthiness she was just like other women.

## NOTES

1. J. P. V. D. Balsdon, *Roman Women* (London, 1962); *Arethusa* 6 (1973) and 11 (1978); Sarah B. Pomeroy, *Goddesses, Whores, Wives, and Slaves* (New York, 1975); Mary R. Lefkowitz and Maureen B. Fant, *Women in Greece and Rome* (Toronto, 1977), a source-collection.

2. Cicero, *Brutus* 211; Quintilian 1. 1. 6; Pliny, *Ep.* 1. 16.

3. Cornelia, Schanz–Hosius 1. p. 219; Sulpicia, ibid. 2. p. 189.

4. Mommsen, *Strafrecht*, p. 636 n. 3.

5. Soranus 2. 6. 10 (ed. Ilberg, Teubner 1927 = *Corpus Medicorum Graecorum* 4).

6. J. P. V. D. Balsdon, *JRS* 61 (1971), 18ff.

7. Dio 55. 22. 5; Aulus Gellius, *Noctes Atticae* 1. 12. 9; Suetonius, *Divus Augustus* 31. 3; Plutarch, *Numa* 10.2.

8. Münzer pp. 351–2; *CIL* 1. 2 27881; K. M. Hopkins, *Population Studies* 18 (1964–5), 309 ff.

9. Richard Duncan-Jones, *The Economy of the Roman Empire* (Cambridge, 1974), pp. 288 ff.

10. Child mortality: J. P. V. D. Balsdon, *Life and Leisure in Ancient Rome* (London, 1969), pp. 85 ff. Girl babies tougher: Soranus 2.21.48. Food schemes: A. R. Hands, *Charities and Social Aid in Greece and Rome* (London, 1968), pp. 113 ff. See the discussion of infanticide by P. A. Brunt, *Italian Manpower* (Oxford, 1971), pp. 148 ff.

11. K. M. Hopkins, *Comparative Studies in Society and History* 8 (1965), 124 ff.; John T. Noonan, Jr., *Contraception* (Harvard, 1965), ch. 1. On conception before the first menstruation, compare Geza Vermes, *Jesus the Jew* (London, 1973), p. 218; on amenorrhea, E. LeRoy Ladurie, *The Territory of the Historian* (English translation, Hassocks, 1979). On the time of conception, even Marie Stopes agreed with Soranus: present-day belief is that conception in the paramenstruum is possible but unlikely.

12. Soranus 1. 19. 64; Ovid, *Amores* 2. 14. 27, *Fasti* 1. 621–4.

13. *Digest* 48. 19. 38. 5, 47. 11. 4; foetus not a person, 35. 2. 9. 1, 25. 4. 1. 1. Tacitus, *Ann.* 14. 63 does not (*pace* P. A. Brunt, *Italian Manpower*, p. 147) suggest that abortion was a crime against the husband in Nero's time: Octavia was accused of aborting someone else's child, i.e., of adultery. Cicero, *pro Cluentio* 31–2 has to fall back on a law from Miletus.

14. Cf. Pliny, *Natural History* 7. 42–3.

15. Gellius 12.1; Tacitus, *Dialogus* 28, *Germania* 20. 1. Musonius p. 11, and *ILS* 8541 count breastfeeding a virtue.

16. The fairy-story, Juvenal 6. 602 ff.; in real life, Suetonius, *de Grammaticis* 7 and 21; inscrip-

tions by grateful foster-children, Balsdon, *Life and Leisure*, pp. 86–7.

17. Beryl Rawson, *CPh* 61 (1966), 71ff. The *lex Aelia Sentia* (A.D. 4) allowed slaves under 30 to be freed without appeal to a *consilium* if, among other reasons, they were about to die, or a relative wished to free them: Gaius, *Institutes* 1. 19.

18. *CIL* 6. 3926ff. (Livia's household), 6213ff. (the household of the Statilii Tauri). Factories, Columella 12 pr. 1.

19. Susan Treggiari, *Roman Freedmen in the Late Republic* (Oxford, 1969), p. 88.

20. *Digest* 25. 7. 1 pr., 23. 2. 44; Ulpian 13. 1; Cicero, *pro Sestio* 110. See F. Schulz, *Roman Classical Law* (Oxford, 1951), p. 138.

21. J. LeGall, *REL* 47 bis (1970), 123f. Doctors, *ILS* 7802–5; midwives, Soranus 3. 1. 3.

22. Asconius, *in Milonianam* 43C; Suetonius, *Divus Augustus* 64. 2.

23. S. F. Bonner, *Education in Ancient Rome* (London, 1977), pp. 136ff.

24. Pliny, *Ep.* 5. 16; Plutarch, *Moralia* 453d; Musonius, pp. 13ff.

25. Statius, *Silvae* 3. 5. 63ff.; Soranus 1.4.23. Dancing; *ORF* I p. 133; Sallust, *Catiline* 25. 2; Horace, *Odes* 3. 6. 21–2, with Nisbet and Hubbard, *A Commentary on Horace Odes 2* (Oxford, 1978), pp. 181–2.

26. Pliny, *Ep.* 5. 16. The epitaph *ILS* 1030 says she lived *ann. XII men. XI d. VII*; Pliny that she died just before her fourteenth birthday, which seems to me a more likely time for her wedding (see below).

27. Amundsen and Diels, *Human Biology* 41 (1969), 125ff.; Soranus 1. 4. 20, 1. 5. 25.

28. *Digest* 23. 2. 4; cf. Dio 54. 6. 7; *Digest* 23. 1. 9. Republican precedent, *Digest* 12. 4. 8; adultery, 48. 5. 14. 8.

29. On the age of Octavia, daughter of Claudius, who is sometimes cited as a pre-pubertal bride, see R. M. Geer, *TAPhA* 62 (1931), 65–7.

30. Rufus ap. Oribasius (ed. Bussemaker-Daremberg), 3. p. 87.

31. Places to go: Ovid, *Amores* 3. 633ff., Tibullus 1. 6. 15ff., Martial 11. 7. Decorum: Seneca, *Controversiae* 2. 7. 3. Dinner-parties: Ovid, *Ars Am.* 1. 565ff., *Amores* 1. 4; Horace, *Odes* 3. 6. 21ff., Varro ap. Nonius p. 372L; Suetonius, *Divus Claudius* 32.

32. *ILLRP* 973; *ILS* 8393 line 30; Tacitus, *Ann.* 5. 1.

33. *RE* Tullius 60; K. Hopkins, *Population Studies* 20 (1966), 245ff.

34. Gordon Williams, *JRS* 48 (1958), 16ff.; *Tradition and Originality in Roman Poetry* (Oxford, 1968), pp. 370ff.

35. I. Kajanto, *Arctos* 7 (1972), 13ff.

36. Marriage-law, J. A. Crook, *Law and Life of Rome* (London, 1967), pp. 100ff. Divorce by women married *cum manu*, Gaius, *Institutes* 1. 137a (against, Alan Watson, *The Law of Persons in the Later Roman Republic* [Oxford, 1967], ch. 6); control of property, Gellius 17. 6.

37. Digest 24. 1. 1, 24. 1. 40 and 42; 48. 5. 23–4. On changing patterns of marriage and parental control, see S. B. Pomeroy, *Ancient Society* 7 (1976), 215ff.

38. Dowry problems, Cic. *Att.* 14. 14. 1, *ad Fam.* 6. 18. 5; penalties, Cic. *Topica* 4. 19ff., Seneca, *Controversiae* 2. 7. 1. Divorce at a lower economic level, I. Kajanto, *REL* 47 bis (1970), 99ff.

39. Balsdon, *Roman Women*, p. 55.

40. F. Schulz, *Roman Classical Law*, p. 103. The then state of English divorce law does much to explain this remark.

41. Dionysius of Halicarnassus, *Roman Antiquities* 2.25.4.

42. *Tutela mulierum*: Gaius, *Institutes* 1. 190, Cicero, *pro Murena* 27; Schulz, op. cit., pp. 188ff.

43. J. A. Crook, *CQ* 17 (1967), 113ff.; Watson, op. cit., chs. 5 and 6.

44. Dio 48. 34. 3, 55. 10. 4; 48. 44. 4–5. Plutarch, *Antonius* 54. 2, 57. 3.

45. Tacitus, *Dialogus* 28. 8–9; Plutarch, *Tiberius Gracchus* 1. 4–5, *Gaius Gracchus* 4. 3–4; Pliny, *Natural History* 34. 31; Suetonius, *Divus Augustus* 61. 2; Nicolaus of Damascus, *FGH* 70 fr. 127.

46. Jolowicz and Nicholas, *Roman Law*$^3$ (Cambridge, 1972), pp. 246ff.; Alan Watson, *The Law of Succession in the Later Roman Republic* (Oxford, 1971), pp. 29ff.

47. Elizabeth Rawson, *Studies in Roman Property* (ed. M. I. Finley, Cambridge, 1976), p. 97.

48. Cicero, *Topica* 4. 18; *Digest* 4. 5

49. Fifty was taken to be the age of menopause: Amundsen and Diels, *Human Biology* 42 (1970), 79ff. Whether the *ius trium liberorum* (*FIRA* p. 457 ff., A.D. 9) was a real incentive to bear enough children to earn freedom from *tutela* would vary with character and circumstances.

50. *Digest* 3. 1. 5; Quintilian 1. 16, Appian, *Bell. Civ.* 4. 33.

51. Gaius, *Institutes* 1. 144; Cicero, *pro Murena* 27; Seneca, *Controversiae* 1. 6. 5; Seneca, *ad Marciam* 1. 1; Valerius Maximus 9. 1. 3.

52. Compare the provisions of the *senatusconsultum Claudianum*, which went against the *ius gentium* by reducing the status of the freeborn mother of a slave's child instead of letting her status determine that of the child. P. R. C. Weaver, *Familia Caesaris* (Cambridge, 1972), pp. 162 ff. argues that its motive was financial.

53. A. Motto, *Classical Weekly* 65 (1972), 155ff.

54. E. Gabba (ed.), *Appiani Bellorum Civilium Liber Quintus* (Florence, 1969), pp. xliiiff. On women at war, cf. Tacitus, *Ann.* 1. 69, 2. 55. 5.

55. R. Syme, *TAPhA* 104 (1960), 323ff. = *Roman Papers*, ed. E. Badian (Oxford, 1979), vol. 2, pp. 510 ff.

56. On cults, J. Gage, *Matronalia* (Paris, 1963); on the appeal of worship other than the established religion, Averil Cameron, *G & R* 27 (1980), 60ff. = pp. 26–35 in this collection.

57. Suetonius, *Divus Augustus* 63. 1, 64. 2; Tacitus, *Ann.* 5. 1. The *iius trium liberorum*, Dio 55. 2. Scribonia was less tactful than Livia: Suetonius, *Divus Augustus* 62. 1, 69. 1. On *univirae*, see Niall Rudd, *Lines of Enquiry* (Cambridge, 1976), pp. 42ff.: but I do not think the main point (p. 44) was that the *univira* was never divorced. A remarried widow would not be *univira* (see the instances in Seneca, *de Matrimonio* 74–7, fr. 13 Hasse).

58. Gordon Williams, *Tradition and Originality* (Oxford, 1968), pp. 525ff.

## ADDENDUM

There are three changes I would make in this paper. First, I would not be so dismissive of Sulpicia (see Jane McIntosh Snyder, *The Woman and the Lyre* [Bristol, 1989], ch. 5, for a survey of recent writing), and I would be even more wary of using poetry as a source for women's history (see Alison Sharrock, *JRS* 81 (1991), 36–49, with references to earlier discussions). Second, I do not think there was ever a law forbidding the exposure of newborn children: see now J. Boswell, *The Kindness of Strangers* (New York, 1988). Third, recent research suggests that Roman contraceptive medicine was more effective than you might think: see J. Riddle, *Past and Present* 132 (1991), 3–32.

Debate has continued on almost every topic mentioned. For reasons of space, I note only some important books on Roman women which have appeared since 1981: Judith Hallett, *Fathers and Daughters in Roman Society* (Princeton, 1984); Jane Gardner, *Women in Roman Law and Society* (London and Sydney, 1986); Beryl Rawson (ed.), *The Family in Ancient Rome* (London and Sydney, 1986) and *Marriage, Divorce and Children in Ancient Rome* (Oxford, 1991); Suzanne Dixon, *The Roman Mother* (London and Sydney, 1988) and *The Roman Family* (London and Baltimore, 1992); Susan Treggiari, *Roman Marriage* (Oxford, 1991).

# LOVE VERSUS THE LAW: AN ESSAY ON MENANDER'S *ASPIS*

*By* DOUGLAS M. MACDOWELL

I fell in love, not of my own free will,  
With your own sister, 'O dearest of mankind!'  
I did no hasty, wrong, unworthy act,  
But asked the uncle whom you left her to,  
And my own mother who has brought her up,  
To give her to me lawfully as wife.  
I though I was a lucky man in life;  
But just when I was sure that I had reached  
My very goal, I cannot even see her  
In future! The law gives someone else control  
Of her, and judges my claim worthless now.

(*Aspis* 288–98)

Thus Khaireas, on being deprived of the girl he loves by a legal obstacle. Menander is renowned as an author, perhaps even the inventor, of romantic comedy; and love triumphing over obstacles is a common feature of his plays. Usually the obstacle is a personal one, such as a father who refuses to permit a marriage (as in *Dyskolos*), and in *Aspis* too the difficulties are made by an unpleasant old man, Smikrines. But he has the law on his side, as Khaireas says. This speech, and the play as a whole, presents a sharper conflict between love and the law than we find elsewhere, and I believe that Menander's purpose here is a more serious one than has generally been realized.

My intention in this article is to examine the story of *Aspis* in relation to Athenian family law, and to consider what reaction Menander expected of his audience. The play gives us some excellent evidence about the rules governing family relationships, and, quite apart from its dramatic quality, is an important document for the study of Athenian society. The legal questions arising from it have been discussed in a good article by E. Karabelias;[1] but since his article appeared in a French journal of legal history, which classical scholars seldom read, I think it advisable to repeat some of his points here besides contributing others of my own.[2]

*Aspis* tells us about Kleostratos and his two uncles. Kleostratos is the young man whom the other characters at the beginning of the play believe to have been killed in a battle in Lykia; his faithful slave, Daos, brings home his young master's shield (from which the play takes its name) together with a quantity of money, slaves, and other booty captured on the campaign, and tells the sad story to the elder uncle, Smikrines. But the sombre tone of the opening scene is soon dispelled by the goddess Chance. In her speech (97–148, which is the prologue postponed, as in some other plays, till after the first scene) she tells the audience that Kleostratos has not really been killed at all but will turn up alive later, and she also gives information about the family.

Smikrines and Khairestratos are the brothers of Kleostratos' father. Kleostratos' father is evidently dead, and we are never told what his name was. Smikrines is older than Khairestratos, but we are not told whether Kleostratos' father was the eldest or the middle or the youngest brother. I place him on the right-hand side of the genealogy as if he were the youngest, but that is arbitrary.

Khairestratos has a wife and one daughter.[3] Khaireas is his stepson, the son of his wife by her previous husband. We are not told why she has been married twice. Divorce was quite easy in Athens; any husband could send his wife back to her family, provided that he paid back the dowry as well. However, in this instance we should assume that the previous husband of Khairestratos' wife had not divorced her, but had simply died. The reason for thinking that is that Khaireas has been brought up in Khairestratos' household (263), whereas it would have been his own father's responsibility to bring him up if his father had still been living. A modern divorce court often awards custody of children to the mother, but the *kyrios* of an Athenian child was always his father if the father was alive. We can imagine, if we wish, that the father of Khaireas assigned his wife and son to Khairestratos on his deathbed, just as the father of Demosthenes assigned his wife and son to Aphobos (Dem. 27.4–5).

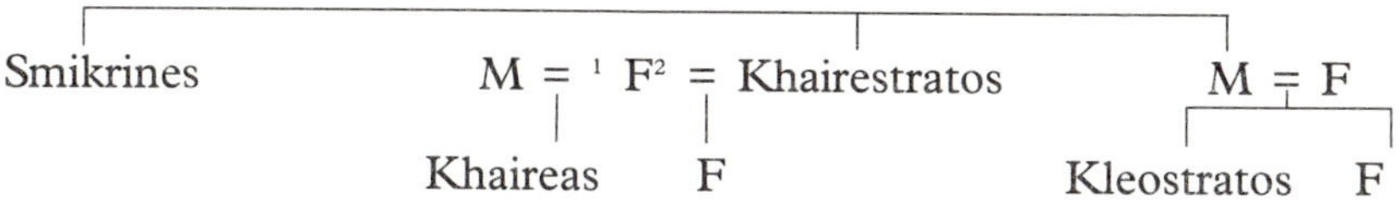


The other member of the family is the sister of Kleostratos, and one of the interesting things about this family is what happened to her when Kleostratos went away to the war. He left her to his uncle Khairestratos (127, 292), who not only brought her up in his house, but took steps some time later to give her in marriage to Khaireas (130–7). What right had he to do that? In Athens the only person who could give a woman in marriage was her *kyrios*, the man in charge of her, who was responsible for providing her home and upkeep and whom in return she had to obey. Until she was married her father was her *kyrios*; or, if he had died, his heir. Kleostratos therefore was *kyrios* of his sister, and he was the man who had authority to make a betrothal (*engye*) for her. *Aspis* 127–37 shows that a man who expected to be away for a long period could transfer this power to someone else, making him the *kyrios* of the woman temporarily.[4] That was not clearly known before the rediscovery of this play.[5]

Neither Smikrines nor Khairestratos has a son to be his heir, but both make reference to the plans which they had for disposal of their property on death. This matter, the inheritance of the property of a man who dies leaving no son, is the subject of a law which has been preserved for us in the text of the speech *Against Makartatos*:

Whoever dies without making a will, his property, together with his daughters if he leaves any, is to be taken over by the following persons: brothers by the same father, if there are any; and if there are legitimate sons of brothers, they are to get their father's share; and if there are no brothers or brothers' sons, . . .

(Law quoted in Dem. 43.51)

This law gives rules for *epidikasia*, adjudgement of an estate to heirs. Any claimant (except a son or grandson of the deceased) had to apply to the arkhon, who made a formal award of the inheritance (*epidikasia*) or in disputed cases referred it to a jury for a decision (*diadikasia*). But the arkhon and jury were not free to decide as they liked; they had to keep to the rules.[6] Unless there was doubt about a person's relationship or legitimacy or about the validity of a will (questions which do not arise in *Aspis*), *epidikasia* was normally just a formality. In *Aspis* there is hardly any allusion to the formal legal proceedings, which do not affect the story. What is of interest is the rules specifying which claims are valid.

Take Smikrines' property first. He is unmarried and has no children, but he has had two brothers, Khairestratos, who is still alive, and Kleostratos' father, who is dead. According to law, therefore, if Smikrines dies, his property should be shared equally by Khairestratos and Kleostratos, as the son of the other brother. But that is not what Smikrines says. When grieving, or perhaps shedding crocodile tears, for the supposed death of Kleostratos, he says:

I do wish he were still alive! He was
The man to manage this and, when I die,
To take control of all my property
According to the laws.

(*Aspis* 168–71)

Why 'all'? According to the law just quoted, Kleostratos should have inherited only half of Smikrines' property. Karabelias has drawn attention to this problem, and the solution which he suggests is simply that Smikrines is not telling the truth: Kleostratos would not have been the heir to all Smikrines' property, but Smikrines wants to create the impression that he would have been, because that will encourage people to think that, in the situation as it actually is believed to be, with Kleostratos dead and

Smikrines still alive, Smikrines should take over all Kleostratos' property.[7] That is an ingenious explanation of the difficult word 'all'. But I am not convinced that it is right. I concede that Smikrines is the sort of character who might well tell a lie, and that Menander might well make him tell a lie, so as to show what a bad character he is. But that point would be lost if the audience did not realize that the remark was in fact a lie, and the passage contains no indication, such as a comment by Daos, to alert the audience to the possibility that Smikrines is lying.

I therefore prefer a different explanation. A man who had no son could adopt one, either during his lifetime or by leaving a will to take effect on his death. (It was not possible to make someone your heir without making him your son.) In the surviving forensic speeches, especially those of Isaios, we read of a number of men who did this, and indeed it may have been the normal practice in the fourth century for a man without sons. So I take Smikrines' reference to 'the laws' (in 168–71) to mean the laws about adoption and wills. In effect he is saying (though perhaps insincerely) 'I intended to adopt Kleostratos as my son and heir'.

Now take Khairestratos. His circumstances differ from Smikrines' because, though he has no son, he does have a daughter, who may eventually produce a grandson for him. This grandson would be his heir; but if Khairestratos should die before a grandson is born or while the grandson is still a child, the boy's father, the husband of Khairestratos' daughter, will have charge of the property until the grandson comes of age in his eighteenth year. That was the rule; but how can it be reconciled with what Khairestratos says to Khaireas?[8]

I always used to think
That you would take this girl, and he himself
My daughter, and that I would leave you both
To take control of all my property.

(*Aspis* 278–81)

The plan was that Khaireas would marry Kleostratos' sister, and Kleostratos would marry Khairestratos' daughter. But that should mean that Kleostratos would take control of Khairestratos' property, not 'you' in the plural; what right would Khaireas have to it? The solution must be, in this case also, adoption: Khairestratos means that he intended to adopt his stepson Khaireas to be his own son. But this leads to a complex situation. Whose is the right to inherit if a man at death leaves an adopted son and also a daughter of his own?

The accepted view hitherto has been: 'If there were daughters but no sons [a man] could adopt a son on condition that he married [him] to one of the daughters.'[9] That would mean that, if Khairestratos adopted Khaireas, Khaireas would have to marry Khairestratos' daughter. But that would be impossible: she was Khaireas' half-sister, by the same mother; marriage with her would have been incestuous and illegal. Could a man with a daughter never adopt his own stepson, then? Yes, he could; the accepted view is wrong, and an exception was allowed to the rule that an adopted son must marry the daughter (if there was one) of his adoptive father. The instance which shows this most clearly is in Menander's *Dyskolos*. There Knemon has no son, but he has a daughter, and he also has a stepson, Gorgias, the son of his wife by a previous husband. Thus his family is exactly parallel to Khairestratos'. When he has just been rescued from the well and thinks that he will quite probably die, he says to Gorgias:

Whether I
Die at once—I think I shall, too; I'm in quite a poorly state—
Or survive, I now adopt you as my son. Regard as yours
All that I possess at present. I transfer[10] this girl to you;
You procure a husband for her. Even in the best of health
By myself I'll never find one; nobody will ever seem
Satisfactory to me. But let me live the way I like;
Do the rest yourself, take over. Thank the gods, you've got some sense.
You're a suitable protector of your sister. Give her half
Of my property as dowry, measuring it equally;
Take the other half, and with it keep me and your mother too.

(*Dyskolos* 729–39)

With these words Knemon adopts Gorgias as his son. But Gorgias is not to marry Knemon's daughter; he cannot do so, because she is his half-sister. Instead he is to find her a husband, and give half of Knemon's property with her as dowry, while taking over the other half himself. I suspect that this half-and-half arrangement was required by law when a man having no son adopted his stepson but also had a daughter of his own. Evidently this was Khairestratos' plan too: Khaireas, as his adopted son, would take over half his property, while Kleostratos, as the husband of his daughter, would take charge of the other half and pass it on eventually to Khairestratos' grandson.[11]

So much for the circumstances and plans of the family in the lifetime of Kleostratos. I pass now to the situation when Kleostratos is believed to have been killed. His death leaves his sister in the position of *epiklēros*, because there is no surviving male descendant of her father (141). The peculiar situation of an Athenian 'heiress' is well known and may be summarized briefly. She did not herself become the owner of the property, in the sense of being able to dispose of it as she wished; it just remained with her, waiting to be inherited by her eventual son. Her deceased father's nearest male relative could claim her as his wife, and so could get control and use of the property until a son came of age, which would be a period of at least eighteen years. (No matter if he was already married; he could divorce his present wife to marry the *epiklēros*.) If the nearest relative did not want to claim the *epiklēros* in marriage, then the next nearest could do so. But the hand of the *epiklēros* and the control of the property went together; it was not possible to obtain either without the other.

Kleostratos had little property when he went away to the campaign (131–2), not even enough to provide an adequate dowry for his sister (8–9). But in the course of the fighting he acquired a quantity of booty, which Daos has brought home: 600 gold coins, silver cups weighing about 40 mnai, a quantity of cloaks, and a crowd of slaves (34–7, 82–9, 138–41), amounting in all to a value of 4 talents (351). All this booty is paraded across the stage in the opening scene before the eyes of the avaricious old man, Smikrines, who at once becomes keen to claim the girl in marriage, so as to get his hands on it. The audience's attention is drawn to this prospect as soon as Daos calls Smikrines *klēronome* (85), a word which should not be translated 'heir' but rather 'estate-holder',[12] since he will not formally be the owner of the property but will merely have control of it. Smikrines' claim takes priority over any claim by his brother Khairestratos. Here we find the solution of a problem which remained unsolved before the rediscovery of *Aspis*. It was known that the nearest male relative of the deceased man had first claim to an *epiklēros* if he wished to claim her, but it was not known who had first claim if there were several relatives equally near, if the deceased man left several brothers, or several uncles, or several first cousins. The suggestion that in such a case the eldest had priority was no more than a guess, since there was no evidence. Now *Aspis* provides evidence showing that the guess was right. Smikrines is stated to have the prior claim to the *epiklēros* because he is older than Khairestratos (142–3, 255).[13] The discovery is interesting, because Athenian law did not otherwise recognize a right of primogeniture; brothers inherited equal shares of their father's property, and there was no advantage in being the eldest. But an *epiklēros* had to be an exception, because she was not divisible, and we note that in this case the Athenians did accept age (rather than other methods of discrimination, such as drawing lots) as the ground of preference. Nevertheless, the primary consideration was proximity of relationship, and age was used only as a tie-breaker.[14]

When Smikrines proposes to claim Kleostratos' sister in marriage, Khairestratos tries to persuade him not to do so but to let Khaireas marry her. Knowing that his brother's desire is really for the property, not for the girl, he offers to let him keep the property, if he will let the girl go (260–9). Smikrines scornfully rejects this suggestion. He knows that, if Khaireas marries the girl and they have a son, the son will have the legal right to the property, regardless of any promises given by Khairestratos or anyone else (269–73). This exemplifies the rule that property passing with an *epiklēros* did not belong to her, and could not legally be disposed of by her or her husband, but belonged to her eventual son. It also enables us to solve another long-standing legal puzzle.[15] Is the woman in such a case, when first her father and then her brother has died, leaving no male descendants, to be regarded as the *epiklēros* of her father's estate or of her brother's? Some scholars have thought the former, believing that only a daughter became an *epiklēros* whereas a sister inherited in her own right. But *Aspis* 269–73 indicates that the other view is correct. The booty which Kleostratos captured in the war is undoubtedly his property, and cannot be regarded as part of his father's estate, since his father died before it was acquired. Yet it is this booty which, as Smikrines knows, can be claimed in due course by the son of Kleostratos' sister. She and Khairestratos (who is her present *kyrios*) would be willing to give it to Smikrines in exchange for her being allowed to have Khaireas as her husband (264–7); but, as Smikrines points out, they have no power to do so. This shows that she does not own it herself; it merely rests with her temporarily until she has a son to inherit it. Thus we have here, for the first time, a clear instance of a woman who is the *epiklēros* of her brother's estate.[16]

Now we come to the plot devised by Daos to get Smikrines to give the girl up. It is pretended that Khairestratos has died. Since he has a daughter and no sons (for his projected adoption of Khaireas has not yet been carried out), that makes his daughter an *epiklēros* too. Smikrines is, in this case also, the nearest male relative, and he will undoubtedly choose the girl with the larger estate:

> *Daos*: Your daughter then becomes an *epiklēros*,
> Just like the girl now to be claimed at law.
> You possess sixty talents, I should think;
> The other girl has four. The old miser has
> The same relationship to both.
> *Khairestratos:* I see now!
> *Daos*: If you're not made of rock! He'll give the one
> Gladly, before three thousand witnesses,
> To the first man who asks, and take the other.
>
> (*Aspis* 348–55)

The plan is based on the assumption that Smikrines can, if he wishes, give Kleostratos's sister in marriage to Khaireas (or to anyone else he chooses). How can he do so? If he forgoes his own right to marry her, can she not be claimed by the next nearest male relative, presumably a cousin of Smikrines and Khairestratos? For an answer to this problem we must turn to the law concerning the position of an *epiklēros* who belonged to the *thētikon telos*, the lowest income-class. This law is referred to by Isaios (1.39) and fully quoted in the speech *Against Makartatos:*

As for all *epiklēroi* of the *thētikon telos*, if the nearest relative does not wish to have her, let him give her away; a *pentakosiomedimnos* is to give with her ⟨as dowry⟩ 500 drachmas, a *hippeus* 300, and a *zeugitēs* 150, in addition to her own property.

(Law quoted in Dem. 43.54)

This is a law designed to protect a poor *epiklēros*, whom no one wanted to claim, and who might otherwise be left unmarried and unprotected; the nearest relative, if he does not wish to marry her himself, must find her a husband and provide a dowry out of his own pocket. Membership of the classes depended on income, not on capital. Kleostratos' booty is a capital gain, but the income-producing property which he has left is very small (131–2). So naturally his sister is an *epiklēros* of the lowest class. Therefore Smikrines, if he does not wish to marry her himself, is not merely able but actually required by law to give her away to another husband. He will also have to give a dowry for her, 500 drachmas if he is himself of the highest class; but he will regard that outlay as trivial, if it leaves him free to claim Khairestratos' daughter and 60 talents.

Daos' plan is that, as soon as possible after Khairestratos' supposed death, Khaireas will ask Smikrines to give him Kleostratos' sister in marriage. Smikrines is expected to agree to that immediately, and also to take the normal legal steps to claim Khairestratos' daughter as his own wife. Once Kleostratos' sister is safely married to Khaireas, Khairestratos will emerge from his hiding-place; he will then be able to reassert his authority as *kyrios* of his own daughter, and refuse to give her in marriage to Smikrines. Even if Smikrines has gone ahead so fast that he has already married her, Khairestratos can still reclaim her; a father had the right to take his daughter away from her husband, effecting a divorce, at least if she had not yet had a child.[17] But will not Smikrines then retaliate by reverting to his original plan, taking Kleostratos' sister away from Khaireas and marrying her himself? Here is another point at which *Aspis* gives us new information about Athenian law. A basic assumption of Daos' plan is that, once the girl is married to Khaireas, Smikrines will not be able to reclaim her when he discovers that he has been tricked. We may draw the conclusion that, unlike a father, a relative who gave away in marriage an *epiklēros* of the lowest income-class did not have the legal right to take her back again.

Most of the later part of the play is lost, but the ending is easily guessed. Kleostratos turns up alive and well; we have some fragments of the scene in which he arrives (491 ff.). He gives his sister to Khaireas, Khairestratos gives his daughter to Kleostratos, and a double wedding is arranged (521). Perhaps the cook and the waiter, dismissed when the earlier wedding was called off (216–49) are now summoned back to prepare for the new festivities; and Smikrines, who has in the end gained nothing at all, is probably mocked in some way, like Knemon at the end of *Dyskolos*.

The plot of *Aspis* is very neatly constructed, in a manner characteristic of Menander. It tells a story of contemporary life, consisting of incidents which really could have occurred in Athens at the end of the fourth century. The particular incident which sets the train of events in motion, the wrong identification of a body after a battle, though doubtless unusual, was certainly not impossible. This is Mr Puff's kind of drama: 'A play is not to show occurrences that happen every day, but things just so strange, that though they never *did*, they *might* happen.'[18] It is, in its way, instructive to the spectators. It broadens their experience by showing them events which might happen to themselves one day.

But it is also Miss Prism's kind of story: 'The good ended happily, and the bad unhappily. That is what Fiction means.'[19] Menander is not a neutral writer. He wishes his audience to regard some characters and some actions as good, and others as bad, and he so contrives his plot that the good ones succeed in the end. In particular, Smikrines is presented as being wholly bad, the worst character in all Menander's extant plays. Just in case anyone in the audience is uncertain how to judge him, Menander provides an assessment with the goddess's authority: 'in wickedness, he's beaten all mankind' (116–17). But what does he do in the play to deserve this sweeping condemnation? He simply attempts to exercise his legal rights. His attempt to claim Kleostratos' sister as his wife, on the assumption that Kleostratos is dead, is in perfect accord with the rules of Athenian law.

The implication, that it is wrong to act in accordance with the law, is astonishing. Perhaps we should be less astonished if we found it in Aristophanes. The mischievous heroes of Old Comedy do sometimes try to evade the law; the aim of Strepsiades in *Clouds*, for instance, is to avoid paying his debts. But in the douce families of New Comedy we expect to find ourselves siding with law-abiding characters. And what Smikrines does is to try to uphold the law about *epiklēroi*. This law was not a recent and controversial innovation. It was a custom of immemorial origin, and its purpose was the preservation of families and their property. But it took no account of love.

Menander has set up a confrontation between this law and love. He has drawn his characters in such a way as to make the audience side with love and against the law, and he makes love victorious in the end. He wants the audience to regard the law as stupid and wrong; love is a better reason for making a marriage. This view was new, as far as we can tell; there is no evidence that the law about *epiklēroi* had been publicly criticized before. Surely one of Menander's purposes in writing this play was to make the

Athenians consider seriously whether the law ought to be changed. Perhaps he was more of a social and moral revolutionary than has hitherto been realized.

## NOTES

1. E. Karabelias, 'Une nouvelle source pour l'étude du droit attique: le *Bouclier* de Ménandre', *Revue Historique de Droit Français et Étranger* 48 (1970), 357–89. There is also an article by J. E. Karnezis, 'Misrepresentation of Attic law in Menander's *Aspis*', *Platon* 29 (1977), 152–5, but his approach seems to me wrong: when we find in Menander a legal feature not mentioned elsewhere, we should use that as new evidence, not pillory it as an error or distortion by Menander. The present article shows how I believe everything in *Aspis* can be interpreted in accordance with Athenian law.

2. Some of these points were presented at the Glasgow-Edinburgh seminar on ancient drama in March 1977, and briefly in my book *The Law in Classical Athens* (London, 1978), pp. 97–8. The translations here are my own, but to anyone wishing to read the play in English I commend W. G. Arnott's version in the Loeb series (Cambridge, Mass. and London, 1979).

3. Khairestratos had his daughter by his present wife, not by a previous wife, for it seems that she is a half-sister of Khaireas, as argued later in this article; cf. note 11.

4. Cf. Karabelias, 366–8. But it remains obscure how this is to be reconciled with the text of the law about ἐγγύη, which is preserved in Dem. 46.18. Possibly it is covered by the last clause of the law: ὅτῳ ἂν ἐπιτρέψῃ, τοῦτον κύριον εἶναι. However, that clause appears to be subject to the condition ἐὰν μηδεὶς ᾖ τούτων, so that it refers only to a woman who has no father or brother (by the same father) or paternal grandfather alive. So it seems more likely that temporary transfer of the power of a κύριος was authorized by another law which has not been preserved.

5. There is a less clear instance in Plaut. *Trin.* 1156. Charmides has been away on a journey to Asia, and during his absence his son Lesbonicus has betrothed his sister, Charmides' daughter, to Lysiteles. This may well have been taken over without alteration by Plautus from the Athenian play on which *Trinummus* is based (Philemon's *Thesauros*).

6. Philokleon's boast that he ignores the rules (*Wasps* 583–6) is Aristophanes' joke, perhaps based on some recent notorious misjudgement, but not on normal practice.

7. Karabelias, 369–70; cf. Gomme and Sandbach, *Menander, a Commentary* (Oxford, 1973), pp. 76–7.

8. The lines are defective in the manuscript, but the general sense is certain. I have translated the supplements adopted by Arnott in the Loeb edition.

9. A. R. W. Harrison, *The Law of Athens* i (Oxford, 1968), 85.

10. The word παρεγγυῶ is worth noting. It may well be the formal term used by the *kyrios* of a woman to transfer her to another *kyrios*, other than a husband (just as ἐγγυῶ is used to transfer her to a husband); we may imagine Kleostratos using it when he entrusted his sister to Khairestratos. Cf. U. E. Paoli, *Altri studi di diritto greco e romano* (Milan, 1976), p. 568.

11. This appears to be the only possible explanation of the plural ὑμᾶς in line 281. It is the reason for believing that Khairestratos' daughter and Khaireas had the same mother; otherwise Khaireas, as Khairestratos' adopted son, would have had to marry his daughter.

12. κληρονόμος is derived from νέμω, which means 'occupy' or 'manage' rather than 'own'.

13. Arnott's translation, generally very accurate, seems to be incorrect in 142–3. τῷ χρόνῳ προὔχων means not 'despite his age' but 'being ahead ⟨of his brother⟩ in age'.

14. It is not correct to say that the law gave the option of claiming an *epiklēros* 'to her male relatives in order of their seniority' (Arnott's note on line 187). An older second cousin would not have priority over a younger first cousin, for example.

15. Karabelias, 372–5, discusses the puzzle, but overlooks the usefulness of lines 269–73 for solving it.

16. An alternative hypothesis might run as follows. Kleostratos' sister does own the property herself, but the law forbids a woman to dispose of property worth more than one medimnos of barley (Isaios 10.10); so, when she dies, her son will claim that she cannot have given it away and that he now inherits it. I reject this hypothesis, because Smikrines in lines 269–73 is clearly not

looking ahead to the time of the woman's death (which would probably be long after his own), but envisages that a claim may be made by (or on behalf of) the son at any time after his birth.

17. Dem. 41.4, Men. *Epitrepontes* 657–8, *Didot Papyrus* 1 (*Menander*, ed. Sandbach, pp. 328–30); cf. Paoli, op. cit., pp. 385–91.

18. Sheridan, *The Critic*, act 2 scene 1.

19. Wilde, *The Importance of Being Earnest*, act 2.

## ADDENDUM

I have left the text of this article unchanged from its original publication in 1982, but readers should note that some of my conclusions have been challenged by P. G. McC. Brown, 'Menander's Dramatic Technique and the Law of Athens', *CQ* 33 (1983), 412–20. He rejects my suggestion that Menander is finding fault with the law about *epiklēroi*, on the ground that Smikrines had another, more acceptable course of action open to him which would not have infringed the law. But I do not find this objection convincing. Menander does not show Smikrines following another course of action; he shows him insisting on his right to marry an *epiklēros*, which was the normal thing for a relative to do according to the law, but which Menander presents as unacceptable.

Brown discusses particularly lines 353–5, where Daos predicts that Smikrines, if he has a choice between two *epiklēroi*, will give the poorer of them, Kleostratos' sister, in marriage to the first man who asks. As I explain above, this will be true only if the girl belongs to the lowest class, the *thētikon telos*. Brown denies that she belongs to that class, because she now has the booty acquired by Kleostratos in the war; he says that there is no evidence that membership of the *thētikon telos* depended on income only. It is true that there is not much evidence about how the four classes were defined, but the main evidence that does exist (Arist. *Ath. Pol.* 7.4) certainly refers to agricultural income, which would not include booty acquired in war, and except for the booty the assets of Kleostratos and his sister are undoubtedly modest (131–2). Thus Brown has not really made good his claim that lines 353–5 are inaccurate.

His main contention, however, is that Menander and his audience were not particularly concerned with legal details. It seems to me that any audience is likely to contain some individuals who are interested and knowledgeable about legal matters and some who are not; but in ancient Athens, where thousands of citizens served regularly on juries, those having some knowledge of the law must have formed a higher proportion of the theatre audience than in most other communities, and they would have been likely to think a play silly if it blatantly contradicted what they knew to be the legal realities. *Aspis*, more than any other surviving Greek play, has a plot which depends on legal rules. Any spectator who did not know what an *epiklēros* was, or which relative had the right to marry her, would not understand this play at all. I believe, therefore, that Menander did expect most of his audience to have a knowledge of the law about *epiklēroi*.

# WIVES AND HUSBANDS

*By* MARY R. LEFKOWITZ

If recently feminist writers have placed too much emphasis on the restrictions and limitations of ancient women's lives, at least they have provided some compensation for the apologetic and uncritical estimations made before the Civil Rights Movement of the 1960s.[1] These earlier studies had tended to single out the accomplishments of certain exceptional women; they tended also to leave the impression that since most ancient women did not appear to have complained about the kind of lives they led, they regarded the customs and laws that governed their lives as equitable and natural. It is easy (at least now) to see that neither premise is acceptable.

First, and most obviously, women's silence about their lot cannot be taken as acceptance, because most of the writing about women in the ancient world was done by *men*. Nor can one assume from the existence of extraordinary achievement that most women found such roles attainable or desirable. For example, Artemisia of Halicarnassus the sea captain (Hdt. 8.87–8) and Cynna the Illyrian strategist (Ath. 13.560F) had 'professions' because their fathers were kings. Cynisca of Sparta in the early fourth century claims to have been the first woman to have won the four-horse chariot race (*A.P.* 13.16), but then she too was the daughter of a king; another female chariot-race winner was Bilistiche, the *hetaera* (or mistress) of Ptolemy Philadelphus, king of Egypt (*P. Oxy.* 2082). If women like Sappho or Corinna were able to be poets, it is in large measure because women could compose verse at home without moving outside of the ordinary routine of women's existence. Aristocratic women in all periods composed poetry: the Argive poet Telesilla was said to have studied music because she was sickly (Plut. *Mor.* 245c); we still have a papyrus fragment of Erinna's epic poem 'The Distaff' (*Gk. Lit. Pap.* 120); epigrams by several Hellenistic women are preserved in the Greek Anthology.

On the other hand, is it really fair to imply, as some of us have done, that ancient women would have wanted to live differently had they had the opportunity? What if any evidence can be found to support such a claim? For many years I doubted whether many intelligent women took pleasure in leading an anonymous life of service to husband and family, but now I wonder if I have not been judging ancient women, as I judge myself, by male standards of accomplishment. Now I would like to re-examine in detail several documents in which it is possible to discern some of the positive aspects of conventional life. Necessarily, much of what I will have to say concerns the nature of the evidence, because as so often in studying the ancient world, we are compelled to rely on scattered and fragmentary information.

To begin with, we had better ask from a man's point of view what kind of women's behaviour wins praise. The basic categories are clearly set forth in Semonides of Amorgos' celebrated satire on women (fr. 7 West). In this poem, as so often, the good is defined primarily by means of the bad. The one laudable type of female, the bee woman, is described after a list of eight despicable ones, and since the bee woman herself is followed by reflections on women's deceptiveness, the poet leaves the impression that a good woman is (to say the least) exceptional, because she occupies only 11 of the surviving 118 lines of his poem:[2]

> Another is from a bee; the man who gets her is fortunate, for on her alone blame does not settle. She causes his property to grow and increase, and she grows old with a husband whom she loves and who loves her, the mother of a handsome and reputable family. She stands out among all women, and a godlike beauty plays about her. She takes no pleasure in sitting among women in places where they tell stories about love. Women like her are the best and most sensible whom Zeus bestows on men. (lines 83-93)

Some of this positive description is expressed in negative terms: 'on her alone blame does not settle' (line 84) and then 'she takes no pleasure in sitting among women in places where they tell stories about love' (*aphrodisious logous*); also, except for the phrase 'she grows old with a husband whom she loves', nothing is said about how *she* feels; the rest is stated from her husband's point of view: she causes his property to increase, he loves her, she had fine children; she stands out among all women (the phrase implies heroic stature).[3] If such women are judged best and 'most sensible', it is because their lives are dedicated to serving their husbands and maintaining their households. It is significant that the bee woman is praised for not talking with other women about sex, first because that would encourage infidelity, and second because it would take her away from work or even send her outside the home in order to meet with other women.

It is easy enough to understand from Semonides' poem why her husband loves her, but why does *she* love her husband? Since the only woman poet we know about who was roughly contemporary with Semonides—Sappho—did not write poetry about women's affection for men, we must turn to poetry by men for information. I suggest that we begin with Penelope and Alcestis; they are the archetypes of good women, at least according to a husband in a fourth-century comedy, who can only come up with those two names to set against a long list of bad women (Eubulus, fr. 116, 117K).[4] Penelope conforms to Semonides' negative criteria: she remains faithful to her husband for twenty years, despite constant temptation; she stays in her rooms in the palace, except for brief public appearances when she is accompanied by maids or her son Telemachus. She does not associate with other women (except for the female slaves who attend her). Everyone acknowledges that she is superior to all other women, particularly for her intelligence:[5]

> Skill in exquisite workmanship, a keen mind, subtlety—these she has beyond anything we have heard of even in the ladies of olden times . . . not one of these had the mastery in devising things that Penelope has . . . (*Od.* 2.116–22)

This description, which is offered by the suitor Antinous, suggests that hers is a special kind of intelligence, involving plotting and planning that seem to men devious because they cannot immediately understand it. As Semonides said 'in the beginning the god (i.e., Zeus) made the female mind separately'. But Penelope uses her particular intelligence to remain faithful to her husband, first by tricking the suitors for three years by unravelling at night the shroud she was weaving (in Antinous' words, 'a trick that went beyond all reason', 2.222) and then by testing Odysseus to see if he really was her husband, by pretending not to know the secret of the construction of their marriage bed (23.177ff.). Certainly by the end of the *Odyssey* we understand why Odysseus was willing to give up Calypso and a promise of immortality to return to Penelope, even though, as he says to Calypso, 'I know that my wise Penelope, when a man looks at her, is far beneath you in form and stature' (5.217). But why does Penelope wait for Odysseus?

In part, it is because Odysseus, as Penelope herself says, was 'peerless'; 'his fame has gone through the length and breadth of Hellas and Argos' (1.344); in part also, it is his house, which he himself helped to build, 'a house so beautiful and so filled with treasures, a house that sometimes, I think, I shall remember, though it be only in my dreams' (21.77–9). But there is also the matter of reputation: she wonders 'if I should stay with my son and keep everything unchanged, my estate, my waiting-women, my lofty-roofed house itself—respecting my husband's bed and the people's voice' (19.524–6). As she says after she has recognized Odysseus, 'there was Argive Helen, child of Zeus, never would she have lain with a foreign lover if she had but known that the warrior sons of the Achaeans were to carry her back again to her own land' (23.218–21). Helen's action was wrong because it caused suffering and death for so many; Penelope also calls it 'folly' (*atē*, line 223) because it seems clear to her that Helen would not have left Menelaus had she been free to remain; as Homer shows in Book 4, Helen has no complaint about her life with Menelaus after the Trojan War in his fine house in Sparta. It is possible to infer from Penelope's remarks that a woman has reason to be faithful if her husband is a person entitled to respect, and if she herself is well-treated; certainly both she and Helen, because of their husbands' wealth and position, live in security and comfort.

What else does Penelope expect (and get) from Odysseus? First of all, proof that she in her way is as important to him as he is to her. She does not demand strict fidelity; neither she nor Helen object to their husbands' liaisons with other women, so long as they are temporary; Odysseus tells Penelope about Circe and Calypso; Menelaus is able jointly to celebrate the marriage of Hermione, his daughter by Helen, and of Megapenthes, his son by a slave woman (4.4). But, as her questions about their bed indicate, it is important that they sleep together; also that he tell her immediately what he knows about his future plans, since that will affect both of them. Odysseus listens to her describing her experiences with the suitors before he tells her about his journey. But Penelope does not question his right to tell her what to do, or seek to persuade him not to set out again for new battles and journeys, since it is success in these that defines his importance in the world, and to her, because she counts on him (in a society without police and law courts) to protect her against their many enemies.

Alcestis, at least as Euripides portrays her, lives in a world that is not presently threatened with human violence; yet her attitude towards her husband Admetus is much the same as Penelope's to Odysseus. She is, of course, classified as 'good' because she offered to die in her husband's stead, when no one else, not even his aged parents, would volunteer. Euripides' drama takes place on the day of her death; like John of Gaunt in *Richard II*, she speaks portentous last words on stage, but Euripides also conveys to us her more private thoughts, by having one of her women slaves report to the chorus what Alcestis said in her own quarters, before she comes out of the palace for the last time to be seen by the community at large. These private words and actions conform to the pattern of behaviour that society (to judge from Semonides) would approve. She washes and dresses in special clothing (like Socrates before he drinks the hemlock, in consideration for the women who must prepare her corpse for burial). Then she prays that her children both make good marriages and live full lives; she sees that the appropriate myrtle boughs are placed on the altars; all this calmly, without shedding a tear. But even when she does break down and cry, her thoughts are for her husband, her children, and her household. First she addresses her marriage bed, 'here I lost my maidenhood to this man, on whose behalf I die; farewell, I do not hate you; you have destroyed only me, for since I was reluctant to betray you and my husband I am dying. Another woman will possess you; not more chaste, but perhaps more fortunate' (lines 177–82). Then she throws herself on the bed, weeping, and walks about the room only to throw herself on the bed again; her children cling to her, and she embraces them;

all the slaves are weeping, but she gives her hand to each and speaks to every one of them, even the most lowly. In all this time she does not confide specially in another woman, not even a sister or a nurse; her sorrow, like Penelope's, is private, and we learn of it only at second hand.

Alcestis' public appearances, like Penelope's, are conducted with dignity and control. After she is carried outside, she addresses Admetus and reminds him of the reasons she decided to die for him, but again without complaint. She could have lived and married another king, but she did not want to live without him, with orphaned children, since she had had 'all she needed to be happy' (line 289). Nor did she want to deprive his parents, who were too old to have children, of their only son. She asks Admetus only one favour, not to marry again, because she does not want to have a stepmother for her children who would wish to put her own children ahead of Alcestis' (lines 305–7). She is not asking him to be celibate or not to take a concubine, but specifically not to acquire another legitimate wife, and Admetus himself readily agrees 'even in death you will be called my wife' (lines 329–30); it is testimony of his remarkable devotion to her that at the end of the play he is reluctant even to accept a concubine, when Heracles appears to be offering him one.

In a society like ours, where male and female lives have under the law at least an equal value, Admetus might seem unduly selfish because he allows Alcestis to die for him. Some have even sensed hypocrisy in his request to her, 'do not betray us' (lines 202, 250, 275), even though that is what survivors might say to the dead person on grave inscriptions (e.g., 'you rush off to the gods, Domnina, and forget your husband').[6] But it is important to note that Alcestis, even behind the scenes, is never represented as having hesitated over or complained about her decision. Admetus himself does not question her decision until after his father has accused him of murder and cowardice and Alcestis herself has been placed in her tomb; then Admetus admits that he now understands (*arti manthanō*, line 940) that he will be unhappy without her wherever he goes; that he cannot bear the thought of another woman, or the criticism that he was a coward. Some scholars have interpreted this speech as a confession of guilt, but Admetus never says that he thought he should have died, just that now Alcestis is dead he does not want to go on living, which is quite a different matter.

Aside from the practical reason (in terms of Athenian inheritance laws) that in his family Admetus was the only surviving son who could serve as guardian of family position and property, why does Alcestis readily agree to die for him? Euripides could have chosen to portray her as a morbid, impulsive psychotic, but instead he makes it clear that her decision was undertaken deliberately and rationally. Like Penelope, she would have been able to marry again: 'I could have the man I wanted from among the

Thessalians and live with a ruler in his prosperous home' (line 286). When she says she had from Admetus everything she needed to make her happy, we can assume that Admetus at least fulfilled the basic roles of protector and provider,[7] and Euripides also shows us in the drama that he was justly renowned for his hospitality and generosity. Whether these qualities were in themselves responsible for Alcestis' devotion to him, Alcestis herself does not say; but her dialogue with him indicates that she trusts him to do as he promises, and her actions when she is alone inside the house show that she is reluctant to leave the marriage bed that (in her words) 'has destroyed' her (line 179). It is possible that she was afraid that a second time she might be less fortunate—as Medea puts it, 'everything depends upon whether you get a bad man or a good one' (*Medea*, 235–6), but Alcestis, even in her soliloquy, says nothing like that, nor does she speak (as a Puritan woman might) of doing her duty.

Euripides apparently could count on his audience being able to believe that married couples could be as devoted to one another as Admetus and Alcestis; inscriptions from gravestones indicate that such sentiments were at least conventionally expressed, if not actually felt. There is, for instance, the inscription on a fourth-century stele that shows a woman holding out her hand to her husband, with verses that awkwardly represent a dialogue between them:

> Farewell, tomb of Melite, a good (*chrēstē*) woman lies here. Your husband Onesimus loved you and you loved him in return (*philount' antiphilousa*). You were the best (*kratistē*), and so he laments your death, for you were a good woman: And to you farewell, dearest (*philtate*) of men; love (*philei*) my children.
>
> (Kaibel 79)

Alcestis' last request is virtually the same. Admetus implores her: 'lift up your head, do not leave your children.' Alcestis replies: 'I would not if I could help it; children, farewell' (lines 388–9; cf. 302–3).

It is understandable that children would provide the principal reason for a married couple's devotion to one another. But even when there are none, or their presence seems to be unimportant, strong ties of affection exist, and even sexual attraction (though some contemporary scholars imply that ancient Greek men had little physical interest in their wives).[8] In the *Suppliants* Euripides describes Evadne and Capaneus virtually as lovers. She refuses to abandon him in death (*prodousa*, line 1024, the same word Admetus used of Alcestis), and throws herself on Capaneus' funeral pyre: 'I will join my body to my husband in the burning flame, placing my beloved flesh next to his (lines 1020–1) . . . hallowed is the bridegroom who is softened by the guileless attraction (lit. breezes, a word that denotes a sudden, powerful sensation) of his noble wife' (lines 1029–30).

There are indications that similar devotion existed outside the context of the ideal marriages of myth, even in the ordinary marriages arranged by Athenian fathers for their children. In a fragment of a lost comedy, a young husband who thinks his wife has betrayed him explains that 'since the night I was married . . . I have not been away from bed a single night, away from my wife . . . I wanted (*ērōn*) her, honestly ... I was tied to her by her noble character and her unaffected ways; she loved me (*philousan*) and I cared for her (*ēgapōn*)' (*P. Antinoop.* 15). Three of the Greek words for love occur in this passage, *eraō*, denoting sexual passion, *phileō*, love for family and friends, and *agapaō*, affection. In his commentary on this fragment, Professor Lloyd-Jones observed that this appears to be the only instance in extant Greek literature where the three words 'recur at such short intervals, in each case referring to love between a man and a woman, and indeed between a husband and a wife';[9] but it is possible that if more literature about ordinary life had survived, the concurrence even in the context of marriage of all forms of love would no longer appear unique.

Another papyrus fragment indicates that a wife can display extraordinary affection for a husband who seems to lack what we might have deduced from myth was the single most important male virtue—wealth. The fragment preserves part of a speech by a wife to her father; she is begging him not to take her away from her husband, who is bankrupt, in order to marry her to a richer man:

> Explain to me how, by whatever he has done, he has done me wrong. There is a covenant between man and wife; he must feel affection for her (*stergein*) always till the end, and she must never cease to do what gives her husband pleasure. He was all that I wished with regard to me, and my pleasure is his pleasure, father. But suppose he is satisfactory as far as I am concerned but is bankrupt, and you, as you say, now want to give me to a rich man to save me from living out my life in distress. Where does so much money exist, father, that having it can give me more pleasure than my husband can? How can it be just or honourable that I should take a share in any good things he has, but take no share in his poverty?
>
> (*Gk. Lit. Pap.* 34)

Since the rest of the play is lost, we do not know anything about this wife's circumstances other than what she tells us in this speech; here she is deferential to her father, and disparages her own intelligence, and suggests that perhaps only in the case of her own affairs a woman may know what is right. To judge from her own words, much of the 'pleasure' she derives from marriage comes from obedience and an opportunity to serve; also she makes it clear that her husband has been good to her in respects other than financial.

This wife's attitude reflects a new emphasis—at least in drama—on human relationships. Among families with property marriages had been arranged primarily to ensure the safe transmission of property: a man in his will could leave his wife to a freedman or a daughter to a close friend;[10] if a man died without male issue, his daughter was required to marry his closest male relative, even if that man had to leave his wife to do so. Euripides in his *Andromache* demonstrated that marriages arranged for political or financial purposes could be less than successful: 'a sensible man will arrange to marry children from a noble house to noble people, and not have any desire for base marriages, not even if they bring vastly rich dowries to his house' (lines 1279–82). The devoted wife in the papyrus fragment, instead of discussing inheritance laws, speaks of 'a covenant (*nomos keimenos*) between man and wife; he must feel affection for her always, till the end, and she must never cease to do what gives her husband pleasure'. The Greek word *nomos*, here translated as 'covenant', is usually translated 'law'; but *nomos* does not so much denote a law in our sense of the word, i.e., a statute or the carefully documented precedent of court decision; *nomos* is rather 'practice', and so may be expressed differently in different cases. The *keimenos nomos* or enduring practice that the wife here describes positively is expressed in tragedy in negative terms, and we can understand what she means by 'a husband must always feel affection for his wife' by comparing how Hermione and Deianeira complain that their husbands have ignored them and given a wife's status to a concubine; 'husbands who want to live in a happy home show affection (*stergousin*) by keeping their eyes on one Cypris (i.e., sexual relationship) in their marriage' (*And.* 179–80). In reply to Hermione, Andromache describes the second half of the covenant, how 'a wife must never cease to do what brings her husband pleasure': 'a woman must, even if she has been given in marriage to a poor man, feel affection (*stergein*) for him, and not hold a contest of wills' (lines 213–14); 'it is not beauty, but excellence that makes a husband happy' (lines 207–8, *terpousi*). Andromache claims that she 'shared Hector's sexual misadventures with him (*synērōn*), and often nursed his bastards herself, so as not to show him any bitterness 'and by so doing I won my husband over by my excellence' (lines 222–7). Euripides' Andromache is perhaps exaggerating in order to emphasize the justice of her cause against Hermione – in the *Iliad* it is the priestess Theano, not Andromache, who brings up her husband's bastard son 'in order to please him' (5.70). But still a wife had no choice under the law (or *nomos*) other than to be tolerant of her husband's sexual relations with other women, so long as her status as wife was recognized. As for deference to her husband's will, the wife in the papyrus fragment illustrates that this is the *nomos* by her insistence that her father knows best, and must decide, even though she does not agree with him. That she is able to express her point of view within the context of that *nomos* suggests that the heroines of tragedy, like Andromache or Alcestis, are not stepping out of line when they politely, but eloquently, speak to the men in their families.

The male speaker of Lysias' orations recounts how a widow not only knew the terms of her husband's will, but was able effectively to argue before her male kinsman how her own father had failed in his duties as guardian (32.13–18).

These passages from drama and comedy suggest that more upper-class women at least managed to express themselves and influence their male relatives under Athenian 'law' or *nomoi* than simple restatement of the laws, as they are expressed in trials or treatises, would lead us to believe.[11] Law by nature emphasizes prohibition and so fails to emphasize the positive; the arguments for chastity, for example, are always stated negatively: 'if she breaks the law (by committing adultery) she wrongs the gods of her family and provides her family and home not with its own offspring but with bastards. She wrongs the true gods, etc. . . . she wrongs her own fatherland because she does not abide by its established rules. . . . She should also consider this, that there is no means of atoning for this sin; no way she can approach the shrines or the altars of the gods as a pure woman, beloved of god . . .'[12] Between the lines one can discern the practical reason why adultery could cause a serious problem in a society without sure contraception, and where citizenship (especially in Athens) is determined by the citizenship of one's parents. The 'law' about adultery implies that a wife by her chastity performed a valuable service to the state; in Athens a woman caught in adultery must not only be repudiated by her husband, but is forbidden to offer public sacrifice; a foreign woman and a prostitute are similarly excluded (we learn this from the case of the notorious Neaera's daughter Phano, who was both, Dem. 59.38). Fifth- and fourth-century law forbids a woman to make a will or to own (at least in Athens) property other than her own clothes and jewelry, but the system also guarantees her financial protection and guardianship by her male relatives.[13]

That I have had to rely primarily on tragedy and comedy in the preceding discussion suggests yet another reason why we have so little detailed information about what non-mythical fifth- and fourth-century husbands and wives felt about each other. The only other sources of evidence, grave inscriptions, offer only very limited information. In the fifth century, epitaphs tend to emphasize the general archetypal forms of excellence: e.g., 'of a worthy wife this is the tomb here, by the road that throngs with people—of Aspasia, who is dead; in response to her noble disposition Euopides set up this monument for her; she was his consort.'[14] In the fourth and third centuries, there is more emphasis on the relationship of individuals to their family (a pattern that is also represented in the arrangement of their tombs).[15] The cause of death is mentioned, or some distinguishing feature; Melite was 'the best'; Dionysia 'did not admire clothes or gold when she was alive but her husband', who in return for her youth adorns her tomb (*IG* II$^2$. 11162);[16] Nicephorus left four children, 'and died in the arms of his good wife' (Kaibel 327).[17] But even these epitaphs are brief and general, and the sculptures that accompany them represent stereotypical scenes, with no attempt at realistic portraiture. We may learn more about the intensity of family affection from the consistency with which family members desire to be together: Aristotle's will ends with a request that the bones of his wife be exhumed and buried with his, 'in accordance with her own instructions' (D.L. 5.16).

We appear to have more specific information about 'real' people in the Hellenistic age and after because of an increasing emphasis on individuality in literature as well as in art. In a world greatly expanded by Alexander's conquests, it was less possible to define oneself as a member of a particular small community; a fifth- or fourth-century epitaph might speak of a woman's *hēlikia*, the group of contemporaries with whom she was educated in dance and song (e.g., Kaibel 73, 78). Fourth-century epitaphs and inscriptions mention a woman's occupation, but particularly from the point of view of the bereaved: 'Phanostrate, a midwife and physician, lies here; she caused pain to none and all lamented her death' (Kaibel 45/Pleket 1); 'Hippostrate still misses you. "I loved you while you were alive, nurse, I love you still now even beneath the earth"' (Kaibel 481; *IG* II$^2$. 7873). But in Greco-Roman Egypt and in Rome itself information is given on inscriptions that clearly distinguishes one person from another: a mother describes how she went from Athens to Alexandria when her daughter, one of Cleopatra's attendants, was sick, but arrived too late and brought her remains back to Athens (Kaibel 118).

As concerns women's relations to their husbands, one gets the impression that in Hellenistic Egypt women were freer to move about, and were no longer closely restricted to the house by custom. In Theocritus' *Idyll* 15, set in suburban Alexandria, a woman calls on a woman friend and they go together to the festival of Adonis; but their conversation tells us that their husbands still do the shopping and make the decisions about where they are to live; the wife can complain, but cannot change the decision. A woman was able to make wills in her own name, and could decide how to dispose of the property she inherited from her father, but as in fifth- and fourth-century Athens, the document must be approved by a male guardian (*SB* x.10756). Legal documents protect the status of both wives and concubines, in the case of divorce or transfer, or rate of payment of a dowry;[18] perhaps such contracts always existed, at least verbally, but we know about them only from Egypt, because the climate was able to preserve them. Roman law, particularly in the Empire, spells out the rights of women in detail, drawing many subtle distinctions and allowing for exceptions with a precision and flexibility that was not possible in classical Athens, where individual cases were subsumed into the general *nomos*.

Roman law thus gives the impression that there was a considerable improvement (from our point of view) in women's status. But in practice, notions of the proper role of wives do not seem to have undergone any radical change.

In the Roman Empire, epitaphs in Greek, perhaps because of the conventions established in classical models, continue to emphasize the standard qualities, chastity, care for husband and children, management of the *oikos*, as in, for example, this second-century inscription from Pergamum:

> Farewell, lady Panthia, from your husband. After your departure, I keep up my lasting grief for your cruel death. Hera, goddess of marriage, never saw such a wife: your beauty, your wisdom, your chastity. You bore me children completely like myself; you cared for your bridegroom and your children; you guided straight the runner of life in our home and raised high our common fame in healing—though you were a woman you were not behind me in skill. In recognition of this your bridegroom Glycon built this tomb for you. I also buried here the body of (my father) immortal Philadelphus, and I myself will lie here when I die, since with you alone I shared my bed when I was alone, so may I cover myself in ground that we share. (Pleket 20)

Again, as in fourth-century Athens, though now it is stated explicitly, the pattern of burial represents the unity of the family of life. Custom now permits a fuller description of the *oikos*; it is sustained not by farming, like most *oikoi* in Attica, but by the practice of healing, in which both husband and wife share. The statement 'though you were a woman you were not behind me in skill' sounds condescending, but (like so many condescending remarks) was meant as a compliment; like Admetus, Glycon assumes his own priority, both as head of household and as a man.

Latin inscriptions, especially from the Empire, provide even more detail; some record whole eulogies which, like Roman portraits, lead us to believe that we might be able literally to recognize the people they describe: specific incidents from the past are mentioned, appearances are described, conversations remembered. We learn why a person has claim to the standard virtues ascribed to him or to her. One of the most famous of these long inscriptions is the eulogy by a husband for a woman who is not named but has been traditionally identified with the heroic Turia (*ILS* 8393).[19] The husband records how his wife helped avenge her parents' deaths, after they were murdered during the Civil War (I. 3ff.), how she raised some young female relatives and gave them dowries from her own inheritance (I. 42ff.), how she helped bring her husband back safely from exile during the proscriptions in 42 B.C. (II. 2aff.), when the triumvir Marcus Lepidus objected to her husband's return: 'when you prostrated yourself at (Lepidus') feet, he not only did *not* raise you up, but dragged you along and abused you as though a common slave; your body was all covered with bruises, yet with unflinching steadfastness of purpose, you recalled to him Caesar's (i.e., Octavian's) edict of pardon and the letter of felicitation on my return that accompanied it. Braving his taunts and suffering the most brutal treatment, you denounced these cruelties publicly so that Lepidus was branded as the author of all my perils and misfortunes' (II. 14–18). The husband even claims that her protest was instrumental in bringing about Lepidus' downfall (II. 19ff.). This wife's performance was not unique: the historian Appian recalls other cases of wives interceding for their husbands, or determining, despite great hardship, to go into exile with them. Wartime conditions demanded that women go to extremes to preserve the unity of their families (Appian 4.39–40).

But 'Turia's' sacrifices for her husband were not limited to wartime. Her husband explains that when they found that they were unable to have children, 'You did not believe you could be fertile and were disconsolate to see me without children; you did not wish me by continuing my marriage to you to give up hope of having children, and to be on that account unhappy so you proposed divorce, that you would vacate the house and turn it over to a woman more fertile; your only intention was that because of our mutual affection (*concordia*) you yourself would search for and provide me with a worthy spouse, and that you would affirm that you would have treated the children as your own; and you said that you would make no division between inheritances which we had heretofore held in common,[20] but that it would continue to be left in my control, or if I wished in your management; nothing would be sequestered, and you would have nothing separate, and that you would henceforth render to me the services and devotion of a sister or mother-in-law' (II. 31–9). Most interestingly for us, the husband records his response to this extraordinary offer, and it is not at all what one would expect him to say from a Marxist or a feminist point of view: 'I will admit that I was so irritated and shocked by such a proposition that I had difficulty in restraining my anger and in remaining master of myself. You spoke of divorce before the decree of fate had forced us to separate, and I could not comprehend how you could conceive of any reason why you, while I was still alive, should not be my wife, you who while I was in exile virtually from life had always remained most faithful (II. 40–3). How could my desire to or need for having children have been so great, that for that reason I would have broken my promise to you, and exchanged what I could count on for uncertainties? There is nothing more to say. You remained in my house; I could not have agreed to your request without disgracing myself or causing us both unhappiness' (II. 44–7). The husband concludes the oration by stating 'you deserved all, and I must remain without having been able to give you all; your wishes have been my law, and I will continue to provide whatever still has been permitted for me to do' (II. 67–8). This wife's self-sacrifice and deference to her husband apparently not only set an example for Octavian, but for the husband himself; even though Octavian once he became emperor offered prizes for the begetting of children (Dio 54.10). The husband refused to accept his wife's offer of divorce and remained childless, rather than lose her. So Andromache may not have been overstating her case when she claimed that by extraordinary service (in her case nursing her husband's bastards) she 'won her husband over' by her excellence (lines 207–8).

The 'Turia' inscription indicates that in certain upper-class Roman marriages, wives could and did participate in all important decisions, as one would expect, because the law allowed them to own property, did not deny them access to the outside world, and specified their rights. But *technically* a woman may have been freer to determine the course of her own life than most chose to be in practice. A woman like the notorious Clodia, who entertained a sequence of boy friends, including perhaps Catullus, in her house after her husband's death, was fair game for a lawyer like Cicero, who could effectively destroy her credibility simply by contrasting her lifestyle with approved patterns of behaviour.[21] The highest compliment on epitaphs remained service to home and husband; in another eulogy, composed about the same time, a son praises his mother Murdia for being 'on an equal level with other good women in modesty, propriety, chastity, obedience, woolworking, and industry',[22] as well as for her sound financial judgement and generosity to her children by two marriages.

'Turia's' husband relates that he 'had difficulty in restraining his anger and remaining master' of himself, but that was only in response to his wife's extraordinary generosity. There is a consistent emphasis even in shorter grave inscriptions in this period and after on domestic harmony: (from Naples) for example, 'For Lollia Victorina his sweetest wife Lollianus Porresimus the Procurator bought this monument, because she deserved it. With her he lived 20 years without any fault finding, on either side. That is having loved' (*CIL* x. 1951). In an inscription from Carthage, a wife says she 'set up this monument to her blessed husband, who was most generous and dutiful; "while I lived with him, he never said a cruel word to me, never gave offense to me or any one else".'[23] It would be naive to take these or any eulogies or epitaphs as precise representations of the truth, but at least they offer valid testimony of an ideal. These wives, like the fourth-century Athenian woman who wanted to remain with her bankrupt husband, appreciated their husband's constant 'affection'.

One expects to find lower-class wives to be involved in their husbands' occupations; we find pairs of grocers in both Greek and Latin inscriptions. In first century B.C. Rome a butcher in praising his wife includes financial honesty among the list of traditional virtues, 'she lives as a faithful wife to a faithful husband with affection equal to my own, since she never let avarice keep her from her duty' (*ILS* 7472). His wife, on the same inscription, claims that her husband 'flourished at all times through her diligent performance of duty'. But the 'Turia' inscription and many of the anecdotes about wives' heroism in times of persecution, suggest that political circumstances could encourage close companionship also among upper-class couples. As a final example, I would like to consider a long inscription about a husband and wife in the late fourth century; their account of their lives is of particular interest because the husband, Praetextatus, was one of the last important pagans, who held office not only under Julian the Apostate but several Christian Emperors.[24] What he and his wife Paulina are represented as saying about each other is virtually the last evidence we have of pagan ideals.

The grave monument (*ILS* 4154) of Praetextatus and Paulina is inscribed on all four sides; the front lists their names and their religious offices, and some of Praetextatus' public offices.[25] On the sides of the monument are eulogies in verse to Paulina: on the right side she is said to be 'conscious of truth and chastity, devoted to temples and friend of the divinities: she put her husband before herself, and Rome before her husband, proper, faithful, pure in mind and body, kindly to all, helpful to her family gods'. In earlier inscriptions, a wife or husband's piety might be routinely mentioned (Alcestis before her death prayed to Hestia and decorated all the altars), but here it is explicitly detailed, and there is a striking emphasis on her patriotism. The inscription on the right side of the monument speaks of her devotion to husband and family, but also of 'the experience of our life together, the alliance of our marriage, our pure, faithful, simple concord; you helped your husband, loved him, honoured him, cared for him'.

On the back of the monument Paulina gives (again in verse) an even more detailed eulogy of Praetextatus. She claims that her greatest honour is having been his wife; she praises him for his civic achievement and for his scholarship. But she places even more importance on his religious piety: 'you as pious initiate conceal in the secrecy of your mind what was revealed in the sacred mysteries, and you with knowledge worship the manifold divinity of the gods; you kindly include as colleague in the rites your wife, who is respectful of men and gods and is faithful to you . . . My husband, by the gift of your learning you keep me from the fate of death pure and chaste; you take me into the temples and devote me as the servant of the gods. With you as my witness I am introduced to all the mysteries; you, my pious consort, honour me as priestess of Dindymene and Attis with the sacrificial rites of the taurobolium; you instruct me as minister of Hecate in the triple secret and you make me worthy of the rites of the Greek Ceres . . . Now men, now women approve the insignia that you as teacher have given me.' From this inscription and other evidence we have about Praetextatus, it seems that for him religion was closely bound up with his service to the state; apparently when he was governor of Achaea in 362 under Julian he restored some of the cults that he and his wife were initiated into. Her eulogy of him indicates that he served both as her mentor and teacher; but it is significant that he wanted her to share in the rituals he himself took so seriously. I am inclined to think she means what she said about her gratitude for having been included in this important aspect of his life, first because the monument was put up after his death (whoever composed the elegant verse), and secondly because other aristocratic women are eager to record their participation in some of the same rituals. It seems that members of family groups would be initiated together, especially in rituals like the taurobolium (cf. *ILS* 4154); so perhaps a pagan husband's taking a close interest in his wife's religious education is not as unusual as evidence gleaned from the Christian fathers might suggest.[26]

If in this paper I have sought to show that certain attitudes persisted throughout classical antiquity, despite significant changes in women's legal status and over a great range of time as well as geography, I am not trying to argue that all ancient marriages were happy, or that in contemporary society we should accept ancient values. After all, so far as we know, every document we have considered was written or at least inscribed (since only men were stone-cutters) by a man, and some men may only have been able to hear part of what the women were saying to them. In his treatise *Advice on Marriage*, Plutarch urges the bridegroom to be understanding and faithful; but it is clear from what he says that he expected most of the adjustments were to be made by the wife: he advocates the kind of marriage described in the inscription about Praetextatus and Paulina; the woman should worship the husband's gods; marriage should be a partnership; he believes that a wife ought to be able to say 'dear husband, to me you are guide, philosopher and teacher in all that is beautiful and most divine'; he advocated that women study geometry and philosophy to put their mind on higher things (*Mor.* 145 c–d). He believes that women can and should be educated, though as tradition would dictate within the context of their husband's home. Clearly he means his advice for the best; can we really blame him for not being able to imagine a system in which women could be completely independent? He was an antiquarian and historian and he had studied and read enough to know that the concept of a married woman's role had not changed very much over seven hundred years.

## NOTES

1. On the problems of selecting and interpreting information about women in the ancient world, see esp. J. Gould, *JHS* 100 (1980), 39–42.

2. Translated by H. Lloyd-Jones, *Females of the Species* (London, 1975), p. 52.

3. Ibid., on line 88.

4. Wives are frequently compared to Penelope on grave inscriptions; see W. Peek, *Ath. Mitteil.* 80 (1965), 163–4.

5. Translated by W. Shewring, *Homer, the Odyssey* (Oxford, 1980), p. 156.

6. H. W. Pleket, *Texts on the Social History of the Greek World*, Epigraphica col. II (Leiden, 1969), no. 26. W. Smith, *Phoenix* 14 (1960), 127–45, imagines that certain inconsistencies in Admetus' character indicate that he is being insincere instead of (understandably) distraught.

7. A quality also singled out by Megara in Eur. *H. F.* 494, because of her desperate circumstances.

8. See, e.g., Gould (n. 1), 56–8.

9. *JHS* 84 (1964), 28.

10. E.g., Pasion's will in Dem. 45. 28 and Aristotle's will in D. L. 5. 11–16. Cf. also the concept of *patria potestas* in Roman law; see esp. S. Treggiari, *Classical Views* 26 (1982), 34–44.

11. Cf. Gould (n. 1), 50; S. G. Cole, *Women's Studies* 8 (1981), 137–8.

12. From a neo-Pythagorean treatise of the third-second century B.C.: see H. Thesleff (ed.), *The Pythagorean Texts of the Hellenistic Period* (Abo, 1965), pp. 151–4.

13. Isaeus 10. 10; Gould (n. 1), 50 n. 85.

14. P. Friedländer and H. Hoffleit, *Epigrammata* (Berkeley, 1948), no. 139.

15. See esp. S. C. Humphreys, *JHS* 100 (1980), 114ff.

16. Cf. Eur., *Alc.* 288–9.

17. Cf. *IG* $II^2$. 10954.

18. E.g., *P. Tebt.* 104, *P. Berol.* 1104, *P. Fam. Tebt.* 21. Cf. S. B. Pomeroy, 'Women in Roman Egypt' in H. Foley (ed.), *Reflections on Women in Antiquity* (London, 1981), pp. 308–9.

19. See esp. E. Wistrand, *The So-called Laudatio Turiae*, Stud. Lat. et Graec. Gothoburgiensia 34, Goteborg, 1976; A. E. Gordon, *Epigraphica* 39 (1977), 7–12.

20. 'Turia' turned her inheritance over to her hisband (I. 37), but they both shared in the administration of their joint fortunes; he protected hers and she was guardian of his. The practice was not unusual; see Wistrand (n. 19), p. 40.

21. Cf. Lefkowitz, *Heroines and Hysterics* (London, 1981), pp. 32ff.

22. *ILS* 8394 (end); cf. Lefkowitz (n. 21), pp. 28–9; also 'Turia', I. 30: 'why should I mention your domestic virtues, chastity, obedience, compatibility, reasonableness, industry in working wool, religion without superstition, sobriety of attire, modesty of appearance?' The unique *domiseda* occurs in *CIL* VI. 11602; cf. H. Comfort, *AJA* 64 (1960), 275.

23. See esp. R. Lattimore, *Themes in Greek and Latin Epitaphs* (Urbana, 1962), pp. 277–80.

24. See esp. H. Bloch, 'The Pagan Revival in the West at the End of the Fourth Century' in A. Momigliano (ed.), *The Conflict between Paganism and Christianity in the Fourth Century* (Oxford, 1963), pp. 193–218.

25. See esp. Bloch, *HThR* 38 (1945), 199–244.

26. Cf. P. Brown, *Religion and Society in the Age of Augustine* (London, 1972), pp. 172–3.

# ἐλάχιστον ... ἐν τοῖς ἄρσεσι κλέος: THUCYDIDES, WOMEN, AND THE LIMITS OF RATIONAL ANALYSIS

*By* THOMAS E. J. WIEDEMANN

The comparative infrequency of references to women in Thucydides' history has often been remarked upon, and explained as due in part to the choice of warfare as his theme, and in part to the success of the Greek republics in excluding women from the political arena.[1] As Pericles says in his funeral speech, women ought to give their menfolk the least possible cause to have to take note of them (2.45.2). But the exclusion of women from the subject-matter of historical discourse is peculiarly Thucydidean. Powell's *Lexicon* tells us that Thucydides' contemporary Herodotus uses γύνη 373 times, while the number of references to women/wives, mothers, priestesses, etc. in Thucydides is less than fifty.[2] This does not mean of course that Thucydides has no interest in, or sympathy for, women: frequently he mentions them as the passive objects of military circumstances precisely in order to underline the tragic effects of warfare.[3] But some of the references to women are decidedly curious. There is a clear example in the account of the unsuccessful Theban attack on Plataea in 431 B.C., with which active hostilities began. Thucydides tells us that some of the Thebans who were locked into the town escaped by breaking open a deserted gate without being noticed (2.4.4). Why does he gratuitously mention that it was a woman—presumably a Plataean—who gave her enemies an axe: γυναικὸς δούσης πέλεκυν? Clearly, it is an oversimplification to say that Thucydides ignores women. Where he records their active intervention in events, he repeatedly seems to suggest that the event in question is somehow odd—that it lies outside the 'norms' of his subject-matter. Barbarians may be involved, or the story may be marked out as mythical, or the context may place the occasion outside rational patterns of explanation.

Firstly, women as the objects of political or military circumstances. On twenty occasions we find them associated with children, and in fourteen of these Thucydides puts the children first (παῖδες καὶ γυναῖκες: the order is frequently transposed in the Penguin Classics translation). Thus when the Athenians recapture the tributary city of Scione (5.32), the men are executed and the children and women sold as slaves; in his reference to Cleon's decree to this effect (4.122), Thucydides does not bother to mention the fate proposed for the children and women, but merely says that it enacted Σκιωναίους ἐξελεῖν τε καὶ ἀποκτεῖναι. Similarly, when Melos is conquered (5.116.4), the men are killed, the children and women enslaved. The first Athenian debate about the fate of Mytilene (3.36.2) also concludes with a decision to execute the men and enslave the children and women; it may be worth noting that in his account of the less harsh punishment actually imposed upon Mytilene, the execution of over a thousand of the wealthiest citizens, Thucydides does not refer to the fate of the women and children (3.50.1). The potential enslaving of the children and women of Syracuse was one of the Athenians' aims in invading Sicily, according to Gylippus in his exhortatory address before the decisive naval battle in the Syracusan Great Harbour (7.68.2). The only occasion where Thucydides explicitly says that a massacre extended to the children and women is at the plundering of Mycalessus by Thracian mercenaries (7.29.4), where he wishes to lay stress on the exceptional barbarity of this incident. There are some other occasions where he fails to tell us what happened to the women, e.g., when the Aeginetans captured at Thyrea were executed (4.57.4). The 110 women enslaved by the Peloponnesians when Plataea surrendered (3.68.3) should be referred to in this context: there were no children to enslave because these had all been evacuated. We are not told what happened to the children of the Corcyrean oligarchs when their fathers were killed and their mothers sold into slavery (4.48.4).

There are eight references to the evacuation or expulsion of children and women (in that order). After the defeat of the Persians, the Athenians bring their children and women back from the Peloponnese, where they have been sent during the occupation of Athens (1.89.3). The Messenian revolt ends with the evacuation of Mount Ithome by the Messenians, together with their children and women (1.103.3). In the face of the Spartan invasion, the Athenians evacuate the countryside of Attica, along with children and women (2.14). Later they expel the population of Aegina, including the children and women (2.27). When Potidaea falls, the Athenian commanders allow the citizens to leave with their children and womenfolk and ἐπίκουροι (here mercenaries rather than slaves); the women are allowed to take two ἱμάτια with them, while everyone else is allowed only one (2.70.3). We are told that Brasidas arranged for the children and women from the Chalcidian cities of Scione and Mende to be evacuated to Olynthus (4.123.4). There are three references to the evacuation of the Plataeans' wives and children to Athens: in two cases the children precede the womenfolk (2.72.2 and 78.3).

We may surely assume that Thucydides' tendency to give children priority over women is not without significance. It was after all the fact that they could provide citizens with legitimate children that gave 'wives' a special status above that of other women.[4] It may be worth comparing Thucydides' phraseology with that of other Greek historians. As we have already noted, Herodotus is quantitatively eight times more interested in women than Thucydides: yet he shares his propensity to rank children before women.[5] Powell's *Lexicon* cites 16 cases of τέκνα or παῖδες καὶ γυναῖκες, only 3 the other way round. One of these refers to women and children being enslaved (6.19.3), one to an Egyptian physician who is parted from his wife and children by being sent to the Persian court (3.1.1), one is a list of evacuees which includes women, children, money, and slaves (1.176.1). A significant contrast is provided by Dionysius of Halicarnassus' *Roman Antiquities*. In the first four books, there are three references to children followed by women, but six where the women come first (including 'passive' ones of women and children being enslaved). This suggests that for all Dionysius' attempts consciously to write Thucydidean Greek, he was unable to escape the fact that his social world was quite different to that of Thucydides and Herodotus.

In Thucydides, there are six occasions where women precede children. The evacuation of the Plataeans (2.6.4) and the enslaving of the women and children of Torone (5.3.4) are straightforward 'passive' occasions, and I can see no obvious reason for the normal order to be reversed. One instance appears to be a gloss which has intruded into the text: at 1.90.3, Thucydides explains that when Themistocles had the Athenians rebuild their city walls after the defeat of the Persians in 479, τειχίζειν δὲ πάντας πανδημεὶ τοὺς ἐν τῇ πόλει. The manuscripts add καὶ αὐτοὺς καὶ γυναῖκας καὶ παῖδας, but the Scholiast's comment τὸ πάντας· αὐτοὺς καὶ γυναῖκας καὶ παῖδας makes no sense if these words already stood in his text (characteristically, it did not occur to him that πάντας might not have included children, but certainly would have included slaves, as at the building of the Argive Long Walls at 5.82.6).

At 3.104, Thucydides digresses about the ceremonial purification of Delos by the Athenians in the winter of 426/5. He says (*c.* 3) that the festival of Apollo was attended by the Ionian inhabitants of the surrounding islands with their women and children. The order here hardly indicates that he saw the women as taking a more active part in the proceedings: in the lines from the Homeric hymn to Apollo which he quotes in support of his account, we read (*c.* 4): σὺν σφοῖσιν τεκέεσιν γυναιξί τε σὴν ἐς ἀγυιάν. Perhaps it was just Thucydides' desire for as much stylistic *variatio* as possible which led him to reverse the order.

In his account of the final appeal of Nicias to the Athenian trierarchs before the naval battle in the Great Harbour at Syracuse, Thucydides lists some of the standard rhetorical *topoi* which such an exhortatory speech would be expected to include, and proposes to waste no time repeating them (7.69.2).[6] The list includes references to wives, children, and ancestral gods. If there were any significance in the order in which they are listed, it would be that since gods clearly have the highest status, children must be more important than women; but again, one suspects instead that

Thucydides wished to reverse the order because he had just given an example of the rhetorical appeal to children and women (*sic*) in the speech of Gylippus already referred to (7.68.2). The final instance where women are mentioned first is in another speech, at 8.74.3, where the democrat Chaereas son of Archestratus tells the Athenian sailors at Samos that the oligarchic regime of the Four Hundred was tyrannizing Athens and ὅτι αὐτῶν καὶ γυναῖκες καὶ παῖδες ὑβρίζονται. The rhetorical context of these accusations, and of their denial by the oligarchs at 8.86.3, confirms the impression that not just Nicias, Gylippus, and Chaereas, but Thucydides himself, introduce women and children to engage the emotions of the audience: to make the full brutality of the effects of war clearer to the reader.

Thucydides' other references to women are not so easy to classify. One group of references is to women whose marriages result in political links between rulers on the fringes of the Greek world. Thus Nymphodorus of Abdera's sister marries Sitalces, son of the Thracian king Teres (431 B.C.; 2.29). The Macedonian king Perdiccas promises to give his sister Stratonice to Sitalces' nephew, Seuthes (429/8: 2.101.5). The murder of the Edonian king Pittacus by the sons of Goaxis and his wife Brauro (4.107.3), and the role played by the wife of the Molossian king Admetus in the Themistocles saga (1.136.3), may be included in this dynastic context. All the other references to marriage as the source of power occur in the distant past, either that of Homer or at least that of Herodotus. There is the oath which the suitors of Helen had sworn to her father Tyndareus—according to myth, the source of the successful suitor Agamemnon's authority over his rivals (1.9.1). Cylon's plan to establish himself as tyrant over Athens is explained in terms of his marriage to the daughter of Theagenes, tyrant of Megara (1.126). It is through his mother that Pericles is said to have inherited the curse of the Alcmaeonids who had killed Cylon's supporters (1.127). Pausanias, in one of his letters offering his services to Xerxes, proposes to seal the alliance by marrying one of the Persian king's daughters (1.128). Three women are mentioned in connection with the overthrow of the Pisistratids: Hippias is married to Myrrhine, daughter of Callias (6.55), and his daughter Archedice marries Aeantides, tyrant of Lampsacus; Thucydides explicitly says that the motive for this dynastic alliance was that Hippias wished to win the friendship of Darius (6.59). And there is the anonymous sister of Harmodius, who plays the key (but entirely passive) role in provoking the assassination of Hipparchus (6.56). Finally, there is a reference to the myth of Alcmaeon having killed his mother Eriphyle (who is not named: 2.102.5).

What these cases have in common is that they all lie outside the normal course of the political and military conflict between Athens and Sparta. Some are 'marginal' in the sense that they take place amongst non-Greeks (the Thracian marriages); the others are located in a different age, that described by Homer or by Herodotus. Frequently Thucydides is at pains to dissociate himself from these accounts involving women: such stories, like many in Herodotus, may be introduced by λέγεται (Alcmaeon: 2.102.5), a word which Thucydides elsewhere uses to introduce mythical references (3.96: Hesiod; 4.24: Odysseus). He mentions Helen only to reject the story that she was responsible for Agamemnon's power: on the contrary, it was the wealth which Pelops brought from Asia which gave the dynasty of Mycenae paramount status (1.9.2). Perdiccas does not promise only his daughter to Seuthes as an incentive for Seuthes to persuade Sitalces to support Macedonia: money changes hands as well (2.101.5). The stories of the Cylonian conspiracy and of Pausanias in Book 1 have puzzled many commentators because both their style and their content seem so much more characteristic of Herodotus than of Thucydides: even in antiquity, a Scholiast remarked that 'here the lion is laughing'. But the context suggests a reason why Thucydides included these exceptions to his self-imposed ban on τὸ μυθῶδες: these are the kinds of accusations which governments make to strengthen the pretexts they have for going to war (1.126.1), but they are in no sense the real reasons.[7] In other words, these Herodotean stories are there precisely to warn the reader that, in Thucydides' view, such anecdotes ought not to be taken seriously by political analysts. The marriage of Cylon, Pericles' inheritance of the Alcmaeonid curse through his mother, Pausanias' proposal to marry Xerxes' daughter—and, in this context, Themistocles' trick in winning the favour of king Admetus by taking the queen's advice to place their baby son on his knee (1.136.3–4): Thucydides wants us to perceive all these episodes as digressions from the norms of genuine political historiography. This does not of course imply that he thought they were not 'true' in the sense that they did not happen, but that in his view they did not contribute to an understanding of why the course of events unfolded as it did. The digression on the overthrow of the Pisistratids at 6.54–9 is intended to show that the popular (Herodotean) myth about Hipparchus' insult to Harmodius and Aristogeiton could not explain what happened: in fact, the tyranny fell for a straightforward political reason—Spartan military intervention. A rational account of political events will explain Agamemnon's power in terms of inherited wealth: there will be no place in such an account for the story of the contest for Helen.

Yet as H.-P. Stahl has pointed out, one of the main themes which emerges as Thucydides' work unfolds is that the actual course of political and military events can rarely be controlled by human reason or planning. The weather is one example of a non-rational factor which affects events.[8] Women can be another. Brauro's murder of the Edonian Thracian ruler Pittacus is mentioned because it is the reason why the city of Myrcinus goes over to Brasidas. Throughout his account of Brasidas' campaign in Chalcidice, Thucydides has been at pains to stress how he has been helped by unforeseen, non-rational factors (at Amphipolis, the weather and Thucydides' own unexplained absence; at Torone, the collapse of the wooden tower at fort Lecythus: cf. esp. 4.116.2). The intervention of Brauro is just such a factor. We may note that Thucydides' reference to the marriage of Nymphodorus of Abdera's sister to Sitalces is followed by a mythological digression explaining that Teres had nothing to do with Tereus, husband of Procne (2.29). This is a curiously polemical passage, and Thucydides' intention is not just to correct a popular or poetic misconception,[9] but to insist that there is a clear distinction between the Tereus of myth and the Teres involved in a real political alliance with Athens: *Τηρεῖ δὲ ... προσήκει ὁ Τήρης οὗτος οὐδέν*.

The evidence suggests that Thucydides used these traditional tales precisely to contrast them with the kind of history he saw himself as writing. These are non-rational accounts; they are also accounts in which women have a place. Are women also associated with non-rational action in those parts of Thucydides' narrative where their presence cannot be explained as belonging to the heroic past, or to the Thracian margins of the Greek world?

There are two references to Chrysis, the priestess of Hera at Argos: we are told that the attack on Plataea occurred in the forty-eighth year of her priesthood (2.2), and that she was replaced as priestess by Phaeinis in 423/22 B.C. (4.133.2–3). It is tempting to see the explanation for her disappearance, her responsibility for the fire which burnt down the temple, as due to a subconscious feeling on the historian's part that this is the kind of chance calamity for which women are to blame; and on a more conscious level, Thucydides is perhaps pointing out how non-rational the basis of a conventional chronological system was, compared to his own reckoning by summers and winters. The third reference to a priestess may be more indicative of an Athenian male's prejudices against women. The enemies of the Spartan king Pleistoanax accuse him of having bribed the Pythia at Delphi to produce a series of oracles ordering him to be restored from exile (5.16.2). A Herodotean story, and Thucydides makes no comment on its veracity. In fact, if there was corruption, it would rather have been on the part of the Pythia's (male) interpreters.[10]

There are few such instances in Thucydides of women actively intervening in the male world of politics. There are the 110 women who remained behind at Plataea to cook for the garrison of 480 men (2.78.3), and were subsequently sold into slavery (3.68.3). In 417/6 B.C., the women and slaves join in the building of the Long Walls from Argos down to the coast (5.82.6), as they may have been reported as doing at Athens in 479 (1.90.3). The two other instances are during the attack on Plataea in 431, and the civil war at Corcyra. At Plataea, women and slaves join in the fighting by screaming and hurling missiles from the rooftops (2.4.2). The same happens at Corcyra, and Thucydides explicitly says that this is not appropriate behaviour (3.74): *αἵ τε γυναῖκες αὐτοῖς τολμηρῶς ξυνεπελάβοντο, βάλλουσαι ἀπὸ τῶν οἰκιῶν τῷ κεράμῳ καὶ παρὰ φύσιν ὑπομένουσαι τὸν θόρυβον*. Later, when the democrats massacre their oligarchic prisoners, the women are sold as slaves (4.48.4). Corcyra is of course Thucydides' ideal example of the inversion of proper patterns of behaviour (3.82f.); for women to be participating in the fighting *παρὰ φύσιν* is just one unnatural feature of this civil war. At Plataea a different point is being made. As Stahl has shown,[11] it was Thucydides' intention to use Plataea to illustrate the role of unforeseen factors in starting the war—the Spartans and Athenians had not planned to initiate hostilities in this way, the Boeotian plan goes wrong, and the weather and other extra-rational factors result in a whole series of uncontrolled occurrences. To return to the apparently gratuitous appearance of the Plataean lady who gave the trapped Thebans an axe (2.4.4). There could be no better example of an unforeseen, chance event: and it is an event brought about by a woman. Where Thucydides' women appear in any other than a purely passive role, it is to mark a particular episode as an instance of the non-rational factors whose description he had hoped to be able to leave to the poets, or to Herodotus.

## NOTES

I am particularly grateful to Prof. H. Strasburger and Jürgen Malitz for their advice and criticism.

1. E.g., H. Strasburger, 'Der Geschichtsbegriff des Thukydides', *Studien zur Alten Geschichte* 2 (Hildesheim, 1982), 787f. On the position of women generally, N. R. E. Fisher, *Social Values in Classical Athens* (London, 1976), pp. 7ff.; S. B. Pomeroy, *Goddesses, Whores, Wives, and Slaves* (New York, 1975), chs. 4–6; J. Gould, 'Women in Classical Athens', *JHS* 100 (1980), 38–59. D. Schapps, 'The Women of Greece in Wartime', *CPh* 77 (1982), 193–213, is a useful list of historical writers' representations of the roles typically ascribed to women—though his proposition that 'The women with whom we are dealing are real ones, not literary characters invented by men' (p. 212) is highly questionable. P. Walcot, 'The Funeral Speech, a Study of Values', *G & R* 20 (1973), 111–21, is a reminder that a Greek peasant's ideal of democracy was not that of a western liberal.

2. Cf. J. E. Powell, *Lexicon to Herodotus* (Cambridge, 1938); E. A. Bétant, *Lexicon Thucydideum* (Geneva, 1843; repr. Hildesheim, 1961). I have omitted a consideration of the intervention of goddesses (e.g., 4.116.2), since they involve different problems. It is ironic in view of Thucydides' attitude to Persians, females, and the divine, that his text should end with a Persian sacrificing to a female deity.

3. Cf. J. Malitz, 'Thucydides' Weg zur Geschichtsschreibung', *Historia* 31 (1982), 267–89, esp. 284.

4. Typically, Demosthenes, *Against Neaira*: 59, 122.

5. This point is noted by R. Kassel, *Quomodo quibus locis apud veteres scriptores Graecos infantes atque parvuli pueri inducantur describantur commemorentur* (Würzburg, 1954), p. 76 n. 267.

6. I would prefer to take ἀρχαιολεγεῖν to mean 'speaking in an old-fashioned way' (with

Gomme, p. 446), rather than as 'talking about (great victories of) the past' (with LSJ). The context would surely allow either interpretation.

7. See the introduction to the Bristol Classical Press reprint of E. C. Marchant, *Thucydides: Book I* (Bristol, 1983).

8. For example, at Pylos: H.-P. Stahl, *Thukydides*, (Munich, 1966), pp. 130ff.

9. Cf. Gomme, *Commentary* II, p. 90 n. 1; H. D. Westlake, 'Irrelevant Notes in Thucydides', *Essays on the Greek Historians and Greek History* (Manchester, 1969), p. 12.

10. If we accept the traditional view of the role of the *Prophētēs* in interpreting the Pythia's utterances: cf. H. W. Parke, *Greek Oracles* (London, 1967), pp. 83f. Contra: J. Fontenrose, *The Delphic Oracle* (Berkeley, Los Angeles, and London, 1978), pp. 196ff. (who does not discuss this passage).

11. H.-P. Stahl, *Thukydides*, ch. 4, pp. 65ff.

## ADDENDUM

This article was conceived in the early 1980s, largely under the inspiration of John Gould (for whose 'Women in Classical Athens', see n. 1). During the past decade, considerable attention has been devoted to women in antiquity: for Athens, see R. Just, *Women in Athenian Law and Life* (London and New York, 1989) and R. Sealey, *Women and Law in Classical Greece* (Chapel Hill, 1990); David Harvey analysed Thucydides' material in 'Women in Thucydides', *Arethusa* 18 (1985), 67–90; and N. Loraux, in 'La Cité, l'historien, les femmes', *Pallas* 32 (1985), 7–39, also demonstrated how Herodotus and Thucydides use women in their histories to symbolize *stasis* and *thorubos*. Øivind Andersen, 'The Widows, the City and Thucydides (II, 45, 2)', *Symbolae Osloenses* 62 (1987), 33–49, pointed out that the women to whom Pericles addresses the words enjoining silence which I used in my title were specifically the widows of the fallen.

In n. 2 I suggested that it was 'ironic' that Thucydides should end his account of how war (the Peloponnesian War) increasingly slips out of the control of reason and rational planning with an incomplete sentence in which a Persian goes to sacrifice to a female deity. I would now go further, and believe that Thucydides intentionally ended his analysis in this way. As Konishi Haruo argues in 'Thucydides' History as a Finished Piece', *Liverpool Classical Monthly* 12 (1987), 5–7, there is no valid reason to suppose that Thucydides intended to write anything more. Haruo nevertheless admits that there is 'stylistic incompleteness' in Book 8; I would prefer S. Forde's judgement that the book as it stands is 'polished' (*The Ambition to Rule* [Ithaca and London, 1989], p. 117 n. 2, citing others who disagree with the conventional view that the book is unfinished). But unlike Forde I do not see Thucydides' ending as 'the most optimistic note possible', 'a promising counterpart to the tragic barbarization of the Greeks during the war' (p. 171 n. 53). By Book 8, Thucydides had made his point about how the rational policies the Athenians had thought they could pursue at the start of the war had proved unsustainable, the ever-increasing intervention of Persia being a major factor. Reason, *logos*, proved no longer to be in control (as the absence of speeches, *logoi*, in Book 8 symbolizes). In place of the *logos* of Greek male citizens, the story significantly comes to a conclusion at 8.109 with Tissaphernes sacrificing to Artemis. My thanks to Mr E. I. McQueen for his bibliographical advice.

# GREEK ATTITUDES TOWARDS WOMEN: THE MYTHOLOGICAL EVIDENCE

*By* PETER WALCOT

## I

Students today demand that what they are taught or what they discuss is 'socially relevant'. A topic appears to exhibit social relevance when it is related to some issue currently reckoned important and the subject of controversy. No topic at present is thought more socially relevant than the role of women in society. Extra-mural students can vote with their feet as undergraduates cannot, and it is significant how regularly the brochures of university extra-mural departments in Britain have come to feature courses with titles such as 'Women's Studies', 'New Horizons for Women', 'Images of Women', and 'Women Speak'. Teachers of classics have not been reluctant to devise their own courses on women in antiquity, and it is my impression that no university in North America is without a course of this type, while postgraduate seminars covering the same field of interest seem to have become firmly established throughout western Europe. Books, articles, and notes on women and ancient society abound, and the resultant bibliography grows more and more daunting each year.[1]

A consequent increase in understanding has been inevitable, and the 'facts' are now reasonably clear when it comes to the women of fifth- and fourth-century Athens. The crucial clues to understanding are offered by

(1) the obsession of the Athenian male with his personal honour;
(2) the need of the man of honour to defend against injury or insult any woman under his protection; and
(3) the belief that prevention is much superior to cure.

Although ultimately it is likely to be the threat of physical retaliation which protects women, society will function much more smoothly if violence is just a last resort and not a norm of behaviour. In fact there existed in Athenian society three 'safety-valves' which served to safeguard the integrity of women and so to ease the obligation on the part of male relatives to swing into violent action in defence of their women.

These safety-valves were

(1) the practice of arranging a daughter's marriage as soon as, or not too long after, the girl attained puberty and became sexually aware.[2] This was

more than simply marrying the girl off in her teens so that the responsibility for her protection was extended to another. To put it bluntly, the marriage was arranged when the girl became sexually active since she could then indulge her sexuality within the context of legitimate marriage and experience no compulsion to tempt, or to be tempted by, others.

(2) the dowry system, which it is a mistake to see as merely the ancient equivalent of our wedding presents. A good dowry meant a good marriage and, given the prospect of a good marriage, a girl would have behaved herself and was unlikely to do anything prejudicial to that prospect. But why should a daughter have bothered about her reputation if her parent could not afford a generous dowry and, as a consequence, she had little hope of contracting an adequate marriage? In other words, the dowry was a form of control, being for a daughter what a legacy was for a son, and we all know today how the elderly may exploit what is to be inherited as a means of calling to order potential heirs to the estate.

(3) the confinement of women to the home, a restriction on a woman's freedom of action which we find it most awkward to accept, although we have no way of being certain how far social reality corresponded to the social ideal of female seclusion.

What is certain, however, is that the life of the Athenian woman was not quite as depressing as what has been outlined above might suggest, for the expectations of women in antiquity were considerably more modest than those of their modern counterparts in the western world today, and it is thwarted expectations which lead to frustration and resentment. What is no less significant is the fact that men and women in the Greek world led distinct and separate lives, not demanding, for example, that husband and wife share much in the way of pleasure together, so that the wives were excluded from symposia and males from a number of exclusively feminine festivals. In short, the Greeks anticipated the answer found by those black groups today whose members appear to have achieved self-fulfilling and happy lives by rejecting integration with white society in favour of a policy of separatism which stresses distinctively black qualities.

We may both know and understand more about the position of women in Athenian society than we did until recently, but our knowledge and understanding remain far from perfect. For instance, what evidence we have refers essentially to the mores of what may be termed middle-class Athenians. It might be argued, however, that this limitation is no handicap since the formulation and the maintenance of morality is the preserve of the middle-class. The really wealthy can afford to flout conventional morality, while the poor will have very little interest in a conception of marriage which was remarkably Victorian in its concern for property rights and the necessity to guarantee legitimate male heirs.[3] More serious a weakness in understanding is our failure to explain with total conviction why the Athenians were so mistrustful of women, why they were so suspicious, bothered, and edgy, and why they were always prepared to think the very worst of any woman. Was it because the Athenian male thought women weak and feeble and so held them in contempt? Or was it because he found women to be strong and effective and so regarded them with fear? The Homeric poems reveal which of these alternative answers is to be preferred. The deception of the king of the gods by his wife Hera in the *Iliad* and the words of Hermes in the *Odyssey* when he surveys the lovers Aphrodite and Ares trapped in bed together[4] demonstrate the devastating power of the female and the male's inability to resist that power; the passages also show the nature of woman's power. If even Zeus succumbs and is deceived by passion, and if Hermes is ready to endure the ridicule of all the gods and goddesses provided he can enjoy the charms of Aphrodite, it is because of the immense power that the female wields through her sexuality, and what follows will attempt to illustrate from further evidence offered by Greek mythology how compulsively a fear of woman's sexuality did condition Greek attitudes towards women.

## II

The Greeks believed women to be incapable of not exercising their sexual charms and that the results were catastrophic, irrespective of whether or not women set out to cause trouble deliberately or acted in a blissful ignorance of what they were doing. Such is the picture presented by Greek mythology. But in order to appreciate the mythological evidence a preliminary word must be said about the two ways in which such material is regularly interpreted. For many social anthropologists mythology has the function of explaining and thereby justifying particular customs and attitudes. Thus Greek wives were required to be totally faithful, whereas husbands might amuse themselves outside the home with those other than their wives.[5] The same double standard of morality applied in heaven, Hera remaining chaste if not absolutely devoid of sexual guilt[6] however many the liaisons of her husband Zeus, and so the pattern of human behaviour was validated and sanctioned by the actions of the deities. To the psychologist, however, the purpose of myth is different: the myth is a 'waking dream' and it is under analysis, in actual dreams, or in myths that man gives expression to the basic fears and anxieties which he otherwise keeps suppressed deep in his subconscious. In other words, the study of myth may uncover fundamental emotions, and so it has been suggested that it is a residual fear of giant-like parents who fondly nibble away at the limbs of children 'good enough to eat' which is expressed in the story of that gigantic cannibal Polyphemus.[7] In fact these two ways of looking at myth are not mutually exclusive and, as we shall see, myth may both explain attitudes as well as expose deep-seated traumas.

But where are we to begin a survey of evidence whose richness forces us to be highly selective? That woman's appetite for sex was voracious and therefore pernicious is clearly implied by a tradition which would appear to go back as early as the seventh century B.C., since we first know of it from a fragment ascribed to the poet Hesiod's *Melampodia*.[8] The tradition told how Zeus and Hera had one of their usual squabbles, this time as to whether the man or the woman had the greater pleasure from intercourse, and turned for a solution to the prophet Teiresias as Teiresias possessed the unique qualification of having been at different times variously male and female. The reply of Teiresias did not please Hera, for he claimed that the woman derives ten times as much enjoyment from intercourse as the man. This is a remarkable opinion for more than simply one reason: first, it is man who is popularly thought to enjoy intercourse the more, a prejudice also reflected in the concept of the frigid woman; secondly, even if it is felt that woman's pleasure was the greater, no one surely would be inclined to argue that woman's pleasure was greater to the extent of measuring ten times as much as a man's. Such a story says something staggering about the sexuality of women and is hardly flattering in the light of the Greek virtue of *sōphrosynē* or (basically sexual) moderation. As a comment on women there is only one other remark likely to occasion a comparable offence today. In Aristophanes' *Clouds* Right Logic stresses the value of *sōphrosynē*, pointing out that it was because of his *sōphrosynē* that the hero Peleus won the hand of the goddess Thetis (verses 1067ff.). But she went off and left Peleus, retorts Wrong Logic, 'for he was not a *hybristēs* ('lustful' is the translation of Liddell & Scott) and pleasant to spend the night with in bed: a woman likes it rough!' (verses 1068–70). There could be no more blatant a statement of man's belief that women are to be overwhelmed by brute force, a belief which man adopts in order to compensate for his own instinctive fear of the other sex. 'Get them before they get you' seems the basic principle.

If women are obsessed with sex and deadly for men, it all goes back to Pandora, the first woman, whose story is related by Hesiod in both his poems from the late eighth century B.C. to have survived in their entirety, the *Theogony* (verses 535ff.) and the *Works and Days* (verses 47ff.). This is the story of how Zeus, tricked into selecting the inferior portion of the sacrifice by the Titan Prometheus, retaliated by having the first woman Pandora prepared and presented to Prometheus' stupid brother Epimetheus. Although warned by Prometheus never to receive a gift from Zeus, Epimetheus seems to have succumbed to the woman's wondrous beauty and took her in. She in due time, and for no apparent reason, removed the lid from a storage jar which housed all the evils now afflicting mankind. These escaped and so man's life is wretched and man himself miserable (*Works and Days*, 83ff.).

For Hesiod Pandora is a 'beautiful evil' (*Theogony*, 585), her splendid exterior but corrupt interior matching the share of the sacrifice with which Prometheus had first deceived Zeus (*Theogony*, 535–55), for this consisted of attractively packaged but quite useless bones. Her character is clearly indicated by the 'gifts' she received from the god Hermes, the mind of a bitch and a deceitful nature (*Works and Days*, 67) and lies and stealthy words (verse 78). Typically she is 'tarted up' so that she can exploit her wiles more effectively. Epimetheus is the weak male, and his folly in accepting Pandora confirms the meaning of his name 'Afterthought' and the contrast with his trickster brother Prometheus or 'Forethought'. 'Eve was framed' reads a feminist slogan and so too perhaps was Pandora, for she seems to have had little or no idea of what she was doing when what one can only presume was regarded as an innate tendency on the part of women not to leave well alone led her to take the lid from the jar and release the evils. The consequences for men of her curiosity were devastating and permanent. A number of real-life Pandoras or close sisters of Pandora are featured in the writings of the historian Herodotus, and these and their actions as described by Herodotus certainly confirm the accuracy of Hesiod's portrayal of their ancestress.[9]

With Homer and Hesiod Greek literature begins, but much of our knowledge of mythology is derived not from literary texts but from Greek art which takes many of its themes from this source. Two of the myths which are often to be seen depicted in the sculptural decoration of a Greek temple are the battle between the Gods and the Giants and the fight between the Lapithae and the Centaurs, and both myths have a symbolic force in representing the clash between order and civilization on the one hand and chaos and violence on the other. A third myth of comparable significance available to the artist and one known, for example, from the Parthenon, the temple of Apollo at Bassae, and the Mausoleum was the Amazonomachy or battle between Greeks and Amazons, a race of warrior-women as monstrous in their own fashion as the snake-limbed Giants or half-horse Centaurs and a race just as expressive of the forces which threaten to destroy civilized life. For Aeschylus in his *Supplices* the Amazons are 'flesh-devouring' (verse 287), and the affinity to 'nature' which the Amazons share with the Centaurs is also suggested by their historical counterparts, the Maenads or female worshippers of Dionysos who again function in a wild, isolated setting, devour flesh, and pose a threat to 'culture' as symbolized by the Greek polis.

Wherever the Amazons are located by the Greeks, whether it is somewhere along the Black Sea in the distant north-east or in Libya and the furthest south, it is always beyond the confines of the civilized world. The Amazons exist outside the range of normal human experience and it is, in my opinion, crass folly to attempt an identification with an actual people, be it Hittites, Scythians, or 'bow-toting mongoloids'.[10] The Amazons are fantasy creatures, the type of predatory woman or domina; they are everything a woman ought not to be and they define the norm and the acceptable by setting that norm on its head; they illustrate the appalling consequence of woman usurping what is properly man's role and emphasize man's fear of any attempt at such a usurpation.

In the ancient world men were the warriors—except for the Amazon daughters of Ares and their marginal status is underlined by the fact that they were not equipped as normal soldiers were, that is, as heavily armed infantrymen, but fought as mounted archers. They challenged and defied woman's function as wife and as mother, the first by rejecting the institution of marriage and preferring to mate with neighbouring men just once a year, and the second by inverting the practice by which daughters rather than sons were exposed on birth, for they were reputed to bring up the girls they conceived but to kill or mutilate the boys, a custom guaranteed to arouse castration anxieties in men. The popular etymology of their name would make them 'breastless' and certainly the amputation of the right breast represents a denial of motherhood and an unwillingness to pander to male concepts of feminine beauty.[11] The Amazons were formidable opponents in battle, and it needed Achilles to vanquish the Amazon queen Penthesilea before Troy and the other two renowned victors over the Amazons were none other than the heroes Heracles and Theseus. But to defeat an Amazon by itself was insufficient to re-establish the supremacy of the male, for such a creature must also be sexually humiliated, which is why the ninth labour of Heracles was to secure the girdle of queen Hippolyte, the loss of this garment symbolizing her sexual submission, and why Theseus carried off an Amazon variously named as Antiope and Hippolyte—rape is yet another violent response on the part of the sexually insecure. Such an idea is probably in the background of the story recorded in the lost epic *Aethiopis* that Achilles killed Thersites when abused by that scoundrel because of his reputed love for Penthesilea.

Another eastern queen, the legendary Omphale of Lydia, turned the tables on Heracles, and revealed the depths to which even the greatest of the Greeks might sink when subjected to the control of a woman. Forced to serve as Omphale's slave, Heracles suffered the ultimate humiliation of being made to wear women's clothes. It was a woman, moreover, who finally brought about the hero's death, his wife Deianeira or 'Man-destroyer'. It was sexual jealousy which persuaded Deianeira to send Heracles a poisoned robe. She did this, however, in the hope of rekindling her husband's love and in no way to do him any kind of harm, and her chosen instrument was a garment, that epitome of the woman's task of spinning and weaving. It is, of course, heavily ironic that so superb a sexual athlete as Heracles should in the end be brought to the point of death by a loving wife, but the very innocence of Deianeira reminds us yet again of the perils posed by a woman and that woman need not be a Helen or her sister Clytemnestra. But let us turn now from mortals or the semi-divine to woman writ large in the alluring shape of the goddess Aphrodite.

## III

When Hera deceived Zeus in the *Iliad*, the deception took place on Mount Ida overlooking Troy. This is also the setting of the myth related in the Homeric *Hymn to Aphrodite*, which tells how the goddess of love Aphrodite appeared in the guise of a Phrygian princess to the hero Anchises, how they slept together, and how as a result their son Aeneas was conceived. What we have here is a form of the birth-myth and in relating a birth-myth the *Hymn to Aphrodite* is comparable to the better known *Hymn to Hermes*. These two poems are alike in another respect also; neither is devoid of humour. In the *Hymn to Aphrodite* the goddess is made to fall in love with a mortal man by a Zeus who is having his own back (verses 45ff.); when she puts in her appearance before Anchises she tells a long lying story to explain her presence, claiming to be a Phrygian princess carried off by Hermes, and in this way depicts herself as a virgin anxious for legitimate marriage and a potential bride whose father will supply a lavish dowry (verses 107ff.). All this is highly ironic as surely is also Aphrodite's explanation—she had had a Trojan nurse—of why she knows Trojan speech (verses 113–15), an explanation scarcely required by the demands of realism but yet a further indication of the duplicity of the female in pursuit of sexual adventure. When their union is on the point of consummation Aphrodite persists in posing as a blushing maid (verses 155–7), and there is rather a delicate touch as Anchises gently strips the ornaments and clothes from the goddess (verses 162–6). Subsequently, however, all is very different: when Aphrodite drops her disguise Anchises is terrified (verses 172ff.) and the standard situation is reversed, for here it is the male who has been seduced and is racked with fear, and here it is the female who refuses any permanent arrangement and the male who is not to disclose the secret of a son's birth.

At the beginning of the *Hymn* Athene, Artemis, and Hestia are listed (verses 7ff.) as the three deities able to resist the persuasion and deceit practised by Aphrodite. All three are, therefore, virgin goddesses. Artemis is the huntress goddess and hunting is associated with ritual purity and sexual abstinence as the hunter tries to relieve his sense of guilt at the slaughter of fellow creatures. It is agriculture, the antithesis of hunting, which provides the language of copulation. It is significant that the most 'professional' virgin in Greek mythology, Atalanta, is a huntress. Hestia is the goddess of the hearth and its purifying fire, although Jean-Pierre Vernant is not satisfied to explain Hestia's virginity in terms of the purity of fire.[12] Having reminded his reader that Hestia rejected marriage with Poseidon or Apollo and received in recompense the honour of a place in the centre of the house (verses 24–30), Vernant proceeds to argue that 'through the goddess of the hearth, the function of fertility, dissociated from sexual relations . . ., can appear as an indefinite prolongation of the paternal line through the daughter, without a "foreign" woman being necessary for procreation'. For the French scholar Hestia had a special quality of appeal to the Greek male, and the same I believe to be true of the goddess Athene and possibly to an even greater extent.

As the patron saint of Athens Athene commanded the devotion of the Athenians just as the Mother of God commands the devotion of Orthodox Greeks today. For the Orthodox the Virgin Mary is an ideal to which women must aspire and part of her perfection lies in the fact that she not only gave birth to the perfect son but did so by a process of immaculate conception which eliminated sex from the relationship. The 'macho' Mediterranean male, really terrified of women and seeing sex as a trap, 'sublimates' in the sense that he finds in a female beyond this earthly world, whether that female be Athene in antiquity or the Virgin Mary today, a woman who can satisfy his emotional needs without his being exposed in any way to the temptation and danger offered by sex. It is as if he has attained a state wished for by Jason in Euripides' *Medea* (verses 573–5) and by Hippolytus in Euripides' tragedy of the same name (verses 616ff.), a state in which the deity has not bothered with women, a curse and snare for men, but has arranged the propagation of the human species through some other means. This wish is uttered with an equal fervour by Milton's Adam in *Paradise Lost* (10.888ff.):

> Oh! Why did God,
> Creator wise, that peopled highest Heaven
> With spirits masculine, create at last
> This novelty on earth, this fair defect
> Of nature, and not fill the world at once
> With men, as angels, without feminine,
> Or find some other way to generate
> Mankind?

The words are addressed to Eve, who, like Pandora, was a 'fair defect', and if they sound almost pathological in their intensity, we must bear in mind Milton's succession of marriages (and daughters?), the ambivalence which critics have detected in the poet's appraisal of Eve, and at the same time his dependence for inspiration on the muse Urania, a dependence on a further sexless deity best illustrated by the passionate invocation of Urania with which the seventh book of *Paradise Lost* opens.[13]

Athene had no real mother but was born from the head of Zeus, as Hesiod tells us in his *Theogony* (verses 886ff. and 924–6). She was a goddess of war, a strictly masculine occupation, and her appearance was decidedly martial if not 'butch'. Her preference for the male is most aggressively displayed in Aeschylus' *Eumenides* when she votes out of sheer prejudice in favour of the acquittal of Orestes, claiming

> It is my task to render final judgement here.
> This is a ballot for Orestes I shall cast.
> There is no mother anywhere who gave me birth,
> And, but for marriage, I am always for the male
> With all my heart, and strongly on my father's side.
>
> (verses 734–8, translated by Richmond Lattimore)

The trial of Orestes was held on the Areopagus of Athens or the Hill of Ares, and we also learn from the *Eumenides* that it acquired this name because the Amazons made it their centre when they invaded Attica (verses 685–90). The Areopagus then was both the centre of the defeated Amazons and the place where the deed of Orestes, his act of matricide, was vindicated. On each of these occasions the Areopagus witnessed the frustration of the feminine principle, the victors being Theseus, the national hero of Athens, and Athene, the patron saint of that city, respectively.

In the first poem of Theocritus Anchises appears in a brief list of those brought to a 'sticky end' by the goddess Aphrodite (verses 105–7). The reference, as so often with Alexandrian poetry, is elusive, but it would seem that Anchises was punished, presumably for revealing the identity of his lover (cf. *Hymn to Aphrodite*, 281–8), and that this punishment took the form of his being stung by bees.[14] There is a particular reason why bees should have been incensed by Anchises' dalliance with Aphrodite, and that reason takes us back finally to the Greek male's fear of sex and consequent predilection for the virginal. The Greeks chose to equate the good wife and the bee, and it is misleading for us to believe that this equation applied merely to the work to be completed by the good wife and the bee, such as is implied by Ischomachus in Xenophon's *Oeconomicus* (7.32ff.; cf. Phocylides frag. 2, 6–8). The seventh poem of Semonides of Amorgos shows that the good wife was also like the bee in her indifference to sex. This seventh-century satire on women refers various types of women to corresponding animals such as the sow, vixen, bitch, and so on. But there is in addition one identification of human and animal which is flattering to the human, and that human is the woman related to the bee (verses 83ff.). This kind of wife increases the prosperity of the house, grows old dear to a husband who is likewise dear to her, and is the mother of splendid children. Other women may be obsessed with sex, and the donkey-woman, for example, accept any partner when it comes to sex (verses 48–9) and the ferret-woman be mad for the bed of love (verse 53),[15] but the bee-woman 'experiences no pleasure sitting among women when they tell stories about sex' (verses 90–1).[16] The *sōphrosynē* (see above, p. 94) of bees was proverbial, Lloyd-Jones tells us, and they were prudish to the extent of attacking those who used scent; we learn, moreover, from Liddell & Scott that the word *melissa* was used of priestesses and in Neoplatonic philosophy referred to '*any pure, chaste being*, of souls coming to birth'. And then we remember Virgil's fourth *Georgic* and the *bugonia*, and we begin to appreciate that the ancients, and indeed their successors until well into the Middle Ages, had some most peculiar ideas about the generation of bees[17] and the sex-life and sexual tastes of these insects in general. No less strange were many of their ideas about women, as I have attempted to illustrate, drawing upon the myths of Pandora, the Amazons, Aphrodite, and Athene. This representative rather than exhaustive range of the evidence provided by Greek mythology is sufficient, I hope, to confirm that Greek attitudes towards women were conditioned by man's fear of woman's sexuality.

## NOTES

1. An updated version of the bibliography published in *Arethusa* 6 (1973) is to appear early in 1984 in *Women in the Ancient World: the Arethusa Papers* (S. U. N. Y. Press Classical Series). The two studies since 1973 which students are likely to find most helpful are Roger Just, 'Conceptions of Women in Classical Athens', *Journal of the Anthropological Society of Oxford* 6 (1975), 153–70 and John Gould, 'Law, Custom and Myth: Aspects of the Social Position of Women in Classical Athens', *JHS* 100 (1980), 38–59. *Femme et Mythe* (Paris, 1982) by Georges Devereux consists of a number of papers written from very much the point of view of a Freudian (see *G & R* 31 [1984], 103–4).

2. The evidence is conveniently collected by M. L. West in his note on verse 698 of his edition, *Hesiod, Works and Days* (Oxford, 1978).

3. An example of the wealthy flouting convention is provided by the Athenian Callias who, according to Herodotus (6.122), allowed his daughters to choose their own husbands. As for the poor, note Aristotle's question, 'Who could prevent the wives of the poor from going out when they want to?' (*Politics*, 1300a).

4. *Il.* 14. 159ff. and *Od.* 8.339–42.

5. See Eur. *Medea*, 244–7 and *Electra*, 1036–40.

6. See *Il.* 14.294–6, lines which emphasize the desirability of marrying a daughter off as soon as possible.

7. See Thalia Feldman, *Arion*, Autumn 1965, 493–4 n. 10. Cf. also Justin Glenn, *G & R* 25 (1978), 141–55. On women in Greek myth and psychoanalysis, see Ada Farber, *Psychoanalytic Review* 62 (1975), 29–47.

8. Frag. 275 (Merkelbach–West). This myth is discussed in detail by Luc Brisson, *Le Mythe de Tirésias* (Leiden, 1976); see also Carlos García Gual, *Emerita* 43 (1975), 107–32.

9. See A. Tourraix, *Dialogues d'Histoire Ancienne* 2 (1976), 369ff.

10. Thus K. A. Bisset, *G & R* 18 (1971), 150. The latest consideration of the Amazons by a feminist writer is Page duBois, *Centaurs and Amazons* (Ann Arbor, 1982).

11. For the female breast as an erotic object, see Douglas E. Gerber, *Arethusa* 11 (1978), 203–12.

12. *Myth and Thought among the Greeks* (London, Boston, Melbourne, and Henley, 1983), pp. 127ff. My quotation is taken from pp. 133–4.

13. Cf. Maud Bodkin, *Archetypal Patterns in Poetry* (Oxford, paperback edition 1963), pp. 153ff.

14. See A. S. F. Gow's note on verse 106f. in his edition, *Theocritus* (Cambridge, 1950).

15. See Hugh Lloyd-Jones, *Females of the Species, Semonides on Women* (London, 1975) on line 53 (pp. 77–8).

16. Cf. Helen F. North, *Illinois Classical Studies* 2 (1977), 36–7.

17. Still of interest as a survey of 'ancient apicultural lore' is B. G. Whitfield, *G & R* 3 (1956), 99–117; rather more exciting is Marcel Détienne in *Myth, Religion and Society* (Cambridge and Paris, 1981), pp. 95–109, who remarks that 'the Greek conception of the bee (*melissa*) was based on a model which, in essential features, remained unchanged for over fifteen centuries. The *melissa* was distinguished by a way of life which was pure and chaste and also by a strictly vegetarian diet (compare the Amazons?) . . . the bee showed a most scrupulous purity; not only did it avoid rotting substances and keep well away from impure things, but it also had the reputation of extreme abstinence in sexual matters' (p. 98).

## ADDENDUM

Books on women in antiquity which open with a chapter on women as portrayed in myth continue to appear, as in the case of Eva Cantarella, *Pandora's Daughters* (Baltimore and London, 1987), pp. 11–23, but results tend to be most disappointing. Altogether more convincing is the discussion of 'the savage without' in which Roger Just, *Women in Athenian Law and Life* (London and New York, 1989), pp. 217–79, shows how 'it is often at the simple narrative level that the Greek myths are most revealing in their recurrent association of women with a world of emotions, desires, and nature which threatens man and which man must master' (p. 219). Among much else Just considers the Amazons (pp. 241–52), and the Amazons are also the subject of a paper by Lorna Hardwick, 'Ancient Amazons: Heroes, Outsiders, or Women?', originally published in *G&R* 47 (1990), 14–36 and reprinted in this collection, pp. 158–76. See also on the Amazons Mary R. Lefkowitz, *Women in Greek Myth* (London, 1986), pp. 15ff., a slim volume which promises rather more than it delivers (cf. *G&R* 34 [1987], 105–6), and François Hartog, *The Mirror of Herodotus* (Berkeley, Los Angeles, and London, 1988), pp. 216ff.

Particular topics are covered by Pierre Lévêque, 'Pandora ou la terrifiante féminité', *Kernos* 1 (1988), 49–62, by myself in an assessment of the *Hymn to Aphrodite*, *G&R* 38 (1991), 137–55, and by Nicole Loraux, 'Herakles: the Supermale and the Feminine' in David M. Halperin, John J. Winkler, and Froma I. Zeitlin (edd.), *Before Sexuality: the Construction of Erotic Experience in the Ancient Greek World* (Princeton, 1990), pp. 21–52. On bees now see Maurizio Bettini, *Anthropology and Roman Culture* (Baltimore, 1991), p. 200, and H. S. Versnel, *G&R* 39 (1991), 42–3 (= pp. 192–3 of this volume), and on man's need not only to defeat militarily but also to humiliate sexually the 'militant' female, see the historical example offered by Fulvia at the siege of Perusia as discussed by Maria Wyke in Anton Powell (ed.), *Roman Poetry and Propaganda in the Age of Augustus* (London, 1992), pp. 110–11.

# THE FIVE WIVES OF POMPEY THE GREAT

*By* SHELLEY P. HALEY

For Roman politicians, marriage could be a tool of advancement, a way of forging alliances among the influential and the wealthy. The major figures of the Late Republic used marriage to realize their political hopes and to increase their political power. Such marriages and their consequences have been discussed often and much scholarly energy has been expended in exploring the ramifications of these alliances.[1]

The political marriage implies that political concerns remained the binding force, that affection or romantic love or even passion had no place in such a marriage. This emphasis on the political aspects has caused the modern scholar to lose sight of the woman[2] in such an alliance and to ignore the intimate relationships possible at the heart of such a marriage. The purpose of this paper is to examine these private relationships in the five marriages of Pompey the Great, a politician who made use of marriage in a traditional fashion to further his political career. The political importance of Pompey's marriages has been studied in detail[3] and is not the central concern here. Rather, the aim is to discover, if possible, the intimate qualities of Pompey's marriages and thereby to shed some light, however meagre, on the lives of women in Rome.

In terms of documentary evidence, the most scanty life histories belong to Pompey's first two wives. They are the most characteristic examples of political marriage and perhaps because of this, they are the most pitiful and most pathetic. Antistia, the first wife of Pompey, was the daughter of P. Antistius, a praetor. In 86 B.C., Pompey had been accused of possession of stolen property and his case had come before Antistius, who was so impressed by the great reputation and favour resulting from Pompey's rhetorical ability that he secretly offered his daughter in marriage (Plut. *Pomp*. 4.2). A few days after Pompey was acquitted of the charge, he did indeed marry Antistia.[4]

It was not long before Pompey came to the notice of Sulla, and, as a token of admiration and perhaps a check on Pompey's growing strength, Sulla arranged an alliance. In 82 B.C., the dictator, along with his wife Metella, persuaded Pompey to divorce Antistia and to marry Aemilia, the stepdaughter of Sulla (Plut. *Pomp*. 9.2). Antistia at that point became a truly piteous victim. According to Plutarch (*Pomp*. 9.3), her father had been killed because of his connections with Pompey, an event that apparently drove her mother to commit suicide. After her divorce from Pompey, Antistia disappears from the historians' sight.

To add a further tragic note, the match between Pompey and Aemilia was not welcomed by either of the parties concerned. Aemilia, pregnant by her first husband M. Acilius Glabrio, entered this new marriage with reluctance (Plut. *Sull.* 33.3). For Pompey, as Plutarch notes (*Pomp.* 9.2), 'this marriage was, therefore, characteristic of tyranny, and befitted the needs of Sulla, rather than the nature and habits of Pompey'.[5] The pain and unhappiness caused by this marriage were for naught, since Aemilia died in childbirth soon after becoming Pompey's wife.

In the modern view, the stories of Antistia and Aemilia are grim and point out the lack of control traditional matrons had over their destiny. To the Roman reader of Plutarch, the stories would rather have provoked a decidedly anti-Pompeian reaction. The colour of these stories may have been derived from a source hostile to Pompey, such as Oppius whom Plutarch admits (*Pomp.* 10.4–5) he consulted. The divorce of Antistia and the subsequent marriage of Aemilia parallel the circumstances in which Caesar found himself with Sulla. Given the same choice however, Caesar frankly refused to divorce his wife at all (Plut. *Caes.* 1). The contrast in behaviour shows up Pompey's cold-blooded ambition, despite Plutarch's implications of humanitarian inclinations. This parallelism between Pompey and Caesar could well be evidence that Plutarch's treatment of Pompey's divorce originated with a propagandist for Caesar.

With his third wife, Mucia, daughter of Q. Mucius Scaevola, Pompey gained a variety of political connections, most importantly with the Metellan *gens*. The marriage between Mucia and Pompey, which took place in 79 B.C., was unique for Pompey because of its length, its issue, and its dissolution. The marriage lasted until 62 B.C. and was the longest of Pompey's five. Mucia was the only wife to provide Pompey with living issue: a daughter Pompeia, and two sons Gnaeus and Sextus.[6]

After seventeen years and three children, Mucia was divorced by Pompey, but the search for the proximate and immediate cause of the divorce is beset with problems. Indeed, the sources provide no clear indication of the reasons for the end of the marriage. Three of the sources—Asconius, Plutarch, and Suetonius—comment upon Mucia's infidelity. Asconius (*Pro M. Scaur.* 17) relates that Pompey was angry with Scaurus who married Mucia, thus mocking Pompey's charges of infidelity. Plutarch records (*Pomp.* 42.7) that she 'played the wanton' during Pompey's absence and so he provides only a glancing hint at sexual misconduct. Suetonius (*D.J.* 50.1) names Julius Caesar as her lover, the only account to do so. Plutarch, in the passage already cited, refers his readers to Cicero's letters for the cause of the divorce but Cicero's only direct reference[7] to the matter comes in an epistle to Atticus where he reports 'divortium Muciae vehementer probatur' (*Att.* 1.12.3).

The allegations of Mucia's infidelity recur only in the later sources. Zonaras' account (10.5) follows evidently from Plutarch: 'When he

(Pompey) went back, he experienced a distressing return, because of his wife Mucia who had been guilty of wanton conduct during his stay abroad. On his approach to Italy, he sent her a divorce.' Jerome (*adv. Jovin.* 1.316) relates that Pompey was, as always in such cases, the last to know of Mucia's infidelity and was greatly disturbed by it. Dio (37.49.3) mentions the divorce but not the allegations of infidelity. He reports that Metellus was angry with Pompey for divorcing Mucia and so vigorously opposed him in everything. The only contemporary source is Cicero with his comment on the hearty approval won by the divorce. Yet, 'divortium Muciae vehementer probatur' can hardly be regarded as decisive evidence for the grounds of the divorce. The divorce could have been warmly received in a moral context; it could be seen as a condemnation by a leading Roman citizen of the 'new morality' and its tolerance of infidelity. The dissolution of the marriage could have been welcome in the political arena, since it afforded an opportunity for Pompey to make new connections and more importantly, it provided the ambitious with a chance to be related to Pompey.[8] In an epistle to Metellus (*Fam.* 5.2.6), Cicero refers to Mucia and indirectly provides evidence that she was not adulterous. This is a letter in which discretion and diplomacy are of the utmost importance. Had Mucia been infamous for adulteries committed in Pompey's absence, Cicero's remark would have been tactless in the extreme.

There are, then, two basic grounds for Mucia's divorce: adultery or political expediency. Certainly women did commit adultery and some men did divorce them for that reason alone; but it was possible for adultery to be used as a pretext to get rid of a wife who had become a political liability. In Mucia's case, politics seem to have been the overriding concern, since there is no firm contemporary evidence of misconduct. Pompey had divorced before for political reasons; he could have done so with Mucia. Why, then, is Mucia's fidelity questioned? The crux of the problem is historiographical and lies with the sources. Plutarch's characterization of Pompey, which undergoes a change in the *Life*, may provide an answer.

After showing Pompey to be brutal in his domestic life because of his early ambition, Plutarch begins to delineate him as a home-loving, warm-hearted man instead of a cold, hard-hearted politician. In *Pomp.* 30.6, Plutarch relates this incident: 'Upon learning of his appointment to the Mithridatic command, Pompey said, "Alas for my endless tasks! How much better it were to be an unknown man, if I am never to cease from military service and cannot lay aside this load of envy and spend my time in the country with my wife."'[9] Plutarch goes on to report (*Pomp.* 36.2) that later when Pompey was on campaign, the concubines of Mithridates were brought to him and he did not use any, but restored each to her family, since most were the daughters and wives of generals and princes.

Such a characterization, undoubtedly based on a pro-Pompeian source, presents Pompey as a devoted and faithful husband. His behaviour, especially the rejection of the concubines, contrasts sharply with the misconduct of Mucia which Plutarch reports later. The contrast serves the purpose of enhancing Pompey's virtue and makes the dissolution of Pompey's marriage to Mucia more palatable. It would be difficult to reconcile this image of Pompey with the cold reality of political divorce,[10] but it would be quite acceptable for such a husband to divorce a wife for promiscuity.

Anti-Pompeian colour is provided by Suetonius who discusses the same episode in the *Divus Julius*. Suetonius relates (*D.J.* 50.1) that Caesar was believed to have had affairs with many high-ranking women and Mucia, mentioned by name, was no exception.[11] She succumbed to his charm, and her adultery does not tarnish Caesar as much as Pompey, who comes across as a cuckolded fool. Given the tone and bias of these later sources and the vagueness of Cicero, the only contemporary source, there are no solid grounds for condemning Mucia for adultery; political expediency seems, after all, the primary motivation and Mucia's alleged infidelity reveals more about historiography than about her moral behaviour. All that can be said with certainty is that Pompey divorced Mucia.

For the purposes of this paper, it is unfortunate that this conundrum cannot be definitely solved. If Mucia were divorced for infidelity, such a situation would have revealed a different social attitude towards women who had committed adultery. For Mucia did not suffer in reputation from the divorce; her name never appears among the notorious *femmes fatales* of the Late Republic. In fact, she continued to be a respected Roman matron, which is shown by her life after Pompey. She married M. Aemilius Scaurus and presented him with a son, the uterine brother to Pompeia, Gnaeus, and Sextus Pompey. This child gave Scaurus reason to believe that he himself had a family connection to Pompey and that presumption gave Pompey another reason to be angry with him (Ascon. *Pro M. Scaur.* 17).

Mucia became a political tool once again during the feud between Octavian, Antony, and Sextus Pompey in 40 and 39 B.C. Both Antony and Octavian were seeking to win Sextus as an ally, each against the other. At Dio 48.15.2, Julia, the mother of Antony, is acting as go-between for Sextus Pompey and her son. Learning of this, Octavian sent Mucia off to talk to Sextus on his own behalf. Appian reports (*Bell. Civ.* 5.69) that later in 39, the people threatened to burn Mucia and her house, and sent her as an envoy of peace to Sextus. A short-lived pact among Octavian, Antony, and Sextus did occur in 39 B.C.; but in Dio's account of its inception neither Mucia nor any other woman figures (48.36–8). Mucia was also responsible for saving her son Aemilius Scaurus, after the battle at Actium (Dio 51.2.5; 56.38 reports only that Scaurus was saved). After this episode, Mucia disappears from sight, leaving not even a record of her death.

Following his divorce from Mucia, Pompey remained without a wife for three years. Nevertheless, he appears to have been eager to make a fourth marriage, one with political advantage, since he attempted to contract an alliance with the niece of Cato but was rejected (Plut. *Pomp.* 44.2; *Cat. Min.* 30.2–6). He then was offered Julia, the daughter of Julius Caesar and his wife Cornelia daughter of Cinna. At the time, 59 B.C., Pompey was 47 and had reached his zenith in politics; Julia was 24 and previously betrothed to Q. Servilius Caepio.[12] Caepio was not pleased with the breach of contract and to appease him Pompey offered him his own daughter Pompeia.

Reaction to the marriage of Pompey and Julia ranged from suspicion on the part of Cicero (*Att.* 2.17.1), to disgust on the part of Cato (Plut. *Caes.* 14.4), who strenuously objected to such acquisition of power through women. In his gossipy account, Suetonius adds another dimension by reporting (*D.J.* 50.1) that Pompey called Caesar 'Aegisthus', a veiled allusion to Caesar's seduction of Mucia while Pompey was away in the East being 'Agamemnon'. Plutarch best expresses the general reaction by observing (*Pomp.* 47.6) that the marriage came as a surprise to everyone. Perhaps even more of a surprise was the character of this political match, for all the sources agree that both Pompey and Julia doted on one another, and that strong bonds of affection held them together (Val. Max. 4.6.4; Plut. *Pomp.* 53.1). Plutarch says (*Pomp.* 48.5) that Pompey yielded to the love of his wife and neglected the affairs of the forum. However, this is not the first indication of a preference for home and hearth given by Pompey, as Plutarch implies in *Pomp.* 30.6.

The marriage of Julia and Pompey presents a case where love was stronger than politics. Pompey was at the height of his hostilities with Clodius, as well as embroiled in his feud with the senate and nobility. Along with his political advisors he sought ways to mend his fences with the nobility. One supporter, Q. Terentius Culleo, argued that he must break with Caesar and divorce Julia, but this Pompey could not do and preferred the counsel of those arguing for the recall of Cicero (Plut. *Pomp.* 49.3).

Pompey's devotion was not one-sided, for Julia gave a far more dramatic and tragic sign of her concern for her husband. There had been a riot during which Pompey's clothes were spattered with blood. He changed his clothes and ordered a slave to carry the soiled ones home. At the sight of the blood Julia thought the worst, fainted and, a few days later, miscarried the child she was bearing (Val. Max. 4.6.4; Plut. *Pomp.* 48.5).

Explaining Julia's devotion to Pompey, Plutarch observes: 'The reason for it, however, seems to have lain in the chaste restraint of her husband, who knew only his wedded wife and in the dignity of his manners which were not severe, but full of grace, and especially attractive to women, as even Flora the courtesan may be allowed to testify' (*Pomp.* 53.2). Plutarch's observation about Pompey has been largely ignored by the statesman's biographers and historians. Apparently, Pompey did not take mistresses, even during the longest of his marriages, that to Mucia. The evidence for Pompey's faithfulness is mainly *ex silentio*, apart from Plutarch's anecdote (*Pomp.* 36.2) about Pompey's treatment of Mithridates' concubines. For certainly, if there had been indiscretions on Pompey's part, his critics and historians such as Suetonius would have pronounced them vigorously. Plutarch too enjoys mentioning the amorous and marital habits of his subjects and does so especially with Pompey.

Pompey's 'chaste restraint' cannot be interpreted as coldness, since Plutarch does mention (*Pomp.* 2) that Flora, a courtesan, had an affair with Pompey and had testified to his passionate nature. It is unclear when this liaison occurred but it seems not to have been when Pompey was married. Plutarch generally writes in chronological order and Pompey's affair with Flora precedes his marriage to Antistia. No more mention of Flora is made until her testimony to Pompey's passion. Plutarch ends the section on Pompey's love-life by noting how his critics attacked him: 'Though he was extremely cautious in such matters and on his guard, still he could not escape the censures of his enemies on this head, but was accused of illicit relations with married women, to gratify whom, it was said, he neglected and betrayed many public interests' (*Pomp.* 2).[13] Furthermore, Pompey apparently did not choose to satisfy his 'passionate nature' through homosexual relations, although his critics made some reference to sodomy. This accusation is found only at Plutarch, *Pomp.* 48.7, a clear literary conflation of Cicero, *Q.Fr.* 2.3.2 and Calvus *FPL* 18. Cicero's eyewitness report has Clodius accusing Pompey of causing the grain shortage and no allusion is made to his sexual conduct, nor does Dio 39.19 record charges of sexual misconduct.

Despite such accusations, Pompey's reputation as Julia's devoted husband remained intact and Julia was worthy of the devotion she inspired. She apparently was a lively, jolly young woman who could distract her politician husband from what now must have become the wearisome world of political intrigue. She may have been responsible for interesting Pompey in the world of the *literati* and may have encouraged him in his literary patronage. She was probably with him during the dedication of his theatre in 55 B.C.[14]

Julia was also attractive to other men. C. Memmius, a notorious womanizer, after concluding an affair with Lucullus' wife (Cic. *Att.* 1.18.3), tried unsuccessfully to seduce Julia. Using a freedman, Nicias, as go-between, Memmius sent letters to Julia. She quickly revealed the whole matter to Pompey who evicted Nicias from his circle of supporters.[15] C. Memmius also seems, because of this episode, to have incurred some disfavour which increased as time went on.

In time, Julia conceived another child by Pompey and carried it to term. She did not survive the birth and her baby daughter died a few days later (Plut. *Pomp.* 53.4). Pompey was prepared to bury his beloved Julia at his Alban villa but the people, out of their devotion to Julia, carried her down to the Campus Martius for burial. Plutarch makes it clear (*Pomp.* 53.4–5) that this was done primarily because of their pity for Julia but he also states that an attempt to curry favour with her father was a secondary motive, adding that people gave more honour to the absent Caesar than to Pompey who was present.

The political ramifications of Julia's death are well known. Along with the death of Crassus, it contributed to the end of the so-called First Triumvirate. Furthermore, the death of Crassus, and of his son Publius in Parthia, made possible Pompey's fifth marriage. After unsuccessful attempts by Caesar to keep the alliance alive (Suet. *D.J.* 27.1), Pompey chose as his wife Cornelia, daughter of Metellus Scipio and widow of Publius Crassus (Vell. Pater. 2.54.2; Lucan 3.21–3; Plut. *Pomp.* 55). This marriage had political overtones and advantages, just as Pompey's previous marriages had. Furthermore, this marriage, too, had its critics. Plutarch says (*Pomp.* 55.2) that the marriage was displeasing to some because of the disparity in their ages, since apparently Cornelia was young enough to be a wife for one of Pompey's sons. Yet Cornelia had much in common with Julia, being pretty, young, and interested and well-versed in literature, music, geometry, and philosophy. Plutarch expresses the age-old idea that an intellectual woman is usually neither pretty nor pleasant. Cornelia, however, was different since 'she had a nature which was free from that unpleasant officiousness which such accomplishments are apt to impart to young women'.[16] Cornelia too enjoyed the deep and lasting affection and love of Pompey, which arose despite the political beginning to their marriage. Cornelia's interest in the liberal arts was no doubt a welcome change from the ubiquitous and anarchic problems that the war-weary Pompey endured. Indeed, some critics saw this marriage as the occasion for Pompey to further neglect the city and his political duties. Lucan in his *Pharsalia* (3.21–3) echoes these critics when he has the ghost of Julia (who seems a bit like a jealous wife) blame Pompey's marriage to Cornelia for the beginning of the Civil War.

It is during the Civil War that Cornelia is next mentioned in the ancient sources. Although Pompey had not had Mucia as a companion during his eastern campaigns, he consented to, and was consoled by, the presence of Cornelia during the decisive battles of the Civil War. Lucan romanticizes the relationship between Pompey and Cornelia and paints a distressing scene as Pompey sends her to the island of Lesbos just before the battle of Pharsalus (5.722ff.; also Plut. *Pomp.* 66.3).

During the rest of the war, Cornelia stayed on Lesbos where she followed the course of the war. Yet she did not receive accurate information about the outcome and when she learned that Pompey had retreated and was travelling to Lesbos, she blamed herself, unreasonably, for the ruin of her husband (Plut. *Pomp.* 74.3). Pompey decided to leave Lesbos accompanied by Cornelia and possibly by his son, Sextus (Vell. Pater. 2.53.2; Dio 42.2.3). While consulting with his friends and advisers as to the safest destination, Pompey at one point suggested Parthia, but his friends advised against this so that, as Appian reports (*Bell. Civ.* 2.83; also Lucan 8.275ff.), beautiful Cornelia, the former wife of P. Crassus, would not be put in the power of those 'barbarians'. Rather, they set their course for Egypt and thus made what would turn out to be a tragic decision.

Cornelia watched anxiously as Pompey went ashore to greet the Egyptian dignitaries and stared helplessly as he was stabbed to death. Lucan (9.51ff.) especially emphasizes the unique tragedy of Cornelia, as Pompey was the second husband to whom she had been unable to give proper last rites. Some of Pompey's companions were captured after his assassination, but his wife and son escaped (Livy, *Epit.* 112; Oros. 6.15.28). Eventually, Cornelia obtained a pardon and returned safely to Rome (Dio 42.5.7). She later received the remains of Pompey and gave them burial at his beloved Alban villa (Plut. *Pomp.* 80.6). With that final wifely duty completed, Cornelia disappears from the historical record.

Generally, each wife of Pompey recognized that her duty lay in the traditional role of wife and mother. About Antistia, there is no evidence to say more, since her reactions to her divorce and family circumstances have gone unrecorded. Her situation does reveal that women in arranged alliances did not live happily ever after as quiet partners in a successful business venture. Aemilia, although unwilling to be divorced from her first husband, did obey her stepfather and was married to Pompey. Her doubts alter the belief that women were passive and content with the disruptions of their lives for the political gain of male kin. With Mucia, Pompey enjoyed the years of growing political influence, and she may have introduced him to the joys of domesticity. She had to suffer allegations of infidelity for the sake of her husband's political career and later was divorced on its behalf. Mucia's life provides evidence that a Roman woman could prevail over allegation and rumour. There is no indication that Mucia suffered any ill effects from these allegations, apart from the end of her marriage, and she was not promiscuous, since there is no evidence of any infidelity on her part to her subsequent husband, M. Scaurus. Mucia's situation, finally, leads to the observation that the Romans valued highly the mother-son relationship and they rightly believed that Mucia as a mother had influence and power over her son Sextus Pompey.

Julia and Cornelia have been moulded to the pattern of the good, young wife: the clever, pretty, but modest girl who is devoted to her father-figure husband (cf. Pliny, *Ep.* 4.19). The Roman literary tradition represents the statesman in private life as a country gentleman, farming his estates, travelling around the leisure spots of the Mediterranean, patronizing the arts, and so on. Julia and Cornelia each helped Pompey fit this pattern. At times, naturally, Pompey's critics could distort this picture and Pompey appeared as an uxorious fool but no unpleasant or unattractive invective was ever levelled against Julia and Cornelia. They are devoted wives and each combined family life with intellectual interests. In this they were not unusual. Plutarch's comments (*Pomp.* 55.1) about Cornelia 'being free from that unpleasant officiousness which such accomplishments are apt to impart to young women' imply that it was not unusual for women to engage in intellectual pursuits. Julia and Cornelia reveal also that Roman women could inspire devotion, affection, and respect because of their own personalities and not simply because of their political dowries. It is clear that Pompey felt deep love for both these women and was willing to suffer political setbacks rather than cast either of them aside.

What further conclusions can we draw about Pompey based on his marriages? In the first place, although Pompey used marriage as a traditional politician would, his first three marriages were not marital successes while his last two were personally satisfying for both partners. Secondly, as Pompey grew older, he preferred as wives younger, more filial types of women whose intelligence and intellectual interests he found attractive. Finally, Pompey was a faithful husband, capable of great love and passion for his later wives and preferring their company and interests to politics. Does this mean that the grand old man of Roman politics was weary of his life-long occupation? Could it be that Pompey, at the time of his marriages to Julia and Cornelia, felt more confident politically and gave in to his natural preference for domestic life? Or was he resigned to the fact that there was no hope for the future of the Roman republic? Answers to such questions can never be known. After all, it may just be that Pompey discovered what the love poets already knew and what Vergil later put into words: *Omnia vincit amor.*

## NOTES

1. The connection between marriage and political advancement has been touched upon or implied in nearly every work dealing with the Roman nobility. Among the foremost of such works are M. Gelzer, *Die Nöbilitat der römischen Republik* (1912), translated by R. Seager (Oxford, 1969) under the title *The Roman Nobility*; F. Münzer, *Römische Adelsparteien und Adelsfamilien* (Stuttgart, 1920), pp. 270, etc.; L. R. Taylor, *Party Politics in the Age of Caesar* (Berkeley, 1949), pp. 33f., 39.

2. In recent years, many more studies on the lives of Roman women have appeared. In a partial list one might include J. P. V. D. Balsdon, *Roman Women: their History and Habits* (New York, 1963); C. Hermann, *Le Rôle judicaire et politique des femmes sous la republique romaine* (Brussels, 1964); S. Pomeroy, *Goddesses, Whores, Wives and Slaves* (New York, 1975); T. Carp, 'Two Roman Matrons', *Women's Studies* 8 (1981) and reprinted in H. Foley (ed.), *Reflections of Women in Antiquity* (New York, 1981); A. Richlin, 'Approaches to the Sources on Adultery at Rome', ibid.

3. The life of Pompey has received a bounty of scholarly attention in recent years. The biographies most recently published include J. Leach, *Pompey the Great* (London, 1979); R. Seager, *Pompey: a Political Biography* (Berkeley, 1979); P. Greenhalgh, *Pompey: Republican Prince* (Columbus, Missouri, 1981). Several articles dealing with particular details of Pompey's life and career touch upon the importance of his marriages and their subsequent relations: E. S. Gruen, 'Pompey, the Roman Aristocracy and the Conference of Luca', *Historia* 18 (1969), 71ff.; idem, 'Pompey and the Pisones', *CSCA* 1 (1969), 155ff.; idem, 'Pompey, Metellus Pius, and the trials of 70–69 B.C.: the perils of schematism', *AJP* 92 (1971), 1ff.; B. Twyman, 'The Metelli, Pompeius and Prosopography', *ANRW* I. 1.816ff.; T. P. Wiseman, 'Celer and Nepos', *CQ* 65 (1975), 180ff.

4. Perhaps it is an exaggeration to call the union of Pompey and Antistia a political alliance. Still, Pompey stood to gain by the patronage of Antistius and his family, whatever career he chose.

5. Plutarch may be basing his interpretation upon Pompey's behaviour in his later marriages.

6. Mucia's children receive attention in the ancient sources (Ascon. *Pro M. Scaur.* 17; Suet. *D.J.* 50.1; Dio 37.49.3). Mucia was fruitful also in her subsequent marriage, being delivered of a son to M. Aemilius Scaurus (Ascon. *Pro. M. Scaur.* 17).

7. Cicero (*Brut.* 218–19) mentions an invective by C. Scribonius Curio in 55 B.C., where an affair with Caesar could have been given as grounds for the divorce of Pompey and Mucia. However, Cicero does not explicitly say this; hence it is doubtful that Plutarch is referring to this. There is always the possibility that Plutarch is referring to a letter of Cicero which is no longer extant.

8. M. Deutsch (*Phil. Quart.* 8 [1929], 218–22) argues that the divorce was for infidelity and that Cicero's letter to Atticus with its juxtaposition of Mucia's infidelity and the Bona Dea scandal makes it ample evidence that the divorce occurred because of adultery. Deutsch believes the letter is an account of social gossip, not political intrigue. Gruen, *The Last Generation of the Roman Republic* (Berkeley, 1974), p. 85 argues that the familial connection with the Metelli gained by Pompey's marriage to Mucia had not proved politically advantageous to him and so Pompey was eager for more promising relations. He was now the leading politician and many, even Caesar, would have been eager for an association with him. One wonders, if Caesar did have an illicit liaison with Mucia, was it a plot to break up the marriage so that Pompey would be available for an alliance with Julia!

9. Even if the sentiment is pretended, it reveals a sensitivity to the attractions of quiet domestic life.

10. In keeping with this new image, Pompey did not divorce Julia despite such a recommendation from his advisers.

11. Anti-Pompeian bias is enhanced further by the presence of Lollia in the list of women seduced by Caesar. She was the wife of Aulus Gabinius, a Pompeian supporter.

12. Plut. *Caes.* 14.4, *Pomp.* 47.6; Suet. *D.J.* 21; App. *Bell. Civ.* 2.1.4. For discussion that Caepio is M. Brutus, see R. Syme, *Roman Revolution* (Oxford, 1939), p. 34.

13. Plutarch here provides another reference to Pompey's preference for the company of women over the execution of public duties.

14. W. S. Anderson, *Pompey, his Friends, and the Literature of the First Century B.C.* (Berkeley, 1963), pp. 77–80.

15. Suet. *Grammat.* 14.1. I am aware that there are problems with the dating of the affair between Memmius and a wife of Pompey. Suetonius says that Nicias delivered a letter from Memmius 'ad Pompeii uxorem', proposing a sexual affair. The affair came to nothing and if this attempt at seduction explains the serious breach between Memmius and Pompey after 53 B.C., then the *uxor* being seduced would have to be Cornelia. On the other hand, Nicias does drop out of Pompey's circle in 56 B.C. and Julia thus seems a more likely candidate for Memmius' attentions than does Cornelia as in W. S. Anderson's interpretation. I wish to acknowledge and thank Professor Anderson for his help with this problem.

16. Plut. *Pomp.* 55.1. This idea is echoed by J. Leach (above, n. 3), p. 154. Cornelia is discussed by E. Best, 'Cicero, Livy and Educated Women', *CJ* 65 (1970), 200–1 and by Anderson (above, n. 14), p. 81.

# PLATO'S MOTHER AND OTHER TERRIBLE WOMEN

*By* PETER WALCOT

> A mother is only brought unlimited satisfaction by her relation to a son; this is altogether the most perfect, the most free from ambivalence of all human relationships. A mother can transfer to her son the ambition which she has been obliged to suppress in herself and she can expect from him the satisfaction of all that has been left over in her of her masculinity complex.
>
> (Sigmund Freud, Lecture on 'Femininity')[1]

## I

In the eighth and ninth books of the *Republic* Plato describes the four inferior or corrupt types of government—timocracy, oligarchy, democracy, and tyranny—and the four related types of human personality—the timocratic, oligarchic, democratic, and tyrannical man (544dff.). Closest to the ideal, and first therefore in sequence of decline, is the timocratic state, the term timocracy being employed not in the Aristotelian sense of a polity demanding a property qualification of its ruling class but with 'the peculiar meaning of government by the principle of honour (τιμή)'.[2] The timocratic state, it is claimed (545cff.), develops when its members no longer live in harmony but come into conflict as the guardians join brides and bridegrooms 'inopportunely' (παρὰ καιρόν, 546d), so that their offspring are neither well-born nor blessed by fortune. The result is a form of government which retains some of the features of its good predecessor, anticipates some of the features of its worse successor, and also boasts some features unique to itself, such as a preference for the 'spirited', men better suited for war than for peace. Above all else such a state will be distinguished by a cultivation of competition and a passion for honour: διαφανέστατον δ' ἐν αὐτῇ ἐστὶν ἕν τι μόνον . . . φιλονικίαι καὶ φιλοτιμίαι (548c).

But what of the corresponding type of human personality? What are the characteristics of the timocratic man? He will be, among other things, a lover of office and a lover of honour who bases his claim to office not on any rhetorical skill but on his prowess in war. An enthusiast for exercise and the hunt, he would scorn wealth as a young man but be increasingly attracted to it as he grew older (548dff.). This is really all that Plato has to tell us about the character of the timocratic man, and it is considerably less than his comments on the other types of human personality. Instead, as

more than adequate compensation, we are presented with a truly remarkable account of the family situation which can shape and mould a character of the timocratic variety, thus confirming Plato's earlier indictment of guardians who fail to match bride and bridegroom successfully; and this account of the relationship between wife and husband and between mother and son is so devastating in its insight into family psychology that it must be quoted in its entirety.

The origin of the timocratic youth is as follows:

> He is often the young son of a brave father, who dwells in an ill-governed city, declining its honours and offices, and avoiding its lawsuits and other such business; and quite ready to waive his rights in order that he may escape trouble. The character of the son begins to develop when he hears his mother complaining that her husband has no place in the government, of which the consequence is that she has no precedence among other women. Further, when she sees her husband not very eager about money, and instead of battling and railing in the law courts or assembly, taking whatever happens to him quietly; and when she observes that his thoughts always centre in himself, while he treats her with no special honour and no great disrespect, she is annoyed, and says to her son that his father is only half a man and far too easy-going: adding all the other complaints about her own ill-treatment which women are so fond of rehearsing. The old servants also, who are supposed to be attached to the family, from time to time talk privately in the same strain to the son; and if they see anyone who owes money to his father or is wronging him in any way, and he fails to prosecute them, they tell the youth that when he grows up he must retaliate upon all people of this sort, and be more of a man than his father. He has only to walk abroad and he hears and sees the same sort of thing: those who mind their own business in the city are called simpletons and held in no esteem, while the busy-bodies are honoured and applauded. The result is that the young man, hearing and seeing all these things—hearing, too, the words of his father, and having a nearer view of his way of life, and making comparisons of him and others—is drawn opposite ways: while his father is watering and nourishing the rational principle in his soul, the others are encouraging the passionate and appetitive; and he being not originally of a bad nature, but having kept bad company, is at last brought by their joint influence to a middle point, and gives up the kingdom which is within him to the middle principle of contentiousness and passion, and, in his maturity, becomes arrogant and ambitious. (549c–550b, trans. Benjamin Jowett)

It is not necessary to be trained in applied psychoanalysis in order to appreciate the skill and sophistication with which Plato has set in the context of the family this description of the easy-going father who avoids his wife's constant nagging by simply not listening, the frustrated mother whose resentment is fuelled by other women and her own servants, and, at the centre of the maelstrom, the son subjected to a relentless pressure to succeed where his father is reputed to have failed by a mother who may realize her own thwarted ambitions only vicariously through her offspring.

'This section has a realistic ring' remarks Andersson at one point when discussing the role of the wife in forming the young timocrat.[3] And surely so intimate an understanding owes less to philosophical principle and at least as much to personal experience on Plato's part as the philosopher appears to display in, for example, his portrayal of the democratic state or when he speaks of the superior knowledge of the tyrant to be expected from the person who has lived under the same roof with a tyrant (cf. 577a–b). But what personal experience can explain so graphic a description especially of the mother of the timocratic man? Obviously the timocratic state reflects to some extent contemporary Sparta (cf. 545a), and one recalls Plutarch's collection of 'Sayings of Spartan Women' (*Moralia* 240c–242d); the celebrated remark passed by one Spartan mother as she handed her son his shield—'either with this or on this' (241f)—is a fair indication of the fierce pride of the mothers of Sparta and the pressure which they applied to their sons. But much nearer at home, in fact in Athens itself, Plato knew of one married couple where the husband was certainly a failure when measured by the standards of contemporary society and the wife notoriously a shrew. That couple comprised Socrates and Xanthippe. In choosing service of god Socrates also chose poverty and to avoid public life (cf. *Apol.* 23b–c and 32a–b). He was obviously much older than Xanthippe, since she was accompanied by a young child at Socrates' death-scene (cf. *Phaedo* 60a), whereas Socrates was seventy at the time of his execution. On that sad occasion Socrates preferred the company of his male associates, cutting short his wife's incipient lamentations with an abrupt request that someone take Xanthippe home (*Phaedo* 60a). Xanthippe's actual name, we may also note, with its 'horse' termination reeks of the aristocracy.[4]

Socrates must have infuriated his wife on many occasions just as much as he undoubtedly infuriated the jury at his trial or his fellow prytaneis at an earlier date when he alone resisted the proposal that the generals who commanded at the battle of Arginusae be tried collectively (*Apol.* 32b–c). The eldest son of Socrates and Xanthippe, and he counted as a mere μειράκιον at the time of the trial (cf. *Apol.* 34d), Lamprocles bears eloquent testimony to his mother's temper when, in Xenophon's *Memorabilia*, he claims that no maternal service can compensate for Xanthippe's appalling temper or τὴν χαλεπότητα (2.2.7). When asked by Socrates which he thinks the harder to bear, the savagery of a wild beast or mother, he has no hesitation in opting for that of a mother when it is a mother like his, and it is clear that it was Xanthippe's tongue which so distressed her son (cf. 2.2.8), though there is a suggestion that Xanthippe was also a strict disciplinarian (cf. 2.2.9). And there are further the comment passed by Antisthenes, also recorded by Xenophon, that Socrates lives with a wife who is the most difficult (χαλεπωτάτῃ) of all existent women and, he suspects, of all women that have ever been or there ever will be, and Socrates' answering riposte—Xanthippe offers good practice since if he can tolerate her, toleration of the rest of mankind will be easy (*Symposium* 2.10)!

But there is another possible prototype for the mother of the timocratic man and one yet closer to home for Plato, and in advancing this potential link I am less influenced by factors which are certainly suggestive, e.g., the abolition of the family for the guardians in the *Republic* (457c–d), and much more by the support of Wilamowitz himself, who stated quite baldly some sixty-five years ago that (1) the description of the mother of the timocratic man is the solitary portrait of a woman drawn by Plato, (2) we must believe the description to have been grounded in experience, and (3) it was experience of Plato's own mother Periktione who, after the death of her first husband and Plato's father Ariston, an apparent nonentity, married the politically active Pyrilampes.[5] And if we should be correct in detecting here the person of Plato's own mother, we ought hardly to register surprise, for a whole series of Plato's relatives, admittedly under their own names, figures in the dialogues, Charmides, Critias, Adeimantus, Glaucon, Antiphon, and Pyrilampes.

The evidence that may be pieced together to build up a picture of Plato's immediate family is restricted but not without interest and significance.[6] His mother Periktione came from stock which traced its descent back to Solon; she appears to have been born about the middle of the fifth century B.C. or slightly later, and to have survived to a very considerable age, still being alive in the 360s. Her first husband Ariston could boast an even more impressive pedigree stretching back to Codrus and Melanthus, but otherwise nothing is known of him or of his activities. Periktione and Ariston must have married when Periktione was no older than her middle teens and, while the marriage lasted long enough for three sons, including Plato, and a daughter to be born, probably for about the ten years between the middle 430s and middle 420s, Plato would have been deprived of his father at a very early age. Pyrilampes, Plato's step-father, was Periktione's maternal uncle and some thirty years older than his wife, and when Periktione lost her second husband, she would seem to have remained a widow for more than fifty years. There is no doubt that Pyrilampes was very active politically, perhaps being an ambassador to the Persians when the peace of 449 B.C. was negotiated, but one is entitled to wonder how attractive a husband he was to a wife so much younger and a wife who had already had four children of her own by a previous husband. Finally, we should remember that Plato himself never married.

But what does all this add up to? It does not require an excess of ingenuity for a psychologist to do for Plato what Freud did for Leonardo in his *Leonardo da Vinci and a Memory of his Childhood*.[7] A relative lack of information has not prevented surprisingly detailed psychoanalysis of the Greek philosopher, a prime example having been offered recently by Bennett Simon.[8] If the more speculative and extreme is left to one side, surely some weight is to be attached to such details as Periktione's great age and continuing influence on a son who never married, and Plato's early loss of a father and his replacement by a distinguished but elderly statesman whose political views are likely to have been much more in tune with those of Periclean Athens than those of oligarchs like Charmides and Critias, his mother's brother and his mother's cousin. Pyrilampes, for instance, had a son by his first wife whom he named Demos,[9] whereas Charmides and Critias were, of course, very prominent in the oligarchic revolution at Athens in 404 B.C. If Plato was seeking a father-figure, his true father having died a youngish man and his step-father being of different sympathies, he appears to have discovered a more than adequate substitute in the person of Socrates only to have been cruelly deprived yet again by the execution of his teacher. And so a void was created which, perhaps, only his mother Periktione could attempt to fill and to fill in such a way as to leave positive traces in Plato's depiction of the mother of the timocratic man.

## II

Although we have exhausted our knowledge of Xanthippe and Periktione, a great deal more remains to be said about this type of mother, for the very first mother to be encountered in any Greek source conforms closely to the Platonic sketch of the mother of the timocratic man. That mother is the nereid Thetis as the goddess is portrayed by Homer. Thetis' son the hero Achilles is very much the timocratic man, a superb warrior obsessed with the pursuit of personal glory to such an extent that he will not have his companion Patroclus too successful on the field of battle (*Iliad* 16.80ff.) in case his own opportunity to acquire honour is threatened (cf. verse 90). What is said by Thetis, and what is said about Thetis, in the *Iliad* readily explain the son's choice of a brief life of glory, for already in that epic we are presented with the goddess's wedding to the mortal Peleus (cf. 18. 84–7; 24.60–3) and, more significantly, Thetis' personal view of the marriage—she did not wish to wed Peleus, who now lives in his halls a victim of grievous old age (18.433–5). Clearly marriage between an immortal goddess and an inevitably aging human is no union of equals and hardly destined to prove a lasting success. We may compare, for instance, the affair between Eos and Tithonus, another pair consisting of one divine and one human partner (*Hymn to Aphrodite* 218ff.): Eos secured from Zeus the grant of immortality for

Tithonus but without the crucial gift of eternal youth, and so Tithonus grew older and older and ever more disgusting until Eos was compelled to lock away her erstwhile lover (verses 233–8). A declining Peleus would be no more physically attractive to Thetis, who certainly in the *Iliad* seems to spend all her time apart from her husband and with her father and sisters in the depths of the sea (cf. 1.357–9, 496, and 531–2; 6.135–7; 18.35ff. and 398–405; 24.77ff.), and here one should recall the Aristophanic joke in which the claim that Peleus won Thetis because of his (sexual) moderation, διὰ τὸ σωφρονεῖν, is countered with the reply that she then went off and left him since he was not exciting enough in bed (*Clouds* 1067–70).

Achilles does, however, speak of often having heard his mother 'in his father's halls' telling of the occasion when she alone of the immortals saved Zeus from disaster (1.396ff.; cf. also 18.59–60). The frequency (πολλάκι, verse 396) with which Thetis appears to have regaled an audience with such a story suggests a female conscious of her own abilities and not averse to parading these before all and sundry. At the same time a sense of bitterness and of frustration is also conveyed when Thetis dwells on Achilles' limited expectation of life (*Il.* 1.414–18; 18.52–62 and 436ff.; 24.131–2; cf. 9.410–16; 18.88–90; 24.84–6 and 104–5), leaving us in no doubt as to her concern and, just as much, her ambition for her son. The removal of Briseis sends Thetis dashing off to console Achilles (1.357ff.), and the goddess is not above a resort to emotional blackmail in order to win the support of Zeus on behalf of her son (cf. 1.500ff.). At one point in the narrative of the *Iliad* the poet refers to Achilles not knowing of Patroclus' death and not expecting that Patroclus was dead (17.401ff.), for often he was kept informed by his mother in private conversation and she would tell him of the intention of great Zeus (verses 408–9); and Thetis did more than simply supply her son with advance information (cf. 9.410ff. and 18.9ff.) since, in addition to presenting the case on his behalf before the gods, she can inspire Achilles to action (cf. 18.128–9 and 19.34–6). As Zeus himself remarks, his mother ever stands by Achilles' side by night and by day alike (24.72–3). Obviously Thetis is over-protective towards her son, but that is hardly unexpected behaviour on the part of a mother when the father is either absent or inadequate or both. According to a tradition preserved by Apollonius Rhodius (4.869ff.), Thetis attempted to bestow immortality on Achilles but her efforts were foiled by Peleus whom the goddess then left for good. Thus Thetis was anxious to remedy the inadequacy of her husband, in this instance his mortality, in her son but this resulted in a lasting quarrel between husband and wife. But while Achilles had to serve as compensation for a husband's deficiencies, to go any further, to stress, for example, the affection shared between Achilles and Patroclus and to relate this to the former's excessive dependence on his mother, would be to strain the evidence.[10]

The bitter resentment of a woman married to a social inferior is even more vividly illustrated in fifth-century tragedy and Euripides' presentation of Electra, the daughter of the murdered Agamemnon, in the play of the same name. In order to prevent Electra from giving birth to 'noble' sons who might avenge their grandfather (verses 19ff. and 267–9), the princess has been married off to a mere farmer whose own sense of outraged shame is such that he has not consummated the marriage. For Electra the marriage is a 'deadly wedding' (θανάσιμον γάμον, verse 247), and the message which she wishes to be relayed to the supposedly absent Orestes reveals the intensity of her anguish at the situation (verses 300 ff.; cf. 1004–5 and 1008–10). She revels in her misery, so much so in fact that when she tells her husband that Orestes has sent the strangers as 'spectators' of her woes, the farmer's response is not a little sarcastic: 'some then they see but others, I imagine, you relate' (verse 355). Here, as elsewhere, we recognize that understanding of the human personality and the forces which shape it that has deservedly earned Euripides the title of psychologist.[11]

What Orestes and Pylades did in fact see was an Electra who carried a pot on her head to collect water (though not of necessity but to proclaim the *hybris* of Aegisthus, verses 55–8) and an Electra who looked like a slave with her shorn head (e.g., verses 107–9) and wretched clothes (e.g., verse 185). But Electra certainly does not lack spirit; in a touch of absolutely typical Euripidean 'realism' she complains that the farmer has invited a pair of guests into the house when the larder is bare (verses 404–5), but the asperity of her taunt to the husband (verse 408) is nothing when compared to the fury and loathing directed against Clytemnestra and Aegisthus, those responsible not only for a dear (cf. verse 1102) father's death in the past but also for her own present humiliation: thus Electra gloats sickeningly over the body of Aegisthus (verses 907ff.) and shows no mercy towards her mother (cf. verses 1060 ff.), willingly admitting her role in that mother's death (cf. verses 1183, 1201–5, 1224–5 and 1303ff.). Clytemnestra, like her daughter, has married beneath her station in society (cf. verses 925 ff.) but chose to do so and, more than a little ironically given her own position, Electra can proceed to comment on the disgrace of a marriage when the woman is in control (verses 932–7).

Electra and Orestes are sister and brother and not mother and son, but Electra's relationship to Orestes is quasi-maternal[12] and indeed is made explicitly maternal by Sophocles in this playwright's version of the story, for in this other *Electra* the heroine declares

> Alas for all my nursing of old days,
> so constant—all for nothing—which I gave you;

my joy was in the trouble of it. For never
were you your mother's love as much as mine.
None was your nurse but I within that household.

(verses 1143–7, trans. David Grene)

There is no doubt that in Euripides Electra is much the stronger character, relentlessly goading Orestes to take action (cf. verses 276–81, 646–7, 685ff., and 967ff.), while Orestes, it might well be felt, displays a sad mixture of indecision and hesitation and is far from being the resolute avenger anticipated by Electra (cf. verses 524–6). His opening words are hardly reassuring (cf. verses 82ff.), for Orestes seems to propose either to beat a hasty retreat if recognized or to contact his sister and enlist her assistance (cf. verses 95ff.). His action in cowering down beneath cover in the hope of picking up some information when a woman seeming to be a slave approaches (cf. verses 107ff.) is lacking in that boldness which Electra thinks essential for success (cf. verse 277).

Fifth-century comedy provides a final example of an aristocratic wife who scorns a socially inferior husband and, as a result, indulges their son to a dangerous extent, and here the effects on the son and the consequences for the father are to be clearly seen. The *Clouds* of Aristophanes opens with the farmer Strepsiades bitterly complaining about the debts which he has incurred because of his son's wildly extravagant passion for horses and chariot-racing (verses 12ff.). In this comedy it is the husband Strepsiades who regrets the marriage, a marriage between a 'rustic' and a town aristocrat, a member of the Alcmeonid family, a niece of Megacles, the son of Megacles, and 'a right duchess' (verse 48; cf. 800) and oversexed to boot (verses 41–55).[13] Even the birth of a son led to a quarrel as husband and wife fought over their offspring's name, in the end compromising and settling on 'Pheidippides', a name, of course, combining the contradictory notions of 'thrift' and 'horses' (verses 60ff.). Certainly the ambitions for the son cherished by each parent were very different (cf. verses 68–70 and 70–2), and the influence of the mother proved stronger in time (cf. verses 73–4). Pheidippides refuses to attend Socrates' school with its sickly pupils and charlatan teacher (cf. verses 102ff.); his own companions are rich young men (cf. verses 119–20), and he can always appeal to his mother's rich relatives (cf. verses 124–5). Strepsiades is totally unable to handle his son and, even when allowance is made for comic exaggeration, it is plain how vulnerable the father is when married to a wife with social pretensions, thus strengthening Electra's observation in Euripides' play

O what perversion, when the woman in the house
stands out as master, not the man. I shake in hate
to see those children whom the city knows and names

not by their father's name but only by their mother's.
It marks the bridegroom who has climbed to a nobler bed;
when no one mentions the husband, everyone knows the wife.

(verses 932–7, trans. E. T. Vermeule)

In the arranged marriage, as that between Pheidippides' parents certainly was (cf. verses 41–2), the husband-to-be as 'bride-taker' is under an obligation to the bride's family inasmuch as he is receiving a favour in the form of his wife-to-be from that family; a higher status on the part of the potential husband helps to cancel the obligation, whereas a lower status increases the debt owed the 'bride-givers' or father and mother of the bride.

## III

But Thetis and Achilles, Electra and Orestes, and Strepsiades and Pheidippides in Homer, Euripides, and Aristophanes are characters in literary texts and, unlike Plato's mother, not real, once living persons. For real people we must turn to history, and in turning to history we must believe psychological analysis to be a legitimate tool of historical research, accepting the judgement of Arthur Marwick when he maintains that 'today no historian could write a biographical study without betraying something of the influence of Freud and post-Freudian psychology'.[14] But the proof of the pudding is reputed to be in the eating and a single convincing illustration is worth any amount of theorizing; and Greek history can boast at least one outstanding personality of the timocratic type and timocratic to the extent that he attempted to model his life and exploits on the life and exploits of Homer's hero Achilles and a personality, moreover, one of whose parents was a passionate, even violent mother desperate to secure her son's accession to power. I refer, it goes almost without saying, to Alexander the Great, who more than sixty years ago was exposed to the scrutiny of a psychologist and claimed as a victim of narcissism or excessive self-worship, a state of morbidity traced back to his mother Olympias' unsatisfactory marriage.[15] 'In the narrow confines of a semi-barbaric court Alexander did not have the best opportunity to rid himself of the distorted views inculcated by his mother, and likely enough they were also fostered by the court circle, whose natural trend to sycophancy is well known even in modern times.'[16] Everything—the early estrangement between son and father, a jealousy of the father's achievements even after Philip's assassination, a harsh education, 'the recurrent and haunting desire for godhood', the murder of Clitus (a substitute father?), an intolerance of criticism, a fondness for 'oriental pomp and circumstance', an insatiable desire for further conquest or adventure, an increasing retreat from reality, a boredom which led to lethargy which in its turn led to debauchery—everything provides grist for the psychologist's mill and adds weight to an inexorable conclusion—the brief life and career of Alexander offers an excellent example of a truly colossal narcissism.

In fact it is possible to do rather better (or should it be worse?) than this without too great an effort, as A. R. Burn was to demonstrate some twenty years on. Burn writes with no little imagination when he tells his reader that 'Alexander's first memories were of a house where his mother was very much the mistress, and an affectionate and doting mother to him; while "father" was a rather remote concept, embodied from time to time in a tired, haggard, but still restless man . . . who turned up at long intervals'.[17] And what was the result? Olympias seems to have saddled her son with 'something of a mother-fixation', and Alexander grew up with an Oedipus complex but, luckily, 'a relatively mild one'. As a consequence Alexander 'appears to have developed a certain disgust with sex in general' as is evinced by his failure to provide an established successor to the Macedonian throne.[18] All this evidently embarrassed W. W. Tarn, who included in the second volume of his *Alexander the Great* an appendix which he regretted having to write entitled 'Alexander's Attitude to Sex'.[19] The main purpose of the appendix was to prove that Alexander did not have any attitude to sex, since it is essentially a rebuttal of the opinions that Alexander was a homosexual or promiscuous. If Alexander never had a mistress, Tarn maintains, if his two marriages were purely political, and if the solitary woman he cared for was his mother well then, this was because of Alexander's 'self-control', the subjugation of body to mind and will. Or was it perhaps something more than just that? Thus Tarn's incredibly romantic estimate of Alexander leads to the astonishing suggestion that also 'there was something very like compassion for the whole of womankind; in his day they needed it badly enough'.[20] One is left gasping as indeed presumably was the scholar who justly claimed that 'the assimilation of the court and temper of fourth-century Macedonia to the reign of Queen Victoria is a *tour de force* that only a genius like Tarn could ever have conceived, or imposed on the English-speaking world'.[21] Tarn's suggestion is surely a proposition to be relegated to the same rubbish-tip as the equally sentimental nonsense that would make Alexander, an élitist if ever there was one, an advocate of the brotherhood of mankind.

The sharpest of contrasts is offered by Robin Lane Fox, who speaks of Alexander as 'a man who was to sleep with at least one man, four mistresses, three wives, a eunuch and, so gossip believed, an Amazon',[22] and there is no room for doubt that Alexander did have mistresses such as the Persian aristocrat Barsine captured at Issus, though the great passion of his life was his male companion Hephaestion who was required to play the role of Patroclus to Alexander's Achilles.[23] Lane Fox must be thought correct when he claims that 'no more can be said with certainty than that Alexander respected women rather than abused them'.[24] A refreshingly sane note has similarly been struck by Peter Green, who, in attacking a Freudian interpretation, remarks that 'if he (Alexander) had any kind of Oedipus complex it came a very poor second to the burning dynastic ambition which Olympias so sedulously fostered in him: those who insist on his psychological motivation would do better to take Adler as their mentor than Freud'.[25]

Alexander has yet to attract the attention of the exponents of the kind of applied psychology which has recently acquired the name of 'psycho-history'. The stress placed by psychohistory on childhood experience will be appreciated when it is noted that the *Journal of Psychohistory* was originally founded in 1973 with a main title *History of Childhood Quarterly*, while a founding father of the journal, Lloyd deMause, was the editor of *The History of Childhood*.[26] The titles of both periodical and book reflect the belief that 'the differing childhoods found in history could be an empirical basis for studying the changing personality patterns of individuals and groups in history'.[27] While we are reasonably well informed about Alexander's early years,[28] the inadequacies of psychohistory have been ruthlessly exposed and many would sympathize with David E. Stannard when he argues that 'the psychoanalytic approach to history is—irremediably—one of logical perversity, scientific unsoundness, and cultural naïveté'.[29] If psychohistory is to be fairly evaluated and its implications for the history of the ancient world judged without prejudice, it is only proper that the work of one of its less extreme adherents should be examined, and such a study is provided by Thomas W. Africa's discussion of the tyrannicide Brutus,[30] and Brutus, it will be recalled, was the son of a mother, Servilia, who was the step-sister of the Younger Cato and mother-in-law of Cassius, another of Caesar's murderers, and also, at one period of her life, the mistress of Julius Caesar as well, a liaison which gave birth to a rumour that Brutus was actually the dictator's son.[31] Brutus suggests highly tempting material for the psychologist, since he lost his father at an early age, most probably when he was not yet ten years old, and had a mother up to her neck in the political machinations of the Late Republic and, according to Suetonius, the most loved of his many women by Caesar, the victim of Brutus' dagger (cf. *Jul.* 50.2, 'sed ante alias dilexit Marci Bruti matrem Serviliam').

It requires little effort to interpret Brutus' assassination of his mother's lover for some twenty odd years in Freudian terms—to see here yet again the rebellion of the young against the dominant older male who reserves the women within the group for his own exclusive use. Thus Ronald Syme, discussing Brutus' motivation, claims that 'there were deeper causes still in Brutus' resolve to slay the tyrant—envy of Caesar and the memory of Caesar's amours with Servilia, public and notorious'.[32] Wisely Syme does not probe any more deeply whereas Africa does, even to the extent of noting that Brutus stabbed Caesar a blow in the groin—*καὶ Βροῦτος αὐτῷ πληγὴν ἐνέβαλε μίαν εἰς τὸν βουβῶνα* (Plut. *Caes.* 66.6)—and remarking 'perhaps, it was a chance blow; more likely it was intended'.[33] Elsewhere Africa treads on even thinner ice though protecting himself from possible criticism by exploiting the formula 'a Freudian psychoanalyst might . . .'. Thus he writes at one point

> A Freudian psychoanalyst might identify Brutus as an anal personality—self-disciplined, parsimonious, obstinate, hard-driving, guilt-ridden, and aggressive . . . . The world of scholarship would be poorer and less productive without anal personalities—and Brutus was a bookish man. Although its dynamics contribute to success in many fields of endeavor, the anal personality is a suit of armor, inside of which is an encapsulated child seething with fierce emotions. In emotional crises, particularly those of rejection or opposition, pent-up feelings may burst forth in acts of fury all the more intense and dangerous when rationalized in terms acceptable to the conscious mind.[34]

Elsewhere Africa is able to contend that 'in 49, when the ever-worsening crisis erupted into military confrontation between Caesar and Pompey, Brutus chose to support Pompey. . . . A traditional Freudian might find Brutus' choice obvious, even obligatory, since Caesar was his mother's sexual partner and in terms of Freud's dogma, his unconscious rival.'[35] And where Caesar is concerned, Africa does not hesitate: 'whatever his unconscious feelings toward Servilia, Brutus' attitude toward Caesar was certainly Oedipal, the protective son against a hated father figure.'[36]

Such speculation will not convince all and perhaps not even many, but Africa has made an important contribution in the identification of what he terms 'the Coriolanus syndrome', that is, a family situation in which the mother plays both parental roles (as Coriolanus' mother did in raising a son deprived of his father early in life) and the mother is the dominant force in the growing son's development. As examples of the dominant mother from the Late Republic Africa can cite Cornelia, the mother of the Gracchi (on whom see Juvenal 6.166–9), Aurelia, Caesar's mother, and Atia, whose son was to become the emperor Augustus (cf. Tac. *Dialogus* 28.6) or refer to Sertorius of whom Plutarch wrote in his *Life* the following: 'having lost his father and having been becomingly reared by a widowed mother, he appears to have been exceedingly fond of this mother'—*ὑπερφυῶς δοκεῖ φιλομήτωρ γενέσθαι* (*Sert.* 2). Another pair consisting of mother and son to be considered is Julia and Mark Antony. A modern biographer has this to say about the son:

> In amateur psychology it is all too easy to attribute a man's character to ties with

his mother; but in the case of Antony, it may be fair to ascribe his repeated rebellions against social mores and his dependence on strong-minded women like Fulvia and Cleopatra to a home governed by Julia, over her short-lived, irresponsible husbands.[37]

Any list of dominant mothers can be readily extended to cover the times of the Julio-Claudian dynasty or even later when one remembers the pressure applied by his mother Vespasia Polla to the man who was destined to become the eventual successor of Nero, the emperor Vespasian (Suet. *Vesp.* 2.2). A mention of Nero immediately calls to mind the Younger Agrippina. Could there ever have been a better example of an ambitious mother than Agrippina or a better example of an inadequate husband than Claudius or, thirdly, a better example of a perverted son than the murderous Nero? Agrippina, moreover, would seem not to have been untypical of her generation, at least according to her son's tutor, the philosopher Seneca, for Seneca, it has been noted,[38] can say of his own mother Helvia that she was quite unlike average mothers who, because women cannot hold office, try to realize their ambitions through their sons ('quae, quia feminis honores non licet gerere, per illos ambitiosae sunt', *ad Helviam* 14.2). Helvia, it is claimed, gained nothing from her sons' election to office except pleasure and expense; never did her affection look to self-interest (cf. 14.3). If any woman played the part of thrusting mother on behalf of Seneca, it appears to have been the philosopher's aunt (cf. 19.2).

## IV

The evidence of mythology and occasional reference in literature to Oedipus-type dreams led E. R. Dodds to 'conclude that the family situation in ancient Greece, like the family situation today, gave rise to infantile conflicts whose echoes lingered in the unconscious mind of the adult'.[39] Many years earlier Dodds had written on perhaps the greatest personality from late antiquity, a son ravaged by conflict and a conflict whose origins were to be sought, in the opinion of Dodds, in family history. That personality was Augustine, the offspring of a Christian mother, 'a pious countrywoman' Monica, and 'a small country squire named Patricius, a pagan by tradition and temperament'—'of this ill-assorted union Augustine was the fruit'.[40] 'The recurrent ground-theme' of Augustine's *Confessions*, according to Dodds, was the saint's claim that 'duae voluntates meae confligebant inter se', and there could really be no closer parallel to the competing pressures, from mother and from father, to which Plato's timocratic youth was subjected, and the *Confessions*, of course, is as personal a document as Plato's description of the timocratic youth is suspected to be. And Dodds was able to take advantage of contemporary psychology and to write as follows:

In the meantime, as we learn from a casual parenthesis, Augustine's father had died. From the tone of this and other references to his father, and from the absence in the *Confessions* of all references to his brother and sister, it is apparent that Monica was the only member of his family who counted for him. More and more, on her side, she concentrated upon this son the love which she had never been able to give to his father: 'far more than other mothers,' he says, 'she delighted to be with her son.' On the son's part, revolt seems to have alternated with partial surrender throughout his youth and early manhood; until his conversion to Catholicism brought about complete surrender, and he could say of her, after her death, 'Of her life and mine was one life made.' One need not have studied Freud to recognise in this exceptional relationship to his mother one of the determining factors in Augustine's life-history. From this springs his inability to find happiness in the love of women; from this his desperate pursuit—in philosophy, in friendship, at last in religion—of an elusive substitute for that happiness.[41]

The contrast between Helvia, the mother of Seneca, and Monica, the mother of Augustine, could not be more marked or so it seems.

Dodds's study was 'addressed to the ordinary reader'; a similarly 'simple account of Augustine's personal life and background' was provided a few years later by a non-professional author and, what is more remarkable, by a woman. Rebecca West may have been a woman but that in no way made her over favourably disposed towards Monica, 'a woman', it was observed, 'whose good temper was of the sort that causes bad temper in others'.[42] Again the preoccupations of contemporary psychiatric theory may be detected when, for example, Augustine's lack of sympathy with his father's economic troubles is said to be explicable only 'by his love for his mother Monnica, which was so strong that he was bound to hate anyone who had a competing claim on her'. Equally suggestive of the teachings of Freud are Rebecca West's comments on Monica's attitude towards her son:

It was fortunate that in her religion she had a perfect and, indeed, noble instrument for obtaining her desire that her son should not become a man. Very evidently Christianity need not mean emasculation, but the long struggles of Augustine and Monnica imply that in his case it did. Monnica could have put him into the Church as into a cradle. He would then take vows of continence and annul the puberty she detested.[43]

But all this sounds very elementary and crude when compared to more recent efforts by the medically qualified. For Charles Kligerman, M. D. Augustine 'was possibly the greatest introspective psychologist before Freud' and his *Confessions* 'a psychiatric personal history without the contaminating presence of an interviewer'.[44] When it comes to an assessment of Monica, Kligerman goes straight to the point, remarking

Emotionally alienated from her husband, she had grown especially close to her oldest son and pinned her hopes on him. Augustine tells us how she daily wept over him, praying for his soul. It is not hard to detect an erotic quality in such behavior. Frigid hypermoral women frequently find concealed incestuous gratification in such stormy emotional scenes with their sons. For him it must have been an extremely seductive yet frustrating process, and sheds light on the turbulence of his adolescence.[45]

Unfortunately Augustine tells us of none of his dreams, but one school experience is thought to be of a very special significance, his strong reaction to the story of Aeneas and Dido. Why? According to Kligerman, Augustine's flight from his mother to Rome 'was almost a direct re-enactment of the Aeneas and Dido legend which had so preoccupied him in boyhood. Like Aeneas, Augustine left the seductive blandishments and entreaties of his widowed African queen; he used the same type of trickery and sailed in the night from Carthage to fulfill his destiny in Rome. The parallelism is too striking to be coincidental; it was the compulsive repetition of his boyhood fantasy. . . . Augustine identified Dido with his mother, and himself with Aeneas, who had a great destiny to fulfill in Rome. The bitter tears he shed in childhood for poor slain Dido were the tears of rage, frustration and guilt he felt toward his mother.'[46]

And it is possible to go considerably further. Thus one authority, having listed the various episodes in Augustine's early life which illustrate the constant interference of Monica, proceeds to tabulate the allegedly abundant indirect evidence implying a close relationship between the young Augustine and his mother:

In the first place, there is his preoccupation with things of infancy, especially with his mouth. He devotes a disproportionate amount of his account—three books (1.6–8)—to speculative reverie of his own infancy, especially to his own behavior at the breast. The object on which he focused as a symbol of much of his adolescent turmoil was a pear. His own vocation, first as a teacher of rhetoric—a 'seller of words', in his own language—and later as preacher and prolific writer, may reflect some of the same oral preoccupation. The crisis of the major transition in his life seems especially to have been associated with somatic ailments of teeth and of lungs (IX. 2, 4, 5).[47]

It will have been noted that this is part only of the indirect evidence, and in addition to 'in the first place' there are also in second, third, fourth, and fifth place Augustine as 'a cowering "mama's boy"' at school, a continuing narcissism and indifference to the welfare of others, 'a strong and strongly disturbing conscience', and, in the view of some, 'running through the *Confessions* a persistent thread of homosexuality'.

But how far are we justified in joining those others who regard the *Confessions* as genuine autobiography and, on the basis of the information offered, in seeing Monica, the mother of Augustine, as the last of a long line of terrible mothers stretching all the way back to Thetis in Homer's *Iliad*? Certainly some of the events Augustine thought worthy of inclusion appear highly suggestive. There is, for example, the story he tells of how his father saw at the baths evidence of his son's sexual maturity and, excited at the prospect of grandchildren, was delighted to relay the news to Monica, whose reaction, however, was very different—'illa exsiluit pia trepidatione ac tremore' (2.3)—'fearing the crooked ways in which they walk who present their backs and not their faces' to God. Yet Monica was not in favour of the obvious solution, namely marriage, as this might threaten her hopes of her son's career. Both parents in fact were extremely keen that Augustine should make a success of his studies but for different reasons—the father because 'de te (sc. deo) prope nihil cogitabat, de me autem inania' and the mother because 'non solum nullo detrimento sed etiam nonnullo adiumento ad te adipiscendum futura existimabat usitata studia doctrinae' (2.3). Augustine surely is as unfair to his father as he is undoubtedly too generous in his assessment of his mother's motive.

A terrible mother will never relax her hold on her son, and I doubt whether any other has been quite so persistent as Monica proved to be, especially when it came to bewailing her son and praying for her son (cf. 3.11). The real crunch arrived when Augustine left Carthage for Rome, as Monica would not let him depart without her and the future bishop, like Aeneas, had to resort to deceit, stealing away at night—'sed ea nocte clanculo ego profectus sum, illa autem non; mansit orando et flendo' (5.8). And even Augustine recognized that Monica was being obsessively maternal—'amabat enim secum praesentiam meam more matrum sed multis multo amplius.' It was no accident that Augustine fell grievously ill on his arrival at Rome; although his mother knew nothing of this, she continued to pray on her son's behalf and Augustine recovered. How would it have struck Monica if Augustine had died in a state of sin and not baptized? The son tells us: 'quo vulnere si feriretur cor matris, numquam sanaretur. non enim satis eloquor quid erga me habebat animi et quanto maiore sollicitudine me parturiebat spiritu quam carne pepererat. non itaque video quomodo sanaretur, si mea talis illa mors transverberasset viscera dilectionis eius' (5.9). From Rome Augustine went to Milan and by this time his mother had joined him after no easy journey from North Africa (cf. 6.1). At Milan Augustine was subjected to considerable pressure to force him into marriage—'et instabatur inpigre ut ducerem uxorem' (6.13)—and his mother was, or so it is reported, the prime instigator of a union. And with what result? A girl was found and the parents' consent secured, but the girl herself was nearly two years too young to marry—'aetas ferme biennio minus quam nubilis erat'—though she pleased Augustine and he was prepared to wait. But more immediate action resulted: the mistress with whom he had been living for years (cf. 4.2) and by whom he had a son whose later death Augustine mentions with an evident and deeply felt distress (9.6), this mistress 'avulsa a latere meo tamquam inpedimento coniugii' was sent back to Africa (6.15). There can be no doubt that the parting was an occasion for the greatest anguish on both sides even when every allowance is made for Augustine's habitual exaggeration. Although Augustine very quickly acquired a replacement, his mother might well have felt satisfied at the elimination of so long-standing a relationship and a further diminution of the son's independence.

When Augustine experienced the revelation in the garden and the process of his conversion was completed, his mother was informed at once: 'inde ad matrem ingredimur, indicamus; gaudet. narramus quemadmodum gestum sit: exultat et triumphat, et benedicebat tibi, qui potens es ultra quam petimus aut intellegimus facere, quia tanto amplius sibi a te concessum de me videbat quam petere solebat miserabilibus flebilibus gemitibus' (8.12). But the real climax of Augustine's autobiography has yet to be related, and it comes in the form of an account of Monica's death and an assessment of this exemplary parent by her son. It is long: Augustine may have passed over much else in silence, 'sed non praeteribo quidquid mihi anima parturit de illa famula tua' (9.8). In fact we are told of her childhood (9.8), of her life when married to the hot-tempered Patricius (9.9), and of a last conversation between mother and son in which the former claimed to have no further reason to linger on earth once the latter had become a fully committed Christian (9.10). And we have still not reached a conclusion: there follows the story of the actual death when 'die nono aegritudinis suae, quinquagensimo et sexto anno aetatis suae, tricensimo et tertio aetatis meae, anima illa religiosa et pia corpore soluta est' (9.11). There remains Augustine's account of his immense though suppressed sorrow, the funeral, and the relief offered by private tears (9.12), and then, finally, we read of the saint's prayers for his dead mother (9.13).

Augustine clearly had a great capacity for love and that included a deepest affection directed towards such a friend as the unnamed young man with whom he had grown up at Thagaste and whose death caused him to leave the provinces for the city of Carthage (cf. 4.4–7). Later in the *Confessions* we hear much of two other friends, Alypius and Nebridius. But Augustine also had his mistresses and enjoyed the pleasures of heterosexual love. We must not, therefore, dwell too long on his male companions nor too long on family groupings such as Periktione, Ariston, and Plato or Thetis, Peleus, and Achilles or Olympias, Philip, and Alexander or Agrippina, Claudius, and Nero or Monica, Patricius, and Augustine, if concentration on examples drawn exclusively from the world of antiquity deceives us into believing that we have been considering personality types confined to that period of time. Our opening quotation from Freud's lecture on 'Femininity' with its mention of the mother being able to transfer to her son her own suppressed ambition is sufficient evidence of the persistence of the types given a society which imposes strict restraints upon the freedom of action allowed females. Twentieth-century parallels will spring readily to mind—read any biography of D. H. Lawrence or, better still, this novelist's *Sons and Lovers* with its picture of the Morel family. But it is perhaps better to close with an anthropologist's comment on the 'indestructible' bond between mother and son among the Sarakatsan shepherds of contemporary Greece:

> The bond between mother and son is indestructible. She gave him life; in him she fulfils herself and transcends the moral inferiority of her sex. Although a mother is more in the company of her daughters, it is the sons who are closest to her heart. They are her pride and the significant achievement of her life.[48]

Such an investment of love is certain to produce some terrible women whether in antiquity or the modern world.

## NOTES

1. *The Standard Edition of the Complete Psychological Works of Sigmund Freud* XXII (1932–6), London, 1964, p. 133.
2. Ernest Barker, *Greek Political Theory* (London, 1918), p. 251.
3. Torsten J. Andersson, *Polis and Psyche, a Motif in Plato's Republic*, Studia Graeca et Latina Gothoburgensia XXX (Göteborg, 1971), p. 161.
4. See A. H. Sommerstein's note on verse 64 in *The Comedies of Aristophanes* vol. 3, *Clouds* (Warminster, 1982).
5. U. von Wilamowitz-Moellendorff, *Platon* I. Leben und Werke (Berlin, 1919), p. 429.
6. See J. K. Davies, *Athenian Propertied Families* (Oxford, 1971), pp. 329ff.
7. *The Standard Edition of the Complete Psychological Works of Sigmund Freud* XI (1910), London, 1957, pp. 57ff.
8. *Mind and Madness in Ancient Greece* (Ithaca and London, 1978), p. 314 n. 28; cf. Dorothea Wender in J. Peradotto and J. P. Sullivan (edd.), *Women in the Ancient World: the Arethusa Papers* (Albany, 1984), pp. 213–28.
9. See D. M. MacDowell's note on verse 98 in his *Aristophanes, Wasps* (Oxford, 1971).
10. I am in agreement with K. J. Dover when he argues 'that there is no overt homosexuality in Homer', *Greek Homosexuality* (London, 1978), pp. 196ff.
11. See, most recently, B. M. W. Knox in *The Cambridge History of Classical Literature, 1 Greek Literature* (Cambridge, 1985), pp. 325ff.
12. Cf. Patrick Roberts, *The Psychology of Tragic Drama* (London and Boston, 1975), pp. 164–5.
13. For Coisyra, see T. Leslie Shear, Jr., *Phoenix* 17 (1963), 99ff.
14. *The Nature of History* (London, 1970), p. 109.
15. The article by L. Pierce Clark, M. D., *Psychoanalytic Review* 10 (1923), 56–69 was the third in a series 'Unconscious Motives underlying the Personalities of Great Statesmen and their Relation to Epoch-Making Events'.

16. Ibid., 67.
17. *Alexander the Great and the Hellenistic Empire* (London, 1947), p. 3.
18. Ibid., pp. 7 and 8; cf., twenty years on, R. D. Milne, *Alexander the Great* (London, 1968), p. 20: 'one hesitates to indulge in the technical jargon of modern psychology, but there are many indications in Alexander's life of the notorious Oedipus complex.'
19. Volume II Sources and Studies (Cambridge, 1948), pp. 319–26.
20. Ibid., p. 325.
21. E. Badian, CW 65 (1971), 45.
22. *Alexander the Great* (Omega edition, 1975), p. 58; cf. also N. G. L. Hammond, *Alexander the Great* (London, 1981), p. 265.
23. But compare Lane Fox, *The Search for Alexander* (London, 1980), p. 67, who is content merely to remark that the friendship between Alexander and Hephaestion 'was exceptionally deep and close'.
24. *Alexander the Great*, p. 57.
25. *Alexander of Macedon* (Penguin, 1974), p. 56.
26. First published in the States in 1974 by The Psychohistory Press and then in London two years later.
27. deMause (ed.), *A Bibliography of Psychohistory* (New York and London, 1975), p. viii.
28. Cf. J. R. Hamilton, *G & R* 12 (1965), 117–24.
29. *Shrinking History: on Freud and the Failure of Psychohistory* (New York and Oxford, 1980), p. 156.
30. *Journal of Interdisciplinary History* 8 (1978), 599–626.
31. On the historical background see M. L. Clarke, *The Noblest Roman* (London, 1981), pp. 9ff., a book which also serves as a sober corrective.
32. *The Roman Revolution* (Oxford, paperback edition 1960), p. 58; cf. Syme, *Sallust* (Cambridge, 1964), p. 61.
33. Op. cit., 620.
34. Op. cit., 611.
35. Op. cit., 613.
36. Op. cit., 612.
37. Eleanor Goltz Huzar, *Mark Antony, a Biography* (London, Sydney, Dover, N. H., 1986), p. 21.
38. See Gillian Clark, *G & R* 28 (1981), 205 (= p. 48 of this volume) and Judith P. Hallett, *Fathers and Daughters in Roman Society* (Princeton, 1984), p. 249.
39. *The Greeks and the Irrational* (Berkeley and Los Angeles, 1951), p. 47.
40. *The Hibbert Journal* 26 (1927–8), 461.
41. Ibid., 465–6.
42. *St. Augustine* (London, 1933), p. 27.
43. Ibid., pp. 28 and 34.
44. *Journal of the American Psychoanalytic Assoc.* 6 (1957), 470–1.
45. Ibid., 474.
46. Ibid., 478–9.
47. James E. Dittes, *Journal for the Scientific Study of Religion* 5 (1965–6), 133.
48. J. K. Campbell, *Honour, Family and Patronage* (Oxford, 1964), p. 168.

## ADDENDUM

Eminently sensible remarks on the mother-son relationship among the Greeks are passed by Robert Garland, *The Greek Way of Life from Conception to Old Age* (London, 1990), pp. 149–53, while Mark Golden, *Children and Childhood in Classical Athens* (Baltimore and London, 1990), especially pp. 97ff., is to be consulted on a mother's love for her children and the child's love for a mother. A particular case—the orator Demosthenes and his mother—is considered by Virginia Hunter, *Echos du Monde Classique/Classical Views* 33 (1989), 39–48; see also Hunter, *Journal of Family History* 14 (1989), 291–311. John K. Evans, *War, Women and Children in Ancient Rome* (London and New York, 1991), pp. 192–5 considers *materna auctoritas*, and even more informative, and suggestive, is Suzanne Dixon, *The Roman Mother* (London and Sydney, 1988), pp. 175ff. Dixon, it will be noted, remarks on 'some formidable women', commenting how 'while they were required to defer to their fathers and to an extent to their husbands, such women stood in an authoritative relationship to their sons, in whom they invested their ambitions' (p. 176). For Socrates as an *apragmon* see L. B. Carter, *The Quiet Athenian* (Oxford, 1986), pp. 183–6.

Scholars remain reluctant to indulge in psychological speculation. Thus writing on the family in the Late Empire and drawing heavily on Augustine's writings, Brent D. Shaw, *Past & Present* 115 (1987), 3–51 finds 'most of the extant scholarly work on family life in the *Confessions* is unfortunately marred by a strain of pseudo-psychological musing that is of no historical value' (p. 6 n. 6). For Shaw 'of all relationships within the *domus* the most dominant was clearly that between father and son' (p. 19), and so he barely mentions the mother-son link except to note that 'the children and the mother seem to have stood as a group apart from the father, united in common love and fear' (p. 25). I, however, prefer to stress particular events related in the *Confessions* such as the 'vision' shared by Monica and her son at Ostia (9.10), a happening which Henry Chadwick claims as 'perhaps a unique instance of a mystical experience for two simultaneously', *Saint Augustine, Confessions* (Oxford, 1991), p. xxiii. Crucial, as always, is the availability of evidence, something lacking, for example, in the attempt by Charles D. Hamilton, *Agesilaus and the Failure of Spartan Hegemony* (Ithaca and London, 1991), pp. 7–39 to assess 'the character and personality of Agesilaus'.

# SECLUSION, SEPARATION, AND THE STATUS OF WOMEN IN CLASSICAL ATHENS

*By* DAVID COHEN

It is a commonplace of contemporary classical scholarship that in the classical period the political and social status of Athenian women was deplorably low. Relegated to the ranks of slaves and children, scholars suggest that they were even much worse off than the women of earlier and later periods of Greek history.[1] This paper proposes not to challenge this global judgement as a whole, but simply to focus upon one aspect of women's lives which has played an important role in such scholarly discussions.

It is a cornerstone of the prevailing school(s) of thought that the low status of Athenian women was particularly marked by their confinement to their homes, their exclusion from social, public, and economic life.[2] While it is undeniable that women did not operate in the public and political spheres in the way that men did, it does not necessarily follow that they did not have public, social, and economic spheres of their own. The following analysis will suggest that scholars have too often mistaken separation of spheres and roles for seclusion and isolation. Social anthropological studies of modern Mediterranean societies show that the patterns of male-female role divisions in classical Athens are in fact typical of traditional Mediterranean societies and imply neither seclusion nor exclusion from social, economic, and, to a more limited extent, public life. Classical scholars sometimes write as if ancient Greek society had no relation to the rest of human civilization, or even to the later history of the Greek or Mediterranean world. As a result, some aspects of ancient society appear as unique or bizarre, when in fact, they are normal aspects of certain forms of social organization.

The prevailing views are generally buttressed by evidence like the following well-known passage from Euripides:

> I [who] in Hector's house worked out all custom that brings discretion's name to women. Blame them or blame them not, there is one act that swings scandalous speech their way beyond all else: to leave the house and walk abroad. I longed to do it, but put the longing aside, and stayed always within the enclosure of my own house and court … I gave my lord's presence the tribute of hushed lips and eyes downcast …[3]

While some scholars have recognized that such ideologically laden description must be assessed with caution, others have taken them at face value. Flacelière, for example, argues that 'Whereas married women seldom crossed the thresholds of their own front door, adolescent girls were lucky if they were allowed as far as the inner courtyard since they had to stay where they could not be seen—well away even from the male members of the family'.[4] He admits, though, that Aristophanes presents a very different picture of Athenian women, but concludes that this must represent a change towards greater freedom in the late fifth century—a rather desperate expedient since we have almost no comparable evidence *before* the second half of that century.[5] Gomme, on the other hand, recognized the problem, but swung too far in the opposite direction, concluding that in regard to women and sexuality, classical Athenian society was really no different from Britain of his day.[6] How is one to orient oneself between such interpretations which represent polar opposites? A first step is to recognize that such questions are not uniquely relevant to the study of ancient Greece.

Similar interpretative problems have arisen, for example, in studies of modern Mediterranean communities. As one social anthropologist, in a study of a modern Greek village, puts it

> When we began our field study at Methana it was soon evident that characterizations of Greek women in some of the ethnographic accounts did not fit the women we were encountering. While we had read about powerless, submissive females who considered themselves morally inferior to men, we found physically and socially strong women who had a great deal to say about what took place in the village. The social and economic affairs of several households were actually dominated by older women, including the house of village officials.[7]

A significant body of recent research, particularly by women anthropologists, has confirmed these findings, and Clark's own explanation of the contradiction focuses on the way in which the gender and marital and parental status of the researcher largely determine the information to which he or she has access.[8] A further source of difficulty in anthropological work on Mediterranean societies arises from failing to differentiate first-hand observation from informants' accounts, based as they often are upon the conscious and unconscious manipulation of norms and cultural ideals so as to convey a particular point of view.[9] In assessing the status of women (and the particular question of seclusion) classical scholars have fallen prey to the same trap, failing to distinguish between ideology and (sometimes conflicting) normative ideals on the one hand, and the life of the society on the other.

The two Athenian authors who were most acutely aware of the problem of women in their society, Aristophanes and Euripides, also seem to have been fully cognizant of these different perspectives. Euripides, in *Medea, Trojan Women, Bacchae*, and other plays, repeatedly juxtaposes these conflicting positions. In *Melanippe* one character exclaims, 'The worst plague is the hated race of women'; 'Except for my mother I hate the whole female sex' (Frags. 496,500). In the same play a woman responds:

> Women manage homes and preserve the goods which are brought from abroad. Houses where there is no wife are neither orderly nor prosperous. And in religion—I take this to be important—we women play a large part . . . How then can it be just that the female sex should be abused? Shall not men cease their foolish reproaches, cease to blame all women alike if they meet one who is bad?[10]

Euripides' practice of conscious dramatic manipulation of ideologically determined stances makes him a difficult source to evaluate. The same applies to Aristophanes, who no less brilliantly placed the same antitheses and ambiguities at the centre of some of his most serious comic creations. In *Lysistrata, Ecclesiazusae*, and *Thesmophoriazusae* much of the sexual humour derives from the way in which he exploits the contradiction between the cultural ideal and real life, between woman as men think she should be, woman as men fear she is, and the mothers, maidens, wives, and widows of everyday existence.

Before beginning an assessment of the particular issue of seclusion a few words about the comparative method are appropriate. In the last twenty years, anthropologists like Pitt-Rivers, Bourdieu, Davis, Friedl, du Boulay, Peristiany, Campbell, and others have contributed much to an understanding of Mediterranean societies. Although there have only been a few attempts at genuinely synthetic treatments, notably in the area of Honour and Shame, such efforts can be extremely valuable, as the work of Pitt-Rivers shows. A beginning has been made in extending this comparative Mediterranean sociology to the ancient world in the discussion of individual topics like Dowry (Levy and Friedl), The City and the Country (Baroja), or Peasants (Walcot).[12] Pitt-Rivers sanctions this approach in suggesting the 'permanence in Greek society of certain fundamental principles of family organization'.[13] One cannot, of course, simply assume cultural identity over time, but as Pitt-Rivers, following in the spirit of Braudel's pioneering work, argues, 'The communities of the Mediterranean possess both more similarities between different countries and more diversities within their national frontiers than the tenets of modern nationalism would have us believe.'[14] That such a statement may be amended to include an historical dimension is suggested by the persistence of cultural patterns (ideological and behavioural) defining the parameters of permissible and impermissible sexual roles and conduct.

In traditional Mediterranean societies the general identification of the public sphere with men and the private sphere with women is familiar and requires little elaboration.[15] Men are associated with commerce and politics, the marketplace, cafe, fields, and so on, the women with the home. To put it in schematic terms which do not do justice to the strategic fluidity of these categories, the man's role requires him to be outside—men who stay at home during the day are considered womanish—the woman's requires her to work at home. As Bourdieu puts it, 'The opposition between the inside and the outside . . . is concretely expressed in the clear-cut distinction between the feminine area, the house and its garden, and the masculine area, the place of assembly, the mosque, the cafe, etc. In the Kabyle village the two areas are distinctly separate . . .'[16]

The house is the domain of secrecy, of intimate life, and honour requires that its sanctity be protected. Any violation of the house is an attack on the honour of its men and the chastity of its women, even if the intruder be only a thief. The separation of women from men and the man's public sphere within this protected domain is the chief means by which sexual purity is both guarded and demonstrated to the community.[17]

As is generally recognized, these dichotomies—public/private, inside/outside—are applicable to classical Athens. Xenophon expounds at length on how by their very natures men are suited for the outside, women for the inside, adding that it is shameful for a man to remain around the house.[18] Apart from Andromache's eloquent testimony to the connection of honour and seclusion, husbands in Aristophanes are angry finding that their wives have been out, and immediately suspect sexual transgression (*Thes.* 414, 519, 783ff.). In *Ecclesiazusae* a wife, regaled by her husband when she returns from assisting a friend in childbirth, says, 'Do you think I've been to see my lover/*moichos*?' (520 and cf. 1008).[19] Not only ought women to remain within, but they must also guard themselves from contact with any men who pass by or call for their husbands. Thus, in Theophrastus, insulting a woman by saying she seizes passers-by out of the street, or that she answers the door herself, or that she talks with men, are all roughly equivalent to saying 'This house is simply a brothel', or 'They couple like dogs in the street' (*Characters*, 28).[20] Lysias, in a rhetorical variation on the familiar topos, emphasizes the honour of women who had led such orderly lives that 'they are ashamed to be seen even by their kinsmen' (3, 6).

How is one to distinguish ideology and reality in these various descriptions? Here comparative evidence can play a crucial role. To begin with, there is a marked tendency to confuse separation and seclusion. That is, it does not follow that because man's sphere is public/outside, and woman's is private/inside, that women live their lives in total isolation from all but their slaves and their family. Scholars too often assume this to be the case, misled by the well-known, manifestly ideologically determined texts like Andromache's speech or Xenophon's portrayal of the ideal wife, and do not attempt to test critically the validity of these models. Thus Flacelière states that 'Whereas married women seldom crossed the thresholds of their own front doors, adolescent girls were lucky if they were allowed as far as the courtyard . . . well away, even, from the male members of their own family'.[21] Or, more recently, Tyrrell, in his study of Amazons and women in Athenian mythmaking, uncritically accepts Xenophon's idealized description arguing that

The outer door of the house is the boundary for the free woman. Segregated from women of other households, with only female relatives by marriage and slaves for company [one wonders how the relatives got there!], women tended to the domestic chores of running the house for their husbands.[22]

Like other scholars, Walcot also speaks of the seclusion of women, but he is sensible enough to differentiate, noting that 'we have no way of being certain how far social reality corresponded to the social ideal of female seclusion'.[23]

Confusion about the translation of cultural ideals into social practice also leads to derivative mistakes. In a recent article on problems of interpreting scenes depicting women on Athenian vases, Dyfri Williams argues that since 'respectable, well-to-do women did not go out of doors a great deal, and certainly not to the fountain house', the women depicted on the vases are probably slaves, and perhaps courtesans.[24] First of all there is the equation of respectable with well-to-do, and secondly, one wonders about the vast majority of the Athenian women who were not 'well-to-do', many of whom would not have had slaves to fetch water for them, or might, after all, have wanted to go themselves. There is evidence in Aristophanes that free women gathered at the fountains for conversation (*Lys.* 327, and cf. Euripides, *El.* 109–11, *Hipp.* 130), one of the most common focal points in the woman's world in the Mediterranean from Spain, Italy, and Greece to Lebanon, Turkey, Iraq, and North Africa. In Bourdieu's description of women in the Kabyle (Algeria), for example, the fountain is one of the most important places where women, whose sphere is also in principle that of the private/house/inside, gather for talk. The examples could be multiplied.[25] If one is not blinded by the smokescreen of cultural ideals, vases depicting women at the fountain may simply be scenes of typical events in women's lives, like those portraying weaving and so on.

A considerable body of evidence indicates that Athenian women participated in a wide range of activities which regularly took them out of their houses. These included working in the fields (Aristophanes, *Peace* 535; Demosthenes 57.45), selling produce in the market (Demosthenes 57.30–1, 34; Aristophanes, *Ach.* 478, *Wasps* 497, 1380–5, *Lys.* 445, *Thes.* 405, 440), acting as a nurse or midwife (Demosthenes 57.35, 45; Plato, *Theaet.* 149), and many other economic activities. This is what one would expect in a poor region like the Mediterranean, where the labour of women and children cannot be dispensed with. Indeed, Aristotle, in the

*Politics*, says that in a democracy it is impossible to prevent the women of the poor from going out to work (1300a, 1323a) and Athenian law made it a delict to rebuke any citizen, male *or female*, with selling in the market-place (Demosthenes 57.30–1). There is no need to list all the passages on the economic activities of women for they were collected as long ago as 1907 when Herfst published his book *The Labour of Women in Antiquity*.

Women's activities which took them out of the house were not exclusively economic of course. They might include going to their favourite soothsayer (Theophrastus 11.9–10 and 16.12), participating in a sacrifice (Aristophanes, *Ach.* 253), or in religious festivals. Indeed women met to organize the Thesmophoria (Isaeus 8.19–20; 3.80; 6.49) and historians tend to underestimate what is implied by the fact that the organization (including election of officials, and the like) of this major festival was solely carried out by the women. As is the rule in Mediterranean communities women not from wealthy families were also responsible for bringing water from the well and washing clothes in the fountain (Aristophanes, *Lys.* 327–31; Euripides, *El.* 109–11, *Hipp.* 130). They visited husbands or relatives in prison (Andocides 1.48; Lysias 13.39–41; Plato, *Phaedo* 60a), participated in funeral processions (Demosthenes 43.63; Lysias 1.8), appeared before arbitrators (Demosthenes 40.11), attended the public funeral orations (Thucydides 2.46), and were brought by their fathers, husbands, or sons into court to rouse the sympathy of the judges (Aeschines 2.148, 152; Plato, *Apology* 34c–35b; Demosthenes 19.310, 21.99 and 186, 25.85, 54.35; Aristophanes, *Wasps* 568–9, *Plutus* 380). They participated in wedding feasts where bridesmaids danced and male guests might talk with the bride (Hyperides, *Lycophron* 3–4; Isaeus 8.18; Aristophanes, *Ach.* 1056, 1067–8; Euripides, *I.T.* 1140). Husbands expected their wives to go out and those wealthy enough gave them slaves to accompany them (Theophrastus 22.10–11). The passages just enumerated indicate that women were not confined in their houses in 'oriental seclusion' (as some scholars rather romantically think of it, having little idea that 'oriental seclusion' also includes indispensable activities like carrying water), never seeing anyone outside their immediate family. Indeed, one of the most important activities of women included visiting or helping friends and relatives. As men had their circle of friends, there is considerable evidence to indicate that women formed intimate friendships, particularly with neighbours, and visited one another frequently—whether to borrow salt or a dress (Theophrastus 10.13; Aristophanes, *Eccles.* 460) or simply to chat (Aristophanes, *Lys.* 300; Demosthenes 55. 23–4, 53.4, 58.40; Lysias 32.10; Euripides, *El.* 1130, *Andr.* 950ff., which in its condemnation of such visiting implies that it is a common occurrence).

In short, Athenian women participated in a wide range of activities typical of traditional Mediterranean societies. Common sense (and a great deal of anthropological and social historical evidence) should suffice to suggest that in a society like that of classical Athens there would have been relatively few families which could dispense with the essential economic activities of the woman—activities which necessarily involve going out of the house. For those families who could afford enough slaves so that the woman *could* stay at home, Athenian and comparative evidence suggests that they may well have nonetheless pursued relationships with other women in social and public religious networks extending beyond their families. What Maher, in her excellent study, *Women and Property in Morocco*, terms 'ostentatious seclusion' primarily occurs among a few *nouveaux riches* and other middle-class families where the husband is anxious to demonstrate that he has enough money literally to isolate his wife. Even there, however, this normally only occurs in large cities when a woman has married a man who lives far from the village where she grew up, and hence finds herself isolated from the supportive network which sustains most women.[26]

What accounts for the difficulty in recognizing the rather striking contrast between idealized visions of women and actual practice? Four reasons come to mind: (1) ignoring the little bits of evidence about the details of women's lives because one has already reached conclusions based upon the grand ideological statements; (2) excessive concentration on the wealthy classes, a phenomenon typical in historiography (the rural population and the urban proletariat are dismissed in a sentence or two as having different standards; they are somehow not Athenian society even though, numerically speaking, they probably comprised a very substantial majority);[27] (3) failure to view the sexual division of labour and public space as a typical Mediterranean social pattern; and (4) failure to recognize that separation is not the same as seclusion or isolation. This leads to missing the point that separation does not reduce the status of women to utter subordination in the way that complete isolation might. Here also modern comparative evidence may assist a great deal in clarifying matters.

A number of ways have been suggested in which patterns of sexual relations in ancient Athens are typical of Mediterranean communities; the division of society into a man's sphere and a woman's sphere is one aspect of this. Now while some scholars have recognized this—as Walcot puts it, 'men and women in the Greek world led separate and distinct lives'—confusion of separation with seclusion and isolation has led to misunderstanding of the woman's sphere and role.[28] This is no less true of some modern anthropology than it is of classical scholarship. Before the recent surge of interest in the social anthropology of the Mediterranean, ethnologists who had studied these societies, usually men, commonly made the same mistake. Because the complicated networks of women's relations were not accessible to them (because of the very fact of separation), they often assumed that such networks did not exist and that separation meant virtual isolation.[29] They sometimes wrote about the role and life of woman without ever having spoken with a female informant. Recent studies of Greek, Turkish, Iraqi, Lebanese, and Moroccan societies have shown, however, that such assumptions may be widely inaccurate.[30] The paper by Clark on gender bias quoted above represents an attempt to show some of the reasons for such confusion.[31] To take but one example, one might refer to the article by Lloyd A. and Margaret C. Fallers on sex roles and the public/private dichotomy in Edremit, Turkey. In this paper, while confirming that the 'world of women . . . in Edremit is the private world of the house and the courtyard', they document the wide range of women's activities and relationships and the autonomy of the women's sphere. Their observations serve as the basis for a re-evaluation of the thesis for isolation advanced by Forster in his study of Italian towns:

> What he [Forster] meant to suggest was that men's monopoly of the town's public space made it possible for them to interract . . . unencumbered by the contingencies of their individual ties with women. It must follow from this, he apparently reasoned, that the women were pining away, each in her own home, awaiting the return of their lord and master . . . Now this, as we have shown, is not the case in Edremit. If relations among males are relatively unencumbered by their relations with females, it is also the case that females' relations with each other are similarly, if in lesser degree (since male authority and possession of public space do inhibit women's movements), free of male interference. Our point is not the familiar one that women, submissive in public, manage to influence their fate by domestic scheming, manipulation and henpecking. Our point is rather that women in Edremit have an institutional structure and sense of solidarity of their own, parallel to those of men which give them a substantial field for self-assertion and a psychological independence of men . . .[32]

These conclusions are supported by similar studies of Portugal, Spain, Italy, Greece, Lebanon, Iraq, Morocco, and Algeria.[33] As Bourdieu says of Kabylia:

> The fountain is to the women what the thajmaath (assembly) is to the men. It is there that they exchange news and carry on their gossip . . . It is commonly assumed that in North African society the woman is shut up in the house. In fact this is completely untrue because the peasant woman always works out of doors. Moreover, it should be remembered that the house being the domain of women the men are to some degree excluded from it . . . Men who remain too much in the house during the daytime are suspect . . .[34]

This latter point is no less true in classical Athens (Xenophon, *Oec.* 7.2, 30) and, as a woman of the Marri Belouch says, 'What do the men know about the household affairs? They are away from home a lot . . . What do they know about what their women do?'[35]

This clarification of the meaning of separation of roles and spheres, considered together with the point made above about the distinction between cultural ideals and social practices can do a great deal to illuminate the situation of women at Athens—these women who never cross the threshold yet somehow appear to participate in a wide range of activities and relationships. Women should not leave the house but participation in their independent sphere of social, religious, and economic activities requires that they do so. How is the conflict resolved? It is not resolved, but rather consciously manipulated in a serious game that is played according to a complex set of rules and prohibitions.[36] Some examples may help to clarify the point. Mothers in the Lebanese village of Harouch say of their daughters that they never leave the house. This is the cultural ideal dictated by the code of honour and shame, according to which the honour of a woman is measured by 'the closeness she keeps to her house and the distance she maintains towards strangers'. Thus one mother says, 'We are here in the house and we have nothing to do with anyone; we just stay in the house and see our neighbours'.[37] How did the neighbours get there? As Bourdieu reports, the hour of *azal*, during the heat of the day, is a 'dead' time. The streets are deserted, the men are resting where they work, and

> No one can say whether the public space of the village belongs to man or to woman. So each of them takes care not to occupy it: there is something suspicious about anyone who ventures into the streets at that hour ... Furtive shadows slip across the street from one house to another: the women, equally unoccupied, take advantage of the limited presence of the men to meet together or visit one another.[38]

Statements to the effect that the women never leave the house in practice mean that they never leave the house without a purpose, a purpose that will be regarded as legitimate in the eyes of the community—for example, going to the fountain, going to work in the fields, visiting a neighbour, etc.[39] But, as Williams notes of the girls of Harouch, 'I have watched our neighbour's daughter dump a full water-jar behind the stables so that she can briskly set out for the tower while the boy she likes is on the road'.[40] As another scholar puts it,

> The very fact that there is a well-recognized dividing line between the two sexes engenders an atmosphere of artful intrigue or flirtation in disguise, which in itself provides its own form of village recreation. Young men stand silently on the verandah and look down on the fountain where the girls lean to fill their pitchers. The young girls, in their turn, make more trips to the fountain than necessary.[41]

These reports are reminiscent of the women described by Aristophanes: those in the *Ecclesiazusae* (520,1008) and *Thesmophoriazusae* (414, 519, 783ff.) whose husbands find them out of the house and want to know what they have been doing. The husbands know that they go out, but they should not be *found* to have been out, particularly not at an inappropriate time or without a legitimate purpose;[42] or the woman in *Peace* peering out of the door to see the man she admires walking down the street (978ff.); the young girl waiting at home for her lover while her mother is out (*Eccles.* 920); the man hanging around outside the house of a married woman waiting to catch another glimpse of her at the window (*Thes.* 840); or the daughter in *Acharnians* (253) on the way to a sacrifice with her mother and father but conscious that she is on display to prospective suitors.[43] These are examples from literature, of course, but as Dover notes, such women 'may be much nearer the norm of Athenian life than those cloistered ladies who were embarrassed by the presence even of a male relative'.[44] The fact is that comparative evidence suggests that the world of women described in Aristophanes (allowances being made for comic effects) is far better evidence for the actual life of the society than the idealized statements like those in Xenophon. While a few scholars like Dover have recognized this, they have usually done so in an incidental way, without rethinking conceptual categories or abandoning their preoccupation with the lives of the wealthy.

The same duality, the same manipulation of categories and behaviour as described above for the social sphere, also applies to economic and political activities. Bourdieu shows the way that, among the Kabyle, norms and definitions in the contexts of kinship, marriage alliances, legal disputes, and feuds are articulated in a fluid manner so as to meet the strategic exigencies of the occasion.[45] Similarly, the women of Harouch claim that they only work in the house—a rare occurrence that is a great sign of status. But once Williams met one of the girls who had previously told her that she only worked in the house coming back from a day of labour in the fields: 'Before I even had a chance to speak, she hastened to explain that she had gone out to supervise the hired hands for an hour ... She told me then as she had done many times before, that her work is "only in the house".'[46] *Mutatis mutandis*, in classical Athens Aristophanes was able to deride Euripides because his mother sold produce in the agora (*Lys.* 560; *Thes.* 840).

The point of the foregoing analysis has not been to show that classical Athens was 'exactly the same' as modern traditional Mediterranean societies. Rather, by focusing upon a particular example concerning the 'confinement' of women to the home, I have attempted to show the way in which the more abundant evidence from contemporary societies with similar patterns of social organization can provide an analytical framework that can assist in differentiating the various sorts of descriptions of women's lives that Athenian sources convey.

## NOTES

1. See, e.g., E. Cantarella, *Pandora's Daughters* (Baltimore, 1987), ch. 1–3,7; W. Schuller, *Frauen in der griechischen Geschichte* (Konstanz, 1985), *passim*.

2. See, e.g., R. Padel in A. Cameron and A. Kuhrt (edd.), *Images of Women in Antiquity* (Detroit, 1983), pp. 3–19; E. Keuls, *The Reign of the Phallus* (New York, 1985), pp. 82–112.

3. *Tro.* 645 ff. See P. Vellacott, *Ironic Drama* (Cambridge, 1975), p. 89, but cf. p. 83.

4. R. Flacelière, *Daily Life in Ancient Greece* (London, 1965), p. 55.

5. Ibid., p. 69.

6. A. Gomme, *Essays on Greek History* (New York, 1967), *passim*.

7. M. Clark, *Women's Studies* 10 (1983), 117–33, 122. See also E. Friedl, *Anthropological Quarterly* 40 (1967), 97–108.

8. See T. Whitehead and M. Conawa, (edd.), *Self, Sex, and Gender in Cross Cultural Fieldwork* (Urbana, 1986) for the most recent studies of this question.

9. The most penetrating analysis of the manipulation of such categories is P. Bourdieu's classic study, *Outline of a Theory of Practice* (Cambridge, 1977), pp. 36–43, 58–71. See also M. Herzfeld in J. Dubisch (ed.), *Gender and Power in Rural Greece* (Princeton, 1986), pp. 215–33.

10. Quoted by Vellacott, op. cit., p. 97. Of course, fragments of a play cannot be used to validate a particular interpretation. Here they are simply used as a reflection of the variety of ideological views of women which Euripides manipulated for his dramatic purposes. The ideology of the portrayals of women in drama and myth has been the topic of much recent scholarship, although these authors generally do not deal with issues concerning the social reality of women's everyday lives. See, e.g., H. King in Cameron and Kuhrt (n. 2), pp. 109–27; R. Just, *Journal of the Anthropological Society of Oxford* 6 (1975), 153–70; N. Loraux, *Arethusa* 11 (1978), 43–87.

11. J. Pitt-Rivers, *The Fate of Shechem* (Cambridge, 1977), and see, e.g., J. Peristiany (ed.), *Honour and Shame* (Chicago, 1966) and J. Davis, *People of the Mediterranean* (London, 1977). Of course, over-generalization in this area is a danger, as M. Herzfeld has pointed out (n. 9), pp. 215–17 and *Man* 15 (1980), 339–51.

12. H. Levy in Pitt-Rivers (ed.), *Mediterranean Countrymen* (Paris, 1958), pp. 137–48; E. Friedl and J. Baroja, both in the same collection, pp. 113–35 and 26–40 respectively. P. Walcot, *Greek Peasants, Ancient and Modern* (Manchester, 1970). See also J. Schneider, *Ethnology* 10 (1971), 1–24.

13. In the Introduction to *Mediterranean Countrymen*, p. 15.

14. Ibid., p. 10. This is, of course, one of the major themes in F. Braudel, *The Mediterranean and the Mediterranean World*, 2 vols. (New York, 1972).

15. See, e.g., Bourdieu (n. 9), pp. 41ff.

16. P. Bourdieu in J. Peristiany (n. 11), pp. 193–241. In *Outline of a Theory of Practice*, Bourdieu examines the way in which such categories operate in a fluid manner in the complex pattern of social and political strategies, rhetoric, and action, pp. 41ff., 159ff. See also Herzfeld (n. 9). On men who are ridiculed for staying around the house, see V. Maher, *Women and Property in Morocco* (Cambridge, 1974), p. 112.

17. See J. Campbell, *Honour, Family, and Patronage* (Oxford, 1964), pp. 185–203, 268–74, 301–20; J. du Boulay, *Portrait of a Greek Mountain Village* (Oxford, 1974), pp. 121–200; M. Handman, *La Violence et la Ruse* (Aix-en-Provence, 1983), pp. 71–175.

18. *Oec.* 7.3ff.; Aristotle, *Oec.* 1.3–4.

19. Handman notes that in Pouri the men always suspect their women of lying—but how else to go visit a neighbour for a chat other than saying that one has to borrow something, whether true or false. Most pleasurable activities for women are covered by lies—a necessity which becomes a sort of reflex (pp. 164–5)—a complicated game of sexual politics whereby women preserve a sphere for themselves through the ruse and the lie, which the men know and accept, but through their suspicion and questioning attempt to limit and control. Handman notes that lying in circumstances where there is no apparent benefit at times seems to be a way of leading a life other than her own (p. 166).

20. Cf. a female informant's account in J. Williams, *The Youth of Harouch* (Cambridge, Mass.,

1967): 'A good girl walks in the street and doesn't speak to anyone . . . The bad one, she tries to talk to everybody even if a man doesn't greet her,' pp. 76–7.

21. Op. cit., p. 55.

22. W. Tyrrell, *Amazons, a Study of Athenian Mythmaking* (Baltimore, 1984), p. 45; likewise, R. Padel (n. 2), p. 8, 'confined to the innermost part of the mudbrick domestic house with only limited access even from the private home'.

23. P. Walcot, *G&R* (1984), 37–47 (pp. 91–102 of this volume), S. Humphreys, *The Family, Women, and Death* (London, 1983), p. 16. See also J. Gould, *JHS* 100 (1980), 38–59.

24. 'Women on Athenian Vases: Problems of Interpretation' in A. Cameron and A. Kuhrt (edd.), (n. 2), pp. 103–4.

25. Bourdieu (n. 16), pp. 221–2. See, e.g., J. Pitt-Rivers, *Children of the Sierra* (Chicago, 2nd ed. 1971); Campbell (n. 17), pp. 32, 274; I. Sanders, *Rainbow in the Rock* (Cambridge, Mass., 1962), p. 159.

26. Maher (n. 16), pp. 2–3, 61, 117, 250–1; J. Williams (n. 20), pp. 67, 83.

27. See K. Dover, *Arethusa* 6 (1973), 59–73, 69, who briefly notes the difference that social status could make.

28. Walcot n. 23.

29. See, e.g., M. Berger, *The Arab World Today* (New York, 1962), pp. 119–22; E. Marx, *Bedouin of the Negev* (New York, 1967), pp. 103–7.

30. Greece: Campbell n. 17; du Boulay n. 17; Friedl n. 7; Handman n. 17; Turkey: Lloyd A. and Margaret C. Fallers in J. Peristiany (ed.), *Mediterranean Family Structures* (Cambridge, 1976), pp. 243–60; P. Stirling, *Turkish Village* (New York, 1966); Lebanon: J. Williams n. 20; A. Faller, *Buarij, Portrait of a Lebanese Mountain Village* (Cambridge, Mass., 1961); Iraq: E. Fernea, *Guests of the Sheik* (New York, 1965); Morocco: Maher n. 16; see also Bourdieu, *Outline* and R. Pehrson, *The Social Organisation of the Marri Beluch* (Chicago, 1971).

31. Clark n. 7.

32. Fallers n. 30.

33. See n. 29.

34. Bourdieu (n. 16), p. 222; Maher makes the same point (n. 16), p. 112.

35. Pehrson (n. 30), p. 60. For just this reason, in Athens men are often portrayed as obsessed with the trustworthiness of their wives, the 'guardians of the house': see, e.g., Xenophon, *Oec.* 4.

36. The strategic manipulation of such categories is one of the major themes of Bourdieu, *Outline*.

37. J. Williams (n. 20), pp. 76–7.

38. See also Bourdieu, *Outline*, p. 161; du Boulay (n. 17), pp. 190ff.

39. Ibid., pp. 159ff.

40. (n. 20), p. 77.

41. Fallers (n. 30), p. 47.

42. Cf. Bourdieu, *Outline*, p. 160.

43. Antoun, 'On the Modesty of Women . . .' 'The abandonment of particular actions may be justified explicitly or implicitly by the realization of the same norm in a wider context. Thus, although girls are not allowed to look attractive for fear of tempting males, they are dressed up at an early age by their mothers until puberty in order to attract attention to themselves and secure a husband. . . . Here violation of the norm prohibiting adornment is in order to bring early marriage and in so doing avoid a much more serious breach of modesty . . .' (pp. 682–3). The vocabulary of strategic manipulation of norms is preferable, but Antoun's example helps to explain the contradiction between the norm requiring the most extreme modesty for girls and the kind of behaviour Aristophanes describes. Indeed, here again, Aristophanes derives his humour from just the exploitation of this conflict.

44. Dover (n. 27), 69.

45. Bourdieu, *Outline*, pp. 35–71.

46. Williams (n. 20), p. 67, and cf. p. 79.

# ARISTOPHANES AND MALE ANXIETY: THE DEFENCE OF THE *OIKOS*

*By* JANE F. GARDNER

The therapeutic value of laughter is a commonplace of psychology; it is recognized that one of the functions of comedy is to exorcize our fears by causing us to laugh at them. This is one possible meaning of Aristotle's generalization, with 'many more than one facet',[1] that comedy represented people as 'inferior' to 'men as they are now' (*Poetics* 1448a18). So, in comedy, we should not expect to find realistic portrayals of people as they actually are, but rather stereotypes, embodying the fears and anxieties, the mild, underlying paranoia about what *might* happen, of the audience for whom the author is writing. Aristophanes was writing for an Athenian male audience, and he had to strike a chord in them, if his plays were to be successful and win prizes. What, on the evidence of Aristophanes' plays, were Athenian men worried about?

They worried about several things, one of which was their womenfolk, and particularly their wives—or rather, there were a number of specific worries relating to their wives. First, and most commonly cited in modern discussions of the subject, is fear of adultery by their wives. There are several references in the three 'women' plays, *Lysistrata, Ecclesiazusae*, and especially *Thesmophoriazusae*, to married women taking, or being suspected of taking, lovers,[2] and not in these three plays alone. For example, in *Peace* 979–85 a slave appeals to the goddess:

> Don't do what the women do when they're looking for their lovers. They just open the door a fraction and peep out, and if anyone notices them they pop back in again, and then when he goes away they peep out again.

*Wealth* 168 and *Clouds* 1083ff. refer to some of the more uncomfortable punishments (short of summary killing) meted out to adulterers. At *Clouds* 1076 ff. one of the advantages of oratory, according to Wrong Logic, is that it helps a man to talk his way out of trouble if caught *in flagrante* committing adultery.

A few lines earlier, 1068–70, Wrong Logic expresses the view that women want a man to show some energy and enthusiasm in bed. Women's supposed appetite for sex, apparently an article of belief among Greek men,[3] is a recurring theme in *Lysistrata* and *Ecclesiazusae*.[4] Great play is also made, in all three 'women' plays, of their alleged fondness for drink[5] which, of course, loosens up the inhibitions. Both are factors which, it might be feared, would predispose women to infidelity.

'Fear of adultery' is a general term. But what exactly was it, to judge from Aristophanes, that Athenian men were afraid of? W. K. Lacey quotes, with some paraphrase, a crucial passage from Lysias 1.33:

Euphiletus says that 'the lawgiver prescribed death for adultery' (though not for rape) 'because he who achieves his ends by persuasion thereby corrupts the mind as well as the body of the woman ... gains access to all a man's possessions and casts doubt on his children's parentage'. This was the point; if an Athenian had an affair with a citizen-woman not his wife, a baby would not have any claim on his property or family or religious associations, nor impose on them a bogus claim for citizenship; but the woman would be compelled to claim that her husband was the father, and his kinship-group and its cult was therefore deeply implicated, since it would be having a non-member foisted upon it, and if she were detected, all her husband's children would have difficulty in proving their rights to citizenship if they were challenged.[6]

The clause omitted in Lacey's version (after 'the body of the woman') is: *ὥστ' οἰκειοτέρας αὑτοῖς ποιεῖν τὰς ἀλλοτρίας γυναῖκας ἢ τοῖς ἀνδράσι*, 'thus making the wives of others more closely attached (*oikeioteras*) to themselves than to their husbands', an omission which, as will be seen presently, obscures the point. What Lysias goes on, after the omission, to say, in a closer translation than that provided by Lacey, is: *καὶ πᾶσαν ἐπ' ἐκείνοις τὴν οἰκίαν γεγονέναι, καὶ τοὺς παῖδας ἀδήλους εἶναι ὁποτέρων τυγχάνουσιν ὄντες, τῶν ἀνδρῶν ἢ τῶν μοιχῶν*. 'The whole *oikia* became at their disposal, and it was unclear whose the children actually were, the husbands' or the adulterers'.'

Lacey's comment concentrates on the paternity of the children and on the consequences both legal (claims to inheritance) and political (doubt cast on claims to citizenship, which depended on a man being the offspring of Athenian parents lawfully married).[7] However, a wife's adultery was important in connection with inheritance and citizenship claims only if it was detected—that is, if it became known, or if there were strong grounds for suspecting, that her child was not her husband's. The paternity of children in the household *is* a source of anxiety—and to that we shall return—but not necessarily in connection with adultery. What Lacey passes over without further comment is not only the omitted clause but also 'gains access to all a man's possessions'. How? Not through the child, whether the adultery was detected or not, but through the wife who had become 'more closely attached' (the Loeb translation of *oikeioteras*) to her lover than her husband, and whose adultery was undetected—otherwise the lover would no longer have had access.

The remarks of Euphiletus are relevant to Aristophanes' handling of the theme of wives' infidelity. Euphiletus' main stress is on the alienation of the wife's loyalties, and the consequent danger to the property of the *oikos*. What Athenian men, to judge from Aristophanes, are afraid of, is that they may be being cuckolded—that is, as we shall see, that their wives may, and not merely euphemistically, be 'betraying' them—without their realizing it. A key passage is the long speech of one of the women in *Thesmophoriazusae* 395ff. about suspicious husbands. (In the context, Euripides is blamed for *making* the men suspicious, but that is required by the logic of the situation in the play; other passages rub in the point that they are quite right to be suspicious.)

If men were afraid that they might be being cuckolded without realizing it, what was the nature of this fear? In modern drama, the emotional motivation would be something like jealousy, and a sense of affront to one's virility—slighted in favour of another man. Are these the Athenian motives? These are not the terms one finds in Aristophanes. Some light may be shed by looking at other matters concerning their wives that, according to Aristophanes, seem to worry Athenian men, and two of them, in particular, occur in the context of this very passage of *Thesmophoriazusae*. The two concern (*a*) suspicion of theft from the household and (*b*) babies.

(*a*) *Suspicion that the women may steal from the household*

At *Thesmophoriazusae* 414ff. we read:

> Now we're not even allowed a free hand on our own side of the house any more, we can't even get at the flour or the oil or the wine; our husbands carry the keys around with them—horrid complicated Laconian things with three teeth ... In the old days you could get a ring made for three obols that'd seal any larder door in Athens. (Penguin translation, David Barrett)

The sting is in the tail. The complaint is not just that the husbands keep the keys, but that they have fitted security locks, which the wives cannot circumvent as they used to do the old system.

See also *Thesm.* 558: 'We give the meat from Apaturia to our pimps and say the cat's taken it'; and—what may be a metaphor for adultery, but drawn from the same idea—812–13: 'stealing a measure of corn from one's husband.' Nor should one overlook the brief exchange in the first scene of the *Lysistrata*, at lines 11–12: 'All our husbands think we're such clever villains—Well, aren't we?'

Locking things up to prevent thieving by slaves, or against possible burglars, is understandable, but why should a husband keep things locked away from his own wife? Remember the phrase in the passage of Lysias above—that an adulterer got access to a man's possessions. How? Not through any possible baby, but directly through the wife.

Taking a wife, in the Athenian system of arranged marriages, meant taking a stranger into one's house. Why should her loyalties be with the *oikos* into which she comes, rather than the one which she has left?[8] The betrayed husband in the Lysias speech says:[9] 'When I decided to marry and brought a wife into my house, for some time I was disposed neither to vex her nor to leave her too free to do as she pleased. I kept a watch on her so far as was possible, with such observation of her as was reasonable. But when a child was born to me, thenceforward I began to trust her, and placed all my affairs in her hands, thinking that this was the greatest *oikeiotēs*.'[10] That is, once she had a child, she had, he felt, something to attach her loyalty to his household. Marrying was, for the man, a risk. It meant letting someone from another *oikos* inside the defences of your *oikos*—but it was a necessary risk, both to have heirs and successors, and also to increase the security of your *oikos* by establishing ties of friendship with others. Every other *oikos* was a potential enemy.

Dover[11] described the classical Athenians as having inherited from previous generations the essential structure of a world in which the adult males of separate tribes fight each other to keep what they have and if possible get more. For 'tribe' read *oikos* and this is true, at the *polis* level, of the Athenians. The *polis* was made up of discrete competing units, the *oikoi*, combining together for security and advantages not available to them separately.[12] Athenians were constantly watching each other to make sure that no one tried to get more than a fair share—and constantly trying to get it for themselves. This is apparent in the mechanisms of the Athenian constitution—a multiplicity of small committees, reviews, checks, and audits—devoted to trying not to let anyone get away with anything.

The same applies to the integrity and privacy of the individual's home, property, and family. Going into someone else's house uninvited was simply not done. It would be assumed that one was there for some nefarious purpose—particularly if there were free women inside. In Demosthenes 47, *Against Euergus*,[13] the speaker is at pains to point out that when he entered the house of Theophemus the door was already open (i.e., he did not force an entry), and that he had already ascertained that Theophemus was not married (so he could not have had designs on his wife). Later in the same speech, he describes the irruption into his own house and violent handling of his women-folk by Euergus and Theophemus. This is in contrast to the behaviour of neighbours and passers-by who observe the break-in; none of them is prepared to enter the house himself, while the head of the household is absent.

The *oikos* and its affairs were to be kept private. The correlative was that Athenian men were inquisitive about each other's business—and especially about their womenfolk. See *Thesmophoriazusae* 796–8: if a woman is glimpsed at a window, the man peers and hangs around waiting to see if he can get another look at her. This is part of the point of *Lysistrata* 404ff.:

> Look at the way we pander to the women's vices—we positively teach them to be wicked. . . . Think of when we go to the shops for example. We might go to the

goldsmith's and say—'The clasp of my wife's necklace came unstuck. I've got to go off to Salamis; so, if you've got time, could you go down to my place tonight and put the pin back in the hole for her?' Or we go to the shoemaker's, a great strapping well-hung young fellow, and we say, 'The toe-strap on my wife's sandal is hurting her toe. Could you go down and ease the strap off for her, enlarge the opening a little?'[14]

The *doubles entendres* are deliberate. The assumption is that any man, allowed to be alone with another man's wife, will have sex with her (her willingness seems equally to be assumed); so, of course, no one would dream of suggesting that another man visit his house in his absence. To invite someone to go to your house when you are not there is, Aristophanes is suggesting, tantamount to inviting him to commit adultery.

*(b) Suspicion of importing babies*

Another worry appears in the same speech in *Thesmophoriazusae*, at lines 407–8, and elsewhere: *εἶεν, γυνή τις ὑποβαλέσθαι βούλεται ἀποροῦσα παίδων, οὐδὲ τοῦτ' ἔστιν λαθεῖν*. 'Supposing a woman finds she can't bear her husband a child—she's got to produce one from somewhere, hasn't she?' This is the worry that a man may not be sure that he is the father of the child that his wife presents as hers. This worry could be grounded in two entirely different fears—either the fear that his wife had borne a child as a result of adultery with another man, or the fear that she was fobbing him off with a supposititious child.

In Aristophanes adultery is not usually associated with having a baby as a result.[15] The only reference in Aristophanes to men not knowing whether they are the fathers of their wives' children appears to be *Ecclesiazusae* 635ff.—in the new society, how are fathers going to be able to recognize their own children?—and this is precisely in a context, the communal society, which presupposes the abolition of private property and total breakdown of the *oikos* system. Deprived of their public roles as warriors, legislators, and farmers (that is, providers and defenders, by warlike or civil means, of the property of the *oikos*) men have no longer a clear private role as heads of their households. The serious treatment of the theme, with similar consequences, that parent and child shall not be known to each other, is Plato's description of the social organization of the Guardians in the *Republic*.[16] Socrates (*Rep.* 457 c–d) enunciates the rule:

All women shall be held in common by all men, no woman shall live together with a man, the children shall be in common, and neither parent shall know his own child nor the child the parent.

The abolition of the *oikos*-system is necessary, from Plato's point of view, so that the Guardians may devote themselves exclusively to the good of the community as a whole. However, while the *oikos* and the truly united community, in Plato's view, are incompatible concepts, this contrasts with the fifth-century democratic ideology, in which the *oikos* and the *polis* are mutually necessary.

On the other hand, the motif already found in *Thesmophoriazusae* 407–8 turns up in three other places in the same play. At lines 339–40 the list of those to be cursed includes the man who 'tells a woman's husband that the baby's not *her* own' (*παιδίον ὑποβαλλομένης κατεῖπεν*)—not 'not *his* own'. At 502ff. Mnesilochus tells an anecdote about a woman *pretending* to be pregnant and in labour, who had to keep it up for ten days, while the midwife hunted around town until she found a baby, and at 564–5 he accuses one of the women: *οὐδ' ὡς σὺ τῆς δούλης τεκούσης ἄρρεν εἶτα σαυτῇ τοῦθ' ὑπερβάλου, τὸν σὸν δὲ θυγάτριον παρῆκας αὐτῇ*. 'You had a girl and your maid had a boy and you changed them round and passed the boy off as yours.' The women are indignant, but Mnesilochus has said no more than has already been hinted at twice in the play. In addition, it is worth noticing that at *Peace* 674–8 the standard joke about Cleonymus throwing away his shield is reworked with an elaborate pun about his being a substituted child (*hypobolimaios/apobolimaios*).

From the woman's point of view, what a woman would be doing in substituting a baby would be safeguarding her own position. We have very little direct evidence about divorce, but a man wanting an heir might be inclined, if he could afford to return the dowry, to divorce a barren wife and take another. She would be obliged to return to her own family—and a barren and therefore unmarriageable relative would not have a happy time, specially after her father was dead.

Clearly, the possibility that some trickery went on, and that sometimes wives merely *pretended* to have produced babies themselves, was something that weighed on the minds of Athenian men. What were they worried about? From the male point of view it meant, presumably, that the stranger-women whom they had taken into their households had, merely for their own personal ends, used trickery and deceit in order to take advantage of the material security the *oikos* could offer, and might with equal readiness betray it.

No doubt, also, the importance attached to paternity as such is involved here (there is no question of adultery). Two theories of human reproduction existed in the Greek world.[17] One, found in various forms in the Hippocratic writers, and attributed also to a number of the pre-Socratic philosophers, was that both male and female parents made a genetic contribution to the child, though opinions varied as to the amount. Another theory, put forward by Aristotle in *On the Generation of Animals*, was that the man was the parent and sole contributor of the genetic material, the woman merely providing the container and nourishment for the foetus.

For the fifth century B.C., the one piece of evidence for a theory of the Aristotelian type is Aeschylus, *Eumenides* 658ff. (458 B.C.).

Neither view succeeded in ousting the other in later antiquity, in so far as medical and gynaecological writers provide evidence, but which prevailed among ordinary Athenians in the fifth century is not directly attested. Athenian inheritance and kinship law appears to admit the possibility of genetic transmission through the female, in the provisions for the epiklerate, and for marriage of half-siblings by different mothers but the same father. Both provisions, however, have the practical effect of resisting dispersal of the property of the *oikos*, and suggest that less importance was attached to genetic considerations than to paternity in securing the continuation of the *oikos*.[18]

How, then, are we to explain the insistence of Athenians, in the citizenship law of 451 B.C., that *both* parents should be of citizen origin? The law has sometimes been explained as directed solely against members of upper-class Athenian families, and intended to prevent their forming 'dynastic' marriages with families from other states.[19] This view ignores other factors, such as the benefits—e.g., proxenies—that international contacts could bring; it also overlooks the existence of large numbers of free foreigners within Attica itself—the metics. There was no question of marrying Athenian girls to metic men, anyhow; but Athenian men were not to take wives from metic families. Why not?

It is a question of loyalties again. Metics might be second or even third generation in Attica—but they were hardly ever given citizenship, and were not allowed to own land, something which, in Athenian ideology (if not always in fact), was one of the essential components of the citizen *oikos*. Without land, it was felt, one could not have a proper *oikos*, nor a proper stake in Athenian society, nor full loyalty to the values of the community. That there was some basis to this is perhaps borne out by what we learn about the attitudes of metics from the inscriptions they have left—tombstones, dedications, etc.[20] Those who had been honoured with *isoteleia*—the privilege of exemption from the special taxes paid by metics—mention it on their tombstones—otherwise, in *no* case does Athens feature on inscriptions, either of the dead or the living—metics always refer to themselves as citizens of the *polis* from which they originated. This attitude has its corollary in Athenian linguistic usage—*astoi* (of the city), like *politai*, is used of citizens, not of metics.

This issue of citizenship was clearly one that worried and (except for a brief period during the final years of the Peloponnesian War) continued to worry Athenians. They worried about possibilities such as that of people having got themselves illegally entered on the deme register (like Euxitheus in Demosthenes 57) or having passed off foreign women as citizens and so deceived Athenians into having illegitimate sons and daughters (in Demosthenes 59 the real gravamen of the offence is that Stephanus has introduced the *daughters* of Neaera into other *oikoi*).

Now, there is a remarkably long list in Aristophanes of accusations (levied specially at politicians) that someone is *not* pure-bred Athenian:

(a) *Acharnians.* In 515–19 the Peloponnesian War is blamed on Athenians—'not even real citizens but aliens who had wormed their way in'.[21] At lines 703–5 there is an insinuation that the sharp young man who prosecuted Thucydides son of Melesias was a Scythian.

(b) *Knights.* Slaves were commonly given as names ethnic terms indicating their origins. The two other slaves, meant to represent Nicias and Demosthenes, are not given any names at all in the original Greek text; Cleon is called 'the Paphlagonian'.

(c) *Wasps.* At 1042 the reference to the people crowding to see the polemarch is an insinuation that sycophants were of foreign extraction, and so people went to complain about them to the court that dealt with foreigners.

(d) *Birds.* There are no less than four references. This is not surprising, since the play is about the founding of a new *polis*, and criteria of citizenship are obviously important. In 31–2 we find: 'The Scythian (the Scholiast tells us this refers to Acestor, a tragic poet) keeps trying to find his way into Athenian citizenship.' No less than three times a certain Execestides is the butt. Line 11: 'Even Execestides could find his way back to Athens.' At lines 764–5 this is explained—he is allegedly a Carian slave, who has faked registration in a phratry and the possession of Athenian grandparents. Prometheus assures Peisthetaerus at lines 1525–6 that *of course* there are barbarian gods—even Execestides has a *patrōos*. The consequences in private life (i.e., for inheritance rights) are spelt out near the end of the play, where it is pointed out (1642–70) to Heracles that his mother was an alien, and so he cannot inherit from Zeus.

(e) *Frogs.* At 420ff. Archedemos, the demagogue, is alleged to have got onto the phratry books only rather belatedly; in 679ff. it is hinted that Cleophon the politician is Thracian. Specially notable is the chorus' speech, 686–705. Citizenship was accorded the slaves who helped man the fleet at Arginusae, and, it is said, they deserved it; but the politicians currently in charge of affairs are denounced, with an allusion to the emergency coinage issued towards the end of the war, as 'knaves, newcomers, aliens, copper-pated slaves, all rascals' (721–6).

Why were the Athenians so anxious that citizens should have both parents of citizen birth? This takes us back to the *oikos* again, only this time not in relation to other individual *oikoi*, but in its relation to the whole community, the *polis*. In early Attic society, when government was confined to a few aristocratic families who had the monopoly, the ruling classes were all large landowners. The size of their stake in the prosperity of the country was obvious, and their right to participate in its government unquestioned. Marriage to an outsider could make no significant difference to that. Things were different in mid-fifth-century Athens. There, apart from a property qualification for a few offices, a large amount of real political power was in the hands of each individual citizen, irrespective of how much land he had, or whether he had any at all. Therefore it was necessary to look for something strengthening the bonds of loyalty between individual Athenians and the interests of Athens as a whole. Someone of citizen birth on *both* sides was linked in to the family networks of two *oikoi* and was therefore more fully integrated into the community, and impinged upon at more points by its values and priorities. Someone with half his personal links outside the *polis* had less ground for loyalty, and was therefore suspect. A foreigner, it might be suspected, was merely using the *polis* for what he could get out of it.

Even though not all Athenians in the later fifth century owned land, the old ideology persisted.[22] The ideal was to have land in the territory of the *polis*, and to live so far as possible off one's own resources. There was a mistrust of the market-place. 'Seller' was a term of opprobrium in Athenian mouths—a 'seller' was concerned with personal profit, and his interests were felt not to be identical with those of the *polis*. Some politicians, notoriously, come in for this kind of sneer in Aristophanes, but metics, also, would be vulnerable to such an attitude, since their status did not allow them the ownership of land in Attica.

Another area about which, if Aristophanes is to be believed, adult male Athenians were feeling some perturbation in the last quarter of the fifth century was relationships between the older and younger generation—particularly the failure of the younger generation to show proper respect and duty to their fathers. One should bear in mind that, in a state with no welfare services and no state pensions for the old, this could be very serious—a man relied entirely on his sons to support him in his old age; the correlative was that legitimate sons were the exclusive heirs to the property of their fathers.[23] The seriousness with which the Athenians took the duty of sons towards parents is reflected in the severity of the penalty, under a law attributed to Solon, for sons convicted of maltreatment of parents, i.e., failure to maintain them in old age, use of physical violence, or failure to carry out proper funeral rites. The penalty for such failures to fulfil one's obligations within the *oikos* was disfranchisement.[24] The worry seems to express itself in Aristophanes particularly in the form of envisaging situations of the son using violence against the father—there are references in *Birds*, *Frogs*, and *Ecclesiazusae* as well as a long scene in *Clouds*.[25]

There is another context in which the youth-age conflict repeatedly crops up in Aristophanes. In his first extant play, *Acharnians*, the chorus complains (676ff.) about the way clever young orators keep hauling the old veterans whose 'valour saved the city in naval battles' into court on petty charges, and running rings round them with smart argument—Cephisodemus, whose nationality is impugned, is one of these. In *Knights* we hear (1375ff.) about a group of these apparently well-to-do young men, idling around the perfume-markets in the agora, engaging in admiring and rather pretentious chatter about their peer Phaiax's law-court speech.[26] In *Clouds* 1063–4 Right Logic advises Pheidippides not to be one of those who are always gossiping in the agora or arguing the toss over a trifle in the lawcourt. There is more in the same vein in *Wasps* 686ff., a complaint about a smart young prosecutor ordering the jurymen around. He is called an 'affected young pansy'—the Greek word used (*κατάπυγον*) is that for a passive homosexual. At *Frogs* 1069ff. Aeschylus complains that young men, instead of exercise, practise debating and, he hints, passive homosexuality.

Homosexual desire for a male was held to be entirely natural, and tolerated, but this toleration did not extend to being a passive homosexual, that is, one who took the woman's part, and in particular, male prostitution was held to be incompatible with Athenian citizenship.[27] Throughout Aristophanes, and specially in *Acharnians* and *Knights*, homosexuality—specially passive homosexuality—is pretty well a standard accusation against politicians, and especially, as noticed above, against the smart young orators.[28] Why? The reason perhaps is that there was a feeling that someone in whom such interests continued to predominate into adult life—and especially the pathic—was, by definition, unlikely to subscribe to an essentially democratic ideology[29] which gave central importance to the preservation of the *oikos*. The city-state was, as remarked above, in essence a collection of *oikoi*, banded together of necessity for mutual aid and protection.

Some of these latter themes come together in the *Clouds*, where Pheidippides learns to be a smart young argufier *and* assaults his father. New ways, new education, and the growth of the *city* as the centre of activity and the focus of personal ambition for the young seem to a section of Athenian society, for whom Aristophanes is speaking, to threaten the old values, based, not on the competitive city milieu and on individual ambition, but on the *oikos*—its land, its gods, its family solidarity.

So—not only where women are concerned, but repeatedly the same theme recurs—prominent among the kinds of behaviour, both privately and in the life of the city, that Aristophanes singles out for ridicule or blame are those that threaten the security of the one institution within which—ideally—the Athenian man thought he could be safe, and on whose members he thought he could rely—the *oikos*.

## NOTES

1. K. J. Dover, *Greek Popular Morality* (Oxford, 1974), p. 19.

2. E.g., *Lys.* 107; *Eccles.* 225, 523–5; *Thesm.* 340–4, 395ff., 477–501, 812–13.

3. And later the key factor in one of the accounts of the blinding of Tiresias: Ovid, *Met.* 3.316.

4. *Lys.* 24–5, 107–35, 715–78; *Eccles.* 228, 256–7, 265.

5. *Lys.* 194ff.; *Thesm.* 347–8, 393, 556–7, 630ff., 733–59; *Eccles.* 132–46, 227, 1118–23.

6. *The Family in Classical Greece* (London, 1968), p. 115.

7. The progress of his argument is not entirely clear. In the first part ('if an Athenian ... claim for citizenship') and towards the end ('if she were detected', etc.) he is envisaging a situation in which the affair and the parentage of the baby were known; but what is the situation in the central section ('but the woman ... foisted upon it')? Presumably one in which an affair was *suspected*, but not known for certain; the family would become embroiled because a decision would have to be made on whether or not to accept the suspect baby.

8. In *Clouds* 41ff., Strepsiades' wife, who has married a bit beneath her, urges the values of her well-to-do, aristocratic family on her son.

9. Lysias 1.6.

10. 'Presuming that we were now in perfect intimacy' (Loeb translation, W. R. M. Lamb); 'thinking that this was the strongest family tie' (N. R. E. Fisher, *Social Values in Classical Athens* [London, 1976], p. 48).

11. Op. cit., p. 96.

12. And so there was a basic unity, rather than any structural opposition, between the supposed public (*polis*) interests of men and private (*oikos*) interests of women in Athens: H. Foley, *CP* 27 (1982), 1–21.

13. Discussed in Lacey, op. cit., p. 161ff., and J. P. Gould, *JHS* 100 (1980), p. 47. See especially chapters 38, 58–60 of the speech.

14. *Lysistrata* 404–419 (Penguin translation, Alan H. Sommerstein).

15. The Penguin translation of *Lysistrata* line 139 is: 'All we're interested in is having our fun and then getting rid of the baby.' The Greek, however, actually reads: 'It's Poseidon and little boats' and this is probably a reference to Sophocles' *Tyro*, the story of which, as the Scholiast informs us, concerned the seduction of Tyro, daughter of Salmoneus, by Poseidon, disguised as her lover, the river-god Enipeus, and her subsequent abandonment of the babies, Pelias and Neleus, Moses-fashion, in little *skaphai*. This escapade is usually assumed to have taken place before she became the wife of Cretheus.

16. Plato, *Rep.* 449b–464d.

17. J. G. Landels, *Biology and Human Affairs* 44 (1979), 94–113; G. E. R. Lloyd, *Science, Folklore and Ideology* (Cambridge, 1983), Part II; D. M. Halperin in Halperin, J. J. Winkler, and F. Zeitlin (edd.), *Before Sexuality: the Construction of Erotic Experience in the Ancient Greek World* (Princeton, 1990), pp. 278–9; A. E. Hanson, ibid., p. 314 n. 27.

18. D. M. MacDowell, *The Law in Classical Athens* (London, 1978), pp. 86, 95–8.

19. S. Humphreys, *JHS* 94 (1974), 93–4. The scope of the law and various modern theories as to its purpose are discussed, with references to relevant literature, by P. J. Rhodes, *A Commentary on the Aristotelian 'Athenaion Politeia'* (Oxford, 1981), pp. 331–4.

20. D. Whitehead, *The Ideology of the Athenian Metic* (Cambridge, 1977), chapter 2.

21. Penguin translation, Alan H. Sommerstein; a more literal rendering would be 'little villains, counterfeit coin, valueless (*atima*—probably intended to suggest also 'without citizen rights'), wrongly stamped'.

22. A point well brought out by R. Osborne, *Classical Landscape with Figures* (London, 1987); see specially pp. 23 and 96–7.

23. MacDowell, op. cit., pp. 92–3.

24. MacDowell, op cit., p. 92. See also p. 174: of the grounds on which someone could be challenged as unfit to speak in the Ecclesia, and disfranchised if convicted on *dokimasia*, two relate to service to the state (refusal of military service, or 'throwing away one's shield'), two (maltreatment of parents and wasting of one's inheritance) to obligations within the *oikos*, and one (being a male prostitute) can be seen as an abrogation of one's role both as a citizen and as potential head of an *oikos* (see below).

25. *Birds* 1347–59; *Frogs* 149–50; *Ecclesiazusae* 638–40; *Clouds* 1321–436 (cf. also 911).

26. For such connoisseurship of speeches, represented as usurping the place of a serious concern for political issues and the welfare of Athens, see Thucydides 3.37.3. See also L. B. Carter, *The Quiet Athenian* (Oxford, 1986), pp. 119–25.

27. Dover, op. cit., pp. 213–16; MacDowell, op. cit., pp. 125–6, 174. The laws are detailed in Aeschines 1, *Against Timarchus*.

28. *Acharnians* 79, 119; *Knights* 423–8, 878–80; *Clouds* 1022, 1084–95; *Lysistrata* 1092; *Frogs* 1069 ff.; *Ecclesiazusae* 112–13.

29. Whereas homosexuality was thought characteristic particularly of those institutions of Athens, such as the gymnasium and the symposium, which were the typical pursuits of aristocratic Athenians: O. Murray, *Early Greece* (Glasgow, 1980) p. 207; Carter, op. cit., chapter 3.

# ANCIENT AMAZONS: HEROES, OUTSIDERS, OR WOMEN?

*By* LORNA HARDWICK

The network of associations of the word Amazon still plays a part in the shorthand of modern discourse. Its connotations may vary from a slightly comic praise of sporting excellence in women to underlying insinuations that Amazons are not quite feminine. When applied by politicians and journalists to the women in the Peace Camp at Greenham Common during the 1980s, for example, the epithet Amazon carried the implication that these women rejected men and had developed a society apart (therefore [*sic*] they must be subversives, lesbians, communists, hippies—etc. etc.). Modern usage perhaps emphasizes the unusual or even threatening associations; Amazons are, for whatever reason, outside the 'normal' parameters of life-style and achievements. Ancient usage presupposed an additional element, Amazons as a subject for artistic and poetic interest. The reasons why this was so do much to explain how and why the image of the Amazons communicated certain associations and how these in turn relate to underlying assumptions about the framework of Greek society and its values.

Various scholars have used the methods of anthropology, psychology, and history to assess the ancient evidence. Any one method on its own is likely to lead to reductionist conclusions. In a seminal article on methodology, S. Pembroke has shown the poverty of attempts to use concepts from modern anthropology without reference to the historical and intellectual context in which the ancient descriptions and representations were produced.[1] Equally, assumptions about the historical authenticity of content can be challenged by formal and structural analysis.

The Amazon legends basically draw on the image of a warlike society of women, living on the borders of the known world, renowned for archery and riding skills. Written sources give a considerable amount of information about the supposed geographical location of the Amazons, their customs, and life-style. Such detail does not imply that they actually existed, nor even that the Greeks thought they did. The Greeks, in fact, knew comparatively little about their past, or even their neighbours. Study of descriptions and representations of the Amazons helps elucidate the Greeks' construction of images relating to the little-known. Analysis of structure (and especially the use of implied contrast and polarity) in the various stories and descriptions shows portrayal of the Amazons in a symmetrical relationship with the way the Greeks perceived their own identity. Changes and developments in the description and portrayal of Amazons therefore throw into relief the very characteristics of society and values which were of most significance to Greek writers and craftsmen and help us to chart shifts of emphasis. (Significantly, Amazons are not represented in cultures based on non-Greek emblems and norms.)

S. C. Humphreys has identified a quality possibly common to rational discourse and works of art as 'the structure of communication in such a way that it contains within itself enough information to make it readily comprehensible'.[2] When dealing with myth and legend, the nature of the communication process broadens to include symbols 'the relation between which is not explicitly made in narrative but is supplied by the social experiences of the audience'.[3] It will be the intention in this paper to explore ways in which analysis of the image of the Amazons in Greek writing, painting, and sculpture both provides a thread of cultural continuity of reference and reveals major landmarks in the development of the self-image of the Greeks.

### *Amazons as Heroes*

In *Iliad* 3.171ff. Helen is sitting by Priam watching the Greeks who have come to attack Troy. She identifies some of the leading Greeks for his benefit. Priam points out the outstanding figure of Agamemnon and she identifies him. Priam seems overawed with the number and stature of the Greeks and recalls how he once went to Phrygia and was deeply impressed with the numbers of his allies there, although even this fighting strength is now outranked by the Achaeans. He refers to a specific occasion when he was camped with the Phrygians and the Amazons attacked. The epithet he applies to the Amazons is *antianeirai*, 'a match for men', 'man-like', the implication being that in war they have the appearance and fighting strength of men. The epithet emphasizes their male type, while the context emphasizes their status as opponents.[4] The Phrygians are presented by Priam as second only to the Achaeans in his experience of fighting numbers of men, yet the Amazons took them on.

A second example from the *Iliad* uses a different story to build on this effect.[5] Before they fight, Glaucus tells Diomedes about his family tree and his descent from Bellerophon, who was expelled from Argos by King Proetus as the result of a false accusation from the king's wife. The king sent Bellerophon off to Lycia with a secret death warrant and the king there set him various tasks in order to ensure his death. He had first to fight the Chimaera, then the Solymi, and thirdly the Amazons 'who go to war like men'. When he succeeded in these tasks, the Lycian king realized

Bellerophon was favoured by the gods so he was given the king's own daughter in marriage. The episode reveals again the two aspects cited from the first Homeric example—the epithets likening the Amazons' qualities to those of men and the contextual stress on their military reputation. In addition, a third aspect emerges. This is the status to be acquired from defeating the Amazons and the way this is presented as a task or trial for someone aspiring to heroic achievements and victories. For example, the ninth Labour of Heracles is to obtain the Amazon queen's girdle while the rape and abduction of their queen by Theseus, the Athenian demi-hero, is followed by Amazon invasion of Attica. This is reflected in other episodes from myth.

Some of the aspects stressed by Homer are taken up by Pindar, as we might expect. An example occurs in *Olympian* 13, written for Xenophon of Corinth, whose father won the foot-race at Olympia in 504 and who himself in 464 won the stadium (or short foot-race) and the pentathlon on the same day. Praise of the victor's family is interwoven with that of Corinth and of famous Corinthians, among whom (perhaps inappropriately) he includes Medea and also (more appropriately) Bellerophon. Pindar describes Bellerophon's taming of Pegasus and then his defeat of the Amazons:

> he assailed from the lonely bosom of the chill air that army of womankind, the archer host of Amazons.[6]

This time the Amazons are *gunaikeion straton*, still military but recognizably feminine. Pindar is clearly more interested in the poetic possibilities of the Amazons rather than the Chimaera or Solymi (other tasks of Bellerophon) who receive only a passing reference. Pindar draws on similar associations of ideas in *Nemean* 3.38, where the Amazons with their brazen bows are presented as mighty opponents, the context this time being a celebration of the exploits of Peleus and Telamon (as might be expected since the victor being celebrated came from Aegina). Peleus' achievements are referred to again in a fragment.[7] He went first to the plain of Troy, secondly in quest of the girdles of the Amazon, and then on the expedition of Jason, after which Medea was brought back to Greece.

These examples show that the Amazons had a stock role as an index of heroic achievement. Their figurative importance is the product of an aristocratic way of looking at the world. They were worthy opponents—so they are worth defeating. In Homer their femininity (or lack of it) is hardly a factor but by the fifth century Pindar (working to an anachronistic value system in which aristocratic kudos is still to be gained from heroic associations) exploits the poetic mystery to be found in the association of military prowess, femininity, and remote geographical location. In *Olympian* 8 Apollo rushes off to the Amazons after helping build the walls of Troy. They are described as 'well horsed' and living on the farther (Asian) side of Troy.[8]

*Amazons as Outsiders*

The geographical and ethnographic interest is taken up by Herodotus. Writing in the mid-fifth century not long after Pindar, he includes information about the Amazons in an extended passage discussing the origins of the Sauromatae, one of the tribes bordering the area round the Black Sea, beyond Thrace and Scythia.[9]

Herodotus' version of the legend is that Amazons taken prisoner by Greeks killed their captors on the high seas and, after landing on Scythian territory, founded a new society based on independence and activity with merit proved in battle, since they rejected the secluded life of the Scythian women. Some Scythian young men went with them and a new tribe, the Sauromatae, was founded. Herodotus' account is significant for the specific treatment of the contrast between the Amazonian and the secluded way of life for the women. His comparative ethnography is doubtless spurious, but his choice of special features emphasizes firstly that the Amazons evolved their way of life as a response to capture and escape, and secondly presents their separateness as a form of dissent from the conventions of life for Greek women, which he projects on to the Scythians. 'We' (the young men say) 'have parents and property.' The Amazons reply:

> We are riders; our business is with the bow and spear and we know nothing of women's work; but in your country (sc. Scythia) no woman had anything to do with such things and your women stay at home in their waggons occupied with feminine tasks and never go out to hunt or for any other purpose.[10]

The contrast in approach with Homer is total. This interest in presenting the Amazons and their life style in terms of a direct opposition to the then developed conventions of the Greek *oikos* occurs also in the Ionian historian Hellanicus. Writing near the end of the fifth century he published a history of Attica which refers to the supposed Amazon invasion. According to Hellanicus, the Amazons had crossed over the frozen Bosphorus. He explains the significance of their name. Their right breasts were removed by cauterization (to facilitate archery, presumably). He describes them as 'a golden-shielded, silver-axed, female, male loving, male infant killing host'. Most of the description is in direct contrast to the qualities expected from women in the Greek *oikos*.[11] Herodotus explores the Amazon rejection of seclusion by focussing on their alternative form of social organization. Hellanicus emphasizes their dissent by emphasizing polarity in attributes and values and adds the phrase 'male infant killing'. This practice is not suggested in Herodotus, although he does refer to their Scythian name as the equivalent of man killers. This is implicit in their initiation requirements for marriage:

They have a marriage law which forbids a girl to marry until she has killed an enemy in battle; some of their women, unable to fulfill this condition, grow old and die in spinsterhood.[12]

Writers less interested in patterns of social organization than is Herodotus tend to use attention-compelling epithets to create a stereotype—for example, in the *Prometheus Bound* of [Aeschylus] the image of the Amazons is used as part of the scenery of geographical and cultural distance and strangeness:

The Amazons of the land of Colchis,
Virgins fearless in battle,
The Scythian hordes who live at the world's end ...[13]

The theme is taken up in Prometheus' description of Io's future wandering:

you come to Caucasus itself, the peak
Of all that range, where from the very brows the river
Floods forth its fury. You must cross the topmost ridge
Close to the stars and take the pathway leading south.
There you will find the warlike race of Amazons
Haters of men.[14]

The epithets used in the *Prometheus Bound* are unusual in that they draw attention to threatened masculinity. (It is not clear whether the hatred is to be deduced from the Amazons' social and marital customs or their virginity.)

The more detailed versions of the Amazon legend concentrate on one of two main areas of threat. The first, as shown by Herodotus, draws on the related themes of geographical remoteness, 'otherness', and implicit or explicit rejection of Greek norms of female behaviour and therefore of social structure. The second adds a quasi-historical dimension and is specifically Athenocentric. In this type of reworking the Amazons are not merely 'other' but invaders. The perceived threat is politicized territorially.

A detailed example can be found in the *Panegyricus* of Isocrates, published in or after 380 B.C. The overall context is Isocrates' attempt to persuade the Greeks to unite against Persia or rather to recognize reassertion of Athenian leadership. To raise the morale of Greek readers, Isocrates refers to Greek defeat of earlier invaders from the East and includes that of the Scythians led by the Amazons, daughters of Ares.[15] Isocrates says that not one Amazon lived to return to her own land, and those at home deposed their rulers because of this defeat. (The *politeia* of the Amazons is considered in Greek terms.) Isocrates also refers to the manner in which the Amazons tried to divide the Greeks. In this and other ways the whole sequence is a typical Isocratean use of myth-as-history with the added dimension that he locates current problems and attitudes in the past in order to use the example as an aid to his rhetoric about the present.

In a parallel passage in his very late work the *Panathenaicus*, Isocrates refers to the Amazon invasion as the result of the abduction of their queen Hippolyte by Theseus.[16] He says she came for love and the passage reads like a variation on the Helen/Paris theme. He gives the Amazon incursion status alongside other invasions repulsed by Athens, such as those from Thrace, the Peloponnese, and those led by Darius, King of Persia, and Xerxes. All these, he says, were routed in battle and had their *hybris* put down. Athens thus emerges with her heroic status enhanced.

The important points about Isocrates' usage are firstly his mythical/historical/rhetorical method which enables us to draw inferences about the kind of association of arguments which had persuasive force in the fourth century; secondly his concentration on the Amazons as an invading force, simultaneously a threat to Athens and a yardstick for her heroic status; thirdly the association of the Amazons with the Scythians and by analogy with the Persians, implying a barbarian threat from the East. In Isocrates the function of the Amazons is politicized and is used to highlight both Hellenic values *and* the fourth-century imperatives of a redrawn Athenian imperialism. The frame of reference is in contrast to that found in Herodotus where there is a strong interest in portraying an *alternative* society. However, the change in emphasis from Herodotus to Isocrates does not merely reflect the demands of genre. It is significant that this association of the defeat of the Amazon invasion with the demands of Athenian hegemony does not fully emerge until the fourth century, when the (to the Greeks) more acceptable aspects of the Athenian Empire were being retrospectively justified. (This should alert us to some potential problems in interpreting fifth-century usage. I shall return to this aspect later.)

Isocrates' aim is to enhance the prestige of Athens by merging the associations of historical and legendary victories. A similar theme is explored in a significantly different way in the *Funeral Oration*, attributed to Lysias.[17] The Amazons are described as formidable in their own territory ('considered as men for their courage rather than as women for their physical nature'). However, the speech writer claims that when they encountered the Athenians they found that against *agathoi* not merely their bodies but also their achievements and capability seemed womanish and they were defeated. The inference is that the reputation of the Amazons was gained against inferior men. When they came up against Athenians the limitations of both the Amazons and their previous opponents were exposed.

However, such a conjunction of contempt occasioned by both race and gender is unusual when applied to Amazons. For example, the treatise *Airs, Waters, Places,* one of the less rigorously scientific elements in the Hippocratic corpus, contains a series of anecdotes suggesting that Asians are weaker or more effeminate than Greeks (climate and despotic government are two of the reasons suggested).[18] Discussion of the Sauromatae tribe follows and although the name of Amazon is not used, the characteristics of the female virgin warriors are broadly those attributed to the Amazons by Herodotus. The Hippocratic author makes the specific point that the tribe is both European and different.[19] Any attempt to make a simple identification between the Greeks' view of the Amazons and their attempts to generalize about Asiatics is therefore not well supported by the evidence.

## *Amazons as Women*

The theme of Athenian defeat of Amazons is taken up by Plutarch in his life of Theseus.[20] Plutarch was writing at the turn of the first and second centuries A.D. and his account combines mythical and quasi-historical elements. Geography and topography are important. He locates the Amazons near the Black Sea, and says that some accounts claim Theseus sailed there with Heracles on a campaign and won Antiope as a prize. Others say that Theseus went on his own after the time of Heracles and captured Antiope. Plutarch favours this version (which is hardly surprising given the subject of the work), and adds that she may have been captured by a trick, since the Amazons were well disposed towards other people and did not try to run away. Presumably Plutarch regards this characteristic not as a human virtue but as a feminine attribute, a step on the way towards the female subservience represented by rape and abduction. Whatever the origins of the matter, the expedition resulted in a war which Plutarch says was 'anything but a trivial or womanish affair'.

Plutarch gives the fighting a specific location. According to his account the Amazons overran the surrounding part of Attica and pitched camp outside Athens. Hand-to-hand fighting took place near the Pnyx, and the tombs of those who fell are situated in the street leading to the Piraeic gate. On one flank the Amazons were successful but on the other they were driven back and many killed. After three months a peace was arranged through Hippolyte – this and not Antiope being the name of the Amazon Theseus married in Plutarch's version. Amazon graves were also supposed to have been situated in Megara and Thessaly (presumably along their route to Athens). Plutarch also refers to a story *The Rising of the Amazons* which he dismisses as a fable.

The significant features of Plutarch's treatment are the association with Theseus (combining minor-heroism and Athenian orientation), the Amazons' status as invaders, and his attibution to them of Hellenic feminized characteristics. These include not only their attitude to Theseus when he went to their country but also the behaviour of Antiope on the journey back to Athens, in spite of the attentions of her Greek admirers. Her sexual loyalty to Theseus is a significant Hellenized element in Plutarch's version, grafting echoes of the Penelope theme on to the initial subjugation by sexual force.[21]

Plutarch's Amazons therefore bring together two separate elements in the legend. As an individual the abducted queen is Hellenized, partly to glorify Theseus, partly to reflect the supremacy of the values of Hellenic culture. Yet alongside the idealization of the individual sexual loyalty which follows defeat or capture, Amazons as a group are also presented as invaders of Athens, to be gloriously defeated. Although Plutarch refers to a number of written sources, now lost, it is a matter of speculation as to how far his interpretation was influenced by presentation of the Athenian version of the legend in painting and sculpture.

Strabo is the one source which self-consciously attempts to bring together several layers of meaning in the legend and to attempt to criticize them. He wrote somewhat earlier than Plutarch, at the beginning of the first century A.D. The key passages are in Book 2.[22] He gives a good deal of apparently precise geographical information, concluding that the territory the Amazons were said to inhabit lies in the mountains above Albania or in part of the Caucasus mountains. Their occupations are ploughing, planting, pasturing cattle, and training horses. The élite (*malista*) mostly hunt on horse back or practice war-like exercises. They specialize in throwing the javelin and to allow free use of the arm the right breast is seared off in infancy. They also use the bow, sagaris (a single edged weapon), and a light shield. They use the skins of wild animals to make helmets, clothing, and girdles. These activities occupy ten months of the year, but there are two special months in spring when they go up into the neighbouring mountains with Gargarians for sacrificing and mating (this is done at random and in darkness). Female children are retained, the males go back to the Gargarians (contrast Hellanicus). The Gargarians are supposed to have made an expedition with the Amazons, then revolted from them. (The word used by Strabo *apostantas* implies *political* strife.) Then they made war, which ended with a pact that both sides would live independently and only have dealings in matters concerning children.

Strabo points out that accounts of other peoples should usually keep a clear distinction between mythical and historical elements—things *ancient* and *false* and *monstrous* are to be called myths. But the Amazons, he says, are unique in that the same stories are told now as in early times, although, he says, they are beyond belief. He finds the tales incredible on two grounds:

1. an 'army of women' could never be organized without men, either into a polis or an ethnos (i.e., he rejects the idea because females lack political skills);
2. such a group could never make gains in the territory of others, not only close neighbours but even into Ionia and across the sea to Athens (i.e., he rejects the idea of military prowess because they are female *and* remote outsiders from Greece).

Strabo recounts a number of stories associating the Amazons with the founding and naming of cities (including Ephesus, Smyrna, Kyme, and Myrine), and adds Alexander to the list of those whose semi-heroic status is claimed by association with them. Strabo also refers to the Amazon expeditions of Priam and Bellerophon. Much of his information seems to be derived from Herodotus, but the main significance of his account lies in his attempt to assess the credibility of the very detailed stories in his possession. He at least makes us more aware of the blurred distinctions between myth, tradition, and history and the variety of ways in which the same mythological framework could communicate. Yet the core of his rejection of the stories is not lack of historical evidence, but because 'to believe these stories is the same as saying the men of those times were women and the women men'—in other words the Amazon stories challenge the received categories of the Hellenic world view.

Thus a chronological study of the written sources reveals two key changes in perspective. In the heroic episodes the function of the Amazons is not just to make a good story, although of course they do, but to point up or embellish the virtues and achievements of the heroes. Their life style and customs represent an adaptation of the ethos of the warrior élite of Homeric epic. They are to be admired, even if admiration is tinged with a degree of amazement. However, once the Amazons are perceived as a group (in contrast to heroic individuals) and once they leave their remote lands, both their achievements and their life-style begin to be presented as a challenge to Greece. Defeating them in battle and/or abducting their leader begins to be formalized not merely as a sign of the supremacy of the mythical heroes but as a sign of the historical supremacy of the Greeks (and most notably the Athenians) over outsiders.

Then, eventually, defeated individual Amazons are presented as assimilated to the property- and power-orientated framework of exclusive citizenship and the *oikos*, by displaying qualities of submission and loyalty valued in Greek females. But the translation from outsider to woman is not a necessary progression. Outsiders can remain different if they stay away but if they move place, willingly or unwillingly, they must conform or be defeated.

The apparently chameleon-like presence of the Amazons in the written sources in a variety of contexts is explained partly by their status as an artistic *topos*. The balance changes between emphasis on status, race, social organization, or gender, according to the experience of the historical audience, and according to the context and purpose of the source. The resulting difficulties of systematic interpretation can be highlighted by analysis of the presentation of the Amazons in painting and sculpture.

## *Amazons in Art*

C. H. Hallet has usefully restated the view that artistic traditions have their own logic and momentum, and may strike the eye or ear of the ancient viewer or audience in a way which is impossible for us to experience because we are in the tradition of what has followed.[23] Thus when we look at sixth-century and fifth-century vases we have to contend with the fact that the associations made by the Hippocratic authors and in the fourth century by Isocrates (for example) are part of *our* cultural experience, but not necessarily that of archaic and early classical painters. The artist's formal communication may be the best guide to the social and cultural experience which is assumed in the audience. Key questions are whether it is possible to construct a typology common to both vase painting and sculpture and whether the chronological pattern and changes of emphasis correspond to that identified in the written sources. The essential basis for such an enquiry has been provided by D. von Bothmer.[24] His monumental work of scholarship contains a detailed catalogue of virtually every known instance of Amazon representation in Greek art, analysed under almost every possible heading according to chronology, type, numbers represented, with whom, doing what, moving left, moving right, alone, in company, mounted, dismounted, etc.

The earliest recognizable Amazon occurs on a fragmentary terracotta native shield of Argolic shape.[25] The workmanship suggests local Argive make. It has been dated to the turn of the eighth and seventh centuries. The earliest Amazons in Attic Black Figure do not appear until the second quarter of the sixth century. Of course, this does not mean that none existed before—but there are none in surviving Proto-Attic or first generation Attic Black Figure. On Black Figure the legend is mostly told on neck amphorae of ovoid shape.[26] In all there are over seventy examples, most of them battle scenes. Some of these may represent the Trojan battle but in most the lion-skinned Heracles figures prominently. Some of the pots are inscribed and Heracles is named seven times. Among the Amazons, Andromache is the most popular as the opponent of Heracles (named five times). In all there are nine names for Greek heroes and twenty-six for Amazons, of which sixteen are certain. None of the non-Heraclean battles are inscribed.

So two features stand out—firstly the primacy of interest in the Heracles version of the legend and secondly the interest in individual Amazons. This could reflect the influence of the aristocratic concentration on the individual as hero, or respond to the demands of current achievement in drawing and painting technique, or both. The representations which are not battle scenes are mainly statuesque single Amazons (cf. Athene figures). There is an absence of portrayal of social scenes on extant early Black Figure pots. Another striking point is the enormous variety in the type and design of armour and weapons. The Amazons are variously portrayed in Attic and Corinthian helmets and caps, some have greaves, some of the archers wear boots. This suggests Amazons were portrayed in whatever garb was familiar to the painter and that they were not primarily perceived as having a communal identity.

In developed Black Figure (from the mid-sixth century to the end of Black Figure) the Heraclean part of the legend continues to be prominent, with Heracles featuring in single combat against various opponents, some named.[27] Amazon costume seems more consistently Athenian in type. Although there are some exceptions, they are predominantly portrayed as *hoplites*. Social scenes appear, with Amazons shown in the same occupations as male warriors—arming, setting out for battle, returning from battle with their dead, leading horses, riding out, dismounting, harnessing and driving chariots. There are some unexpected scenes, notably an Amazon in *oriental* dress approaching an altar but this characterization is exceptional in Black Figure.[28]

The transition to Red Figure is marked in subject matter by an interest in the abduction of Antiope. For example, a scene on the outside of an Attic Red Figure cup attributed to Oltos (*c.* 510) shows the abduction scene.[29] The chariot waits with its driver. Theseus runs up carrying Antiope. The Amazons are in hot pursuit, one dressed as a hoplite, the others as mounted archers wearing pointed hats and trousered combinations. This is typical of an increased importance for Theseus as the legend becomes more Athenocentric. There is also an increasing tendency to depict Amazons in *eastern* dress—trousers and sleeves and sometimes pointed caps, often armed as archers rather than hoplites. The oriental emphasis testifies to increased knowledge and interest about the East in the second half of the sixth century. It should be noted these scenes date

FIG. 1 Trojan Amazonomachy. Achilles killing Penthesilea, Queen of the Amazons. Attic Black Figure Neck Amphora. Potted by Exekias and attributed to him as painter *c*. 540–30 B.C. (Ht. 41.6 cm. BM. Cat. Vases B 210).
(Reproduced by permission of the Trustees of the British Museum)

FIG. 2 Mounted Amazonomachy. Battle between two Amazons and Theseus and a Companion. Attic Red Figure Stamnos from Gela, Sicily, by Polygnotos *c*. 450–40 B.C. (Ht. 45.6 cm. Cat. 522). (Reproduced by permission of the Ashmolean Museum, Oxford)

FIG. 3 The Abduction of Antiope by the Expedition of Theseus and Herakles. Exterior of Attic Red Figure Kylix, provenance unknown *c.* 510 B.C. by Oltos (Diameter 32.75 cm. Cat. 1927.4065). (Reproduced by permission of the Ashmolean Museum, Oxford)

FIG. 4 Greeks fighting with Amazons. Bassae: Temple of Apollo. Frieze, block 16 *c*. 420 B.C. (Ht. 0.61 cm. BM Cat. Sculpture 537). (Reproduced by permission of the Trustees of the British Museum)

from before Persian wars and there is no evidence of contempt in the presentation.

Oriental themes are also depicted in Amazon scenes on white ground alabastra. The finest (from Delphi and now in Athens) depicts Penthesilea, who is named.[30] She carries bow and arrows and axe and is dressed in sandals (a new feature), a sleeved and trousered combination with Attic helmet and a shirt or apron. A quiver is by her side. A Maenad is portrayed on the other side of the alabastron. An example in London shows an overdressed Amazon by a palm tree.[31] Another, in the Louvre, shows an Amazon approaching an altar on both knees.[32] Her quiver and bow are hung up behind and there is a palm tree behind the altar.

However, the major characteristic of the representation of Amazons in early classical and classical Red Figure is the resurgence of the large set-piece battles. Von Bothmer has identified seventeen vases spanning half a century, which show the large battles on a grand scale, ranging all the way round the vase.[33] These pots cover most of the scenes on which vase painters have drawn for small representations, although the smaller ones show a more limited coverage of the various aspects of the legend, most concentrating on the battles with the Athenians, with some depiction of Trojan Amazonomachy, mostly featuring Penthesilea. Despite the military context, the portrayals of the Amazons reflect the stylistic developments of mature Red Figure and the Amazons are generally depicted in a positively feminine way with breasts exposed and drawn in the correct perspective (although there are still a few examples of drawing in the archaic style). The right breast seems not to be depicted as mutilated. The inference to be drawn is problematic. Was that part of the legend not generally known at that time? If known, was it considered incredible? Or was it simply aesthetically unacceptable to painters? If it was generally known and acceptable might we not expect it to be used as an identifying feature, like Heracles' club and lion skin?

One influential conclusion which both ancient and modern commentators have drawn from the mature Red Figure concentration on set-piece battles is that style and subject matter reflect the monumental Amazonomachies created in Athens between 460 and 438 B. C. by Mikon and Pheidias.[34] However, a causal relationship is difficult to prove from the available evidence. While it may be reasonable to hold that both vase painting and public painting and sculpture draw on the same public interest in battle themes, to prove that vase painting necessarily and narrowly followed public art in style and composition (or, for that matter, in stressing the topicality of the Athenians' own struggle) would require detailed analysis of a range of examples with precise dating and special attention to chronology.

In fact the three distinct types of Amazonomachy (Trojan, Heraclean, Athenian) are more securely identifiable in vase painting than in public art. Significantly, the outstanding extant examples of Trojan Amazonomachy are from private art, while vase painting is also an important source for the 'slide' from emphasis on Heracles to that on Theseus and Athenian Amazonomachy (Theseus appears initially as a member of Heracles' expedition and then becomes more prominent). Identifications are assisted by the use of inscription and by the conventions of iconography.

The problems of identification and interpretation of particular battle scenes in public sculpture can be illustrated by the debate about the representations on the Athenian Treasury building at Delphi. The subjects of the marble metopes and acroteria are the exploits of Heracles and Theseus. Some scholars identify this as the Heraclean expedition to Themiskyra in which, according to some sources, Theseus participated. However, other identifications emphasize the role of Theseus and interpret the scenes as referring to the Amazon invasion of Attica. This is especially so if they follow Pausanias' dating for the building.[35] Pausanias thought the treasury was built out of the spoils of Marathon. Given an early fifth-century date, the representation of a mythological counterpart to the Persian invasion would be appropriate, but if the building dates from the last decade of the sixth century, which has been suggested on stylistic grounds, then the Heraclean emphasis may be just as likely.[36] This would match the emphasis in archaic and transitional sculpture on the Labours of Heracles, for example, on the twelve marble metopes from the temple of Zeus at Olympia. Pausanias describes the subject of the metopes as the Labours of Heracles.[37]

The Heraclean theme was taken up in a number of examples in classical sculpture, notably the metope on the east side of the Hephaisteion which depicts the seventh in the cycle of nine Heraclean Labours. These metopes are generally taken to be earlier than those of the Parthenon but later than Olympia. The Olympia representation may have been influential in choice of subject and perhaps composition and may account for the confusion between Heraclean and Athenian Amazonomachy identification in some of the later examples, since it introduced Theseus as a companion of Heracles. According to Pausanias, Theseus' role was shown on one of the crossbars on the throne of Zeus.[38]

The best preserved of the three friezes on the base of the Mausoleum at Halicarnassus depicts Greeks fighting Amazons. Reconstruction gives an unbroken sequence of twelve figures. There are three single combats between Greek and Amazon. Heracles can be identified by club and lionskin. Another of the Greeks may be Theseus. The example shows the persistence of the Heraclean Amazonomachy through classical sculpture

(Mausolus died about 353 B.C.). (The other battle frieze on the monument shows Lapiths and Centaurs.)

J. P. Barron has argued influentially that the subjects of the various metopes from the Parthenon are all significantly inter-related—battles between gods and giants, Greeks and Amazons, Lapiths and Centaurs.[39] B. F. Cook relates these to conflict between East and West, asserting that 'all seem to refer allegorically to the Persian Wars in the early fifth century'.[40] Barron sets what is represented at a more abstract level, arguing that the battle depicts 'the triumph of reason and order over chaos and the triumph of Hellenism over barbarism', these being 'the laurels upon which the Athens of Pericles now rested'.[41]

However, analysis of the Funeral Speech attributed by Thucydides to Pericles suggests that the Athenian self-image promoted in Periclean Athens took as its 'laurels' military virtues (derived from competitive heroic values) and the ethos of a citizenship exclusive to Athenians.[42] As was shown above, these are precisely the values celebrated by a careful reading of the contexts in most of the written sources referring to Amazons up until the end of the fifth century. Only in the Hippocratic writings and in the post-imperial apologia of Lysias and Isocrates are the Amazons specifically associated with racial generalizations about Hellenism and barbarism and the natural order of (male) Greek supremacy. In the mid-fifth century Herodotus could open his histories by giving equal status to the heroic deeds of Greeks and babarians.[43]

More work needs to be done on the relationship between Athenianism and Hellenism in the fifth and fourth centuries, on typologies of superiority and their chronological and rhetorical contexts, and on the relation between Greek ideas of 'other' and 'inferior'. Interpretations of the Funeral Speech have suffered when distorted by the influence of the cultural (and post-imperial) rhetoric of the fourth century. The same danger may be present in the case of interpretations of fifth-century public sculpture. The dynamic, acquisitive, and aggressive imperialism communicated by Thucydides had no need to present its victory as one for 'reason and order' nor to present the epic triumph of the men of Marathon and Salamis as 'emergence from chaos'. The Athenians celebrated a citizen version of heroic *timē* (hence the association with Heracles and Theseus), and there was little heroic reputation to be gained in setting out to defeat the 'womanish' and 'feeble'.

Recent scholarship has called attention to the manner in which modern imperial powers may stigmatize the traditions of conquered foreign peoples as 'feminine, emotional, naturally submissive'.[44] However, it is a mistake to assume that the use of such ideas can necessarily be projected backwards on to the *fifth-century* Athenians. At the time they defeated the Persians and began to develop their hegemony over *fellow Greeks*, military virtues *were* virtues. The status of the winner was enhanced by merit in the defeated. They had no need to take refuge in cultural apologia, even if contempt for the defeated 'barbarians' developed later. Furthermore, the Amazons are not presented or depicted in terms of the more negative characteristics attributed by Greeks to barbarians. Their lives are not shown as luxurious or effeminate, they do not flee, make a lot of noise, nor live in subjection to a ruling tyrant (to name only those 'differences' which along with more positive qualities were attributed to the Persians in the early fifth-century play by Aeschylus).[45]

Depiction of the Amazons in fifth-century public sculpture, therefore, can be interpreted as a statement of the association of the Athenians with the victories of the heroes and provides further evidence for the persistence of traditional emblems into fifth-century culture. Far from being thought contemptible, the Amazons continue their role as heroic artistic *topoi*; their depiction draws on the association with a network of legendary references to outstanding achievement. And they continue to be celebrated for their own artistic interest. Unfortunately the paintings by Mikon in the Theseum and Painted Porch are lost, but they have been described in sufficient detail by ancient writers to give an adequate idea of the composition, the number of participants, and the possible names of Athenians and Amazons. Pausanias and Arrian mention the subjects and we know from a reference in Aristophanes that Mikon painted Amazons on horseback.[46] Furthermore, evidence from Pliny and from the existence of Roman marble copies of the Ephesian Amazons (which were probably bronze) indicates that *single* Amazons were the subject of a sculpture competition in the fifth century, in which Polykleitos and Pheidias were said to be contestants.[47]

If the role of the Amazons as rhetorical and artistic *topoi* had been changed and they had become historically or ideologically assimilated to fifth-century *debate* about the world, we should expect them to play a much more prominent role in drama. But in the extant plays barbarian threat to Greece is represented in the *Persians*, conflict about values in *Antigone* (for example), alienation of the foreigner in *Medea*. The Amazons recur as fringe motifs, emblems of geographical remoteness (*Prometheus Bound*), yardsticks for heroism (*Heracles*), exceptions to the conventional disgrace entailed by death at the hands of a woman (*Eumenides*),[48] and *exempla* of the capacity of women to achieve male standards of excellence (*Lysistrata*).[49] There is a lack of evidence about whether fifth-century dramatists had any interest in exploring (for example) Antiope's 'dilemma' in deciding on which side to fight when her fellow Amazons came to rescue her from Theseus.

There are more complex implications underlying the simple schematic polarities between the social organization of Greeks and Amazons shown in Herodotus and Strabo. These are explored to some extent by Plato, but his approach draws more from the historical example of Sparta than from the legendary society of the Amazons and his failure to mention them shows that the Amazons had no status as a 'real' alternative society. In *Republic* 5 women are assimilated to Guardian status on the grounds that

> There is therefore no function in society which is peculiar to woman as woman or man as man; natural abilities are similarly distributed in each sex and it is natural for women to share all occupations with men ... They must play their part in war and all other duties of a Guardian.[50]

It follows from this, in view of the duties of Guardians, that the traditional life of the *oikos* is impossible for the female élite and other arrangements have to be made. Just as important, there is no need for these 'Amazonian' qualities in the life of the ordinary people who lack the special duties and privileges of the élite.

M. Lefkowitz assumes a more general application of the *oikos*-based perspective in her reading of the Amazons legend:

> The Amazons and other mythical women who attack men are destructive to themselves as well as to the rest of society; the myth's message is directed both to women and to men and warns that anyone who withdraws from or hates ordinary family life (*sic*) becomes dangerous to society as a whole.[51]

But the sources show that Amazons were not only used as touchstones for implicit comment about the citizens' democracy (to which Lefkowitz's remarks might apply) but also as emblems of heroic achievement. There is more than one kind of society. In Plato's Guardian state Amazonian qualities might be used to promote excellence, not to undermine it. More important, Lefkowitz ignores the crucial point that the Amazons were not always aggressive. They were defiant when attacked (which is a different thing). The polarity in classical thought was conventionally between the ideas of aggressive male and submissive female; the idea of an aggressive female might therefore be a challenge. However, the concept of a holistic psychology relating to attitudes and life-style which could be self-sufficient and *neither submissive nor aggressive without provocation*, is implicit in the sources (including Herodotus) and specifically mentioned by Strabo and Plutarch. It is that possibility, rather than the crude oppositions of traditional gender stereotypes, which represents the real challenge to Greek social and political assumptions. However, that challenge was insufficiently comprehended (then as now) to be formalized in debate about Greek attitudes and practices.

Amazons as such remain 'other'. Some of the tensions and polarities addressed in the written sources were progressively internalized in Hellenic debate in the fifth century. After the fifth century the essential qualities of the Amazons could be either hijacked for Plato's radicalized Utopia or denied them by the contempt for race or gender evident in the post-imperial perspectives of Lysias and Isocrates. But in art they retained something of their individuality and heroic associations. Evidence from painting and sculpture therefore remains a vital check on generalizations about the direction and chronology of development of the coded attitudes presented in the written sources. The ancient evidence both benefits from insights suggested by modern perspectives and also challenges the claims of those perspectives to provide exclusive coherent interpretations.

## NOTES

1. 'Women in Charge: the Function of Alternatives in Early Greek Tradition and the Ancient Idea of Matriarchy', *Journal of Warburg and Courtauld Institutes* 30 (1967), 1–35. Pembroke argues that the similarities in structure in the examples of customs of marriage and sexual intercourse attributed by Herodotus to non-Greeks do not suggest a historical relativism but indicate rather the construction of an image of foreigners, with practices and values alien to those of Greeks, and in symmetrical tension with them.

2. *Anthropology and the Greeks* (London, 1978), p. 241.

3. Discussed in Humphreys, ibid., pp. 265–75 with reference to B. Bernstein, *Class Codes and Control* Vols. 1–3 (London, 1971).

4. *Iliad* 3.189.

5. *Iliad* 6.186.

6. Pindar, *Ol.* 13.87–90 (tr. J. E. Sandys).

7. Pindar Fr.158 (Bergk) = 172 (Loeb).

8. Pindar, *Ol.* 8.47.

9. 4.110–18.

10. 4.114 (tr. A. de Selincourt).

11. Fr. 16, 17 in F. Jacoby, *F Gr H* 3 B 45–46. For the place of the *oikos* in Athenian male psychology, see J. F. Gardner, *G & R* 36 (1989), 51–62, reprinted in this collection, pp. 146–57.

12. 4.117.

13. [Aeschylus], *Prometheus Bound* 410–5 (tr. P. Vellacott).

14. Ibid., 719–24.

15. Isocrates, *Panegyricus* 68–70.

16. Isocrates, *Panathenaicus* 193.

17. Lysias, *Funeral Oration* 18.

18. Hippocratic *Airs, Waters, Places* XVI.

19. Ibid., XVII.

20. Plutarch, *Theseus* 26–8.

21. Compare the attitudes implicit in Shakespeare's *Midsummer Nights Dream* Act 1, scene 1, 16ff.: Theseus to the Amazon queen, 'Hippolyta, I woo'd thee with my sword/*And won thy love doing thee injuries.*'

22. 2.5.1–4.

23. 'The Origins of the Classical Style in Sculpture', *JHS* 106 (1986), 71–84.

24. *Amazons in Greek Art* (Oxford, 1957).

25. Nauplia Museum 4509. Drawing and photo D. von Bothmer, ibid., Plate 1.

26. Ibid., chapter 2.

27. Ibid., chapter 3.

28. Olpe, Munich 1745 (repainted). Bothmer, Plate LXVIII no. 6.

29. Oxford 1927. 4065 = fig. 3.

30. Athens 15002, signed by Pasiades as potter.

31. London B673. Bothmer, Plate LXXIII no. 3.

32. Paris, Louvre CA 1710. Bothmer, Plate LXXIII no. 7.

33. Bothmer, chapter 10.
34. Ibid., chapter 9, p. 147.
35. 10.11.5.
36. Discussed by Bothmer, op. cit., chapter VII, pp. 117–19.
37. 5.10.9.
38. 5.11.4.
39. *An Introduction to Greek Sculpture* (London, 1981), chapter 5.
40. *The Elgin Marbles* (London, 1984), p. 19.
41. Op. cit., pp. 95–6.
42. P. Walcot, 'The Funeral Speech: a Study of Values', *G&R* 20 (1973), 111–21, N. Loraux, *The Invention of Athens: The Funeral Oration in the Classical City* (Cambridge, Mass. and London, 1986), passim.
43. 1.1.
44. Ashis Nandy, *At the Edge of Psychology: Essays in Politics and Culture* (Oxford, 1980) explores (in relation to colonialist domination of India) the polarity of 'warrior' masculine and 'passive' feminine as 'normal' forms of gender, challenged by Gandhi. In a different context D. Cairns and S. Richards, *Writing Ireland: Colonialism, Nationalism and Culture* (Manchester, 1988) chapter 3, 'An Essentially Feminine Race', discuss ascendancy attitudes to the Celtic tradition in Ireland.
45. The usage is discussed by S. Goldhill, 'Battle Narrative and Politics in Aeschylus' *Persae*', *JHS* 108 (1988), 189–93.
46. *Lysistrata* 678–9.
47. *N. H.* 34.53; Amazon statue (marble copy) Met. Museum, New York 32.11.4.
48. Aeschylus, *Eumenides* 625–8.
49. Aristophanes, *Lysistrata* 670ff. and cf. 404.
50. 5.455 (tr. H. D. P. Lee).
51. *Women in Greek Myth* (London, 1986), p. 27.

## ADDENDUM

Since this article was prepared in 1988–9, the Amazons have continued to appear as a motif in studies of the cultural history of the ancient world. On the whole, anthropological approaches are still dominant. For example, in his study of women in Athenian society, Roger Just placed the Amazons firmly in the category of 'The Savage Without', rather than 'The Enemy Within'. (These are the titles of chapters 10 and 9 of his *Women in Athenian Law and Life* [London and New York, 1989].) According to Just, the Amazons belonged to a category of women defined by an alien quality—like Medea, in whom this characteristic is associated with emotional forces which were perceived as threatening 'civilized' conventions (ibid., pp. 241–51). Such women were therefore distanced morally as well as geographically from the dominant Greek male culture.

However, congruence between the images of the Amazons and the figures explored in fifth-century tragedy is far from established. Culturally, the Amazons function more like catalysts for the transformation of perspectives. This has been demonstrated by Edith Hall in her definitive treatment of the 'invention' of the barbarian, *Inventing the Barbarian: Greek Self-Definition through Tragedy* (Oxford, 1989). Hall argued that after the Persian Wars, images of foreigners took over the 'antagonistic' roles from Amazons and monsters. Persian details were overlaid in art and literature on the traditional Amazonomachies, momentarily fusing a familiar motif with contemporary patriotism. This contributed to the 'barbarization' of foreigners which was a necessary foil to the Athenians' assertion of their identity (ibid., pp. 62–8). Once this process was under way, the Amazons slipped out of sight. Hall emphasizes the contrast between these later images and the earlier heroic associations, which were not concerned with ethnicity (ibid., pp. 54–5).

This multiplicity and elusiveness of readings of the Amazon motif have been explored in some detail by Christiane Sourvinou–Inwood in *'Reading' Greek Culture: Texts and Images, Rituals and Myths* (Oxford, 1991). Her analysis of pursuit scenes in vase-painting showed how the stylizing of the Amazons as axe-wielding warriors persisted alongside the prominence of Amazons on alabastra, where the semantic field was that of preparation for marriage. (Of course, there is an irony in that killing in battle, rather than personal beautification, fulfilled this function for the Amazons.) Sourvinou–Inwood has also explained how the culturally ambivalent iconography of the palm tree (especially alongside an altar) may point to an Artemis/*parthenoi* connection rather than merely to the conventional (to twentieth-century western eyes) association with the oriental or 'exotic' (ibid., pp. 112–18).

The problematic readings of the representations of Amazons in art are a useful reminder that the defining characteristic of the Amazons is that they do not consent to any form of domination. (The tension between *Peitho* [persuasion] and cathartic models of artistic representation is discussed by R. F. Sutton, Jr., in 'Pornography and Persuasion on Attic Pottery' in A. Richlin [ed.], *Pornography and Representation in Greece and Rome* [Oxford, 1992], pp. 3–35. The theoretical aspects of Sutton's article are equally relevant to 'reading' the representation of Amazons on vases.) In not 'seeing themselves as they are seen', they resist any discourse which confines their significance solely to gender or solely to ethnicity. This defiance speaks as much to contemporary scholarship as to their own 'history'.

# THE DANCING GIRLS OF CADIZ

*By* A. T. FEAR

Cadiz's main claim to fame in antiquity was its situation at the end of the known world[1] and its temple to Hercules which was visited by many famous personalities of antiquity;[2] however, perhaps surprisingly, given Seneca's and Pliny's insistence on the sobriety of the Spanish character,[3] Cadiz had another well-known attraction, its dancing girls, leading to Martial dubbing the town 'Laughing Cadiz', 'Iocosae Gades'.[4]

The vast majority of our references to this aspect of the town's life are from writers of the Early Imperial period such as Juvenal, Martial, and Statius. Nevertheless our earliest reference to it dates some three centuries before. Strabo gives an account of Posidonius which tells us of the explorer Eudoxus' attempts to find a route to India, avoiding the tax monopoly of the Ptolemies. Convinced that Africa could be circumnavigated, Eudoxus built a 'great ship', πλοῖον μέγα, at Cadiz and embarked, amongst other things, 'slaves trained in music', μουσικὰ παιδισκάρια, presumably to trade at the court of the Indian kings. The voyage failed, though Eudoxus was sufficiently encouraged to attempt a second voyage on which he disappeared, never to be seen again. We are not told of the fate of his human cargo.[5] Although παιδισκάρια could indicate either sex, given our later references, it seems clear that dancing girls are being referred to here. The story shows therefore that they were an established feature of the town well before the Imperial period.

Another feature of the story is the indication that the girls were normally slaves. This is borne out by our later references. Of these Juvenal is the most explicit when he refers to the dancers as possessions, 'mancipia'.[6] Martial speaks of the 'ancilla', i.e., slave dancing girl, Telethusa, 'skilled at performing wanton gestures to Baetican castanets and dancing to Gaditane tunes',[7] who was first sold and then bought back by her former master.[8] The implication here is that the girl was a personal slave; however, it also seems that troupes of Gaditane dancing girls were owned to be hired out. Martial describing the typical low life of Rome lists among the sundry sausage sellers, etc., 'the wicked pimp from Cadiz'.[9] Such a man would have catered to a low class market; however, more refined versions of the same product were also available. The Younger Pliny complaining good naturedly about Septicius Clarus' non-appearance at a dinner party, remarks that Septicius will suffer for his preference to attend others where a variety of exotic food and 'Gaditanae' are on offer.[10] Martial too, when making a virtue of his own poverty, remarks he can only offer a single flute player not a troupe of 'Gaditanae'.[11]

The dancing girls therefore covered the entire social spectrum and were owned individually and as groups for hire. What, however, can we tell about the nature of the entertainment they offered? The dancing involved was of a highly erotic nature and apparently had a devastating effect on its audience.[12] The style of the dance itself appears to have been very similar to that of the present day belly dancers of the Middle East; one 'Gaditana' is said to 'so tremulously move her thighs, so alluringly gyrate';[13] another description refers to 'Gaditanae' 'wantonly shaking without ceasing their lascivious loins in trained measure'.[14] Finally it appears that a trembling descent to the floor, a common feature of belly dancing, normally known as the 'shimmy',[15] was also practiced by the 'Gaditanae'.[16]

The dancers used a form of castanet, or *crusmata*, as part of their performance. Martial's Telethusa, as seen above, was said to be skilled in the use of Baetican castanets, and Statius refers to the 'cymbals and tinkling music of Cadiz'.[17] On another occasion Martial tells us the material these castanets were made of when he speaks of 'Tartessic bronze', 'Tartesiaca aera'.[18] Again this form of accompaniment is paralleled in modern belly dancing where the dancer will often wear small brass cymbals called 'sagat' or 'zills' on her fingers.[19] The dancing was also accompanied by erotic songs.[20] Martial when referring to a transvestite who has learnt to dance in this fashion, ('he moves his depilated arms to varied measures'[21]), also says he murmurs the songs of the Nile and Cadiz.[22] Juvenal too warns a potential guest for dinner that it is no use expecting Gaditane songs,[23] and speaks of hearing the rattle of castanets to the accompaniment of song.[24]

The dress of the dancers is unclear: on a black and white pavement in the Vatican Library there is a picture of a dancer, with *crotalia*, wearing a long diaphanous robe.[25] This too has its parallels in modern belly dancing[26] and could be what Juvenal is referring to with poetic licence when he calls the dancers naked possessions, 'nuda mancipia'.[27] Although this seems the most likely solution, given the mores of Rome at this period, we cannot rule out the possibility that Juvenal, at least on occasions, was being entirely literal in his description.[28] The dancing of Telethusa described in the *Corpus Priapeum* suggests a much shorter dress than that found on the Vatican Library mosaic.[29] If J. P. V. D. Balsdon is right that the women athletes depicted on the Piazza Armerina mosaics are really dancing girls, some sort of Bikini style dress, perhaps made of leather, may be another possibility.[30]

Unfortunately the history of individual girls is almost impossible to trace. Martial twice mentions a Telethusa,[31] and this name also appears twice in the *Corpus Priapeum*, where once she is referred to as a dancing girl, 'circulatrix',[32] and then as a 'girl from Subura' (an area of Rome notorious for its prostitutes).[33] It is tempting to believe that all these references are to one particular girl, who would then have been sold by one master, bought her freedom from a second, and consequently been taken as a lover by her first master. However, Telethusa was probably a common name for such girls; nevertheless the date of the *Corpus Priapeum* could coincide with Martial which would leave this intriguing possibility open.[34] The *Corpus Priapeum* also mentions a Quintia, a 'star of the circus' who was a belly dancer and so could have been a 'Gaditana', but sadly does not refer to her nationality explicitly.[35] From Milan we have an inscription recording a Lesbia, 'whom the fair land of Tarsis bore'.[36] It has been suggested that Tarsis is the Punic spelling of Tartessos and consequently Lesbia is a 'Gaditana'. This is an attractive possibility, but an eastern interpretation is equally possible.[37] Two more certain traces can be found on tombstones from Rome itself. One of these is a small fragment and reads Gaditan[...]. It has normally been restored Gaditan[o], but given the presence of 'Gaditanae' in the city, Gaditan[ae] seems at least equally plausible, if not preferable.[38] The other stone is more explicit and refers to 'Carpima Gaditana' and should be the tomb of a dancing girl.[39]

The origins of the dancing are an intriguing question. As we have seen, the style is very similar to the belly dancing of the Near East. Garcia y Bellido thought that 'Gaditana' was a general reference to Andalucia as a whole,[40] but apart from the reference to Baetican *crusmata* and Tartessian *aera*, all our references are to Cadiz itself; moreover, given the frequent identification of Tartessos with Cadiz in antiquity,[41] this latter reference too may be specifically to Cadiz.

Cadiz was a Phoenician foundation, and it is noticeable that in antiquity the other area famous for this style of dancing was the East. Syrian dancing girls, or *ambubaia*, are frequently referred to in our sources.[42] Automedon's praise of a dancing girl from Asia, who 'quivers from her tender finger tips in wicked postures',[43] shows the similarity of the dance style. The connection is made explicit by a Scholion on the passage of Juvenal quoted above. This explains the reference to 'Gaditanae' as 'that is to say "perhaps you are hoping that beautiful and delightful *Syrian* girls are going to dance" since Cadiz was founded by Syrians and Africans (i.e. Carthaginians)'.[44]

The 'Gaditanae' should therefore represent part of Cadiz's Phoenician heritage, and if they did not hail from Cadiz itself, should have come from the heavily Punicized Mediterranean coast of Baetica rather than other parts of the province. They are in this respect another instance of the staying power of Punic customs in the region.

That the style of dancing described above has some parallels with the flamenco dancing of present day Andalucia has been remarked on by many commentators,[45] but while it is true that flamenco probably has an Eastern origin, it is more likely to have been introduced into the region by the Arabic invasion of the eighth century or migrant gypsies in the fifteenth century A.D. than be an unbroken cultural inheritance from the days of Phoenician settlement.[46] The comments made on the subject vary: Schulten believed that the flamenco of Cadiz was more erotic than the restrained versions found at Seville and Granada;[47] the nineteenth-century traveller Richard Ford, on the other hand, believed 'Seville is now in these matters what Gades was'.[48]

Clearly there is scope for future research in this field. The last word on the subject ought to be left again to Ford who wisely remarked 'every young antiquarian ought to witness this exhibition'.[49]

## NOTES

1. Horace, *Odes* 2.2.11; Juvenal 10.1–2.

2. For a visit by Julius Caesar, see Suetonius, *Div. Iul.* 7, and for a complete survey of the temple, see A. Garcia y Bellido, 'Hercules Gaditanus', *AeA* 36 (1963), 70ff.

3. Seneca, *Controv.* 1.pr.16; Pliny, *Ep.* 2.13.

4. Martial 1.61.9.

5. Strabo 2.3.4–5 and M. Cary and E. H. Warmington, *The Ancient Explorers* (London, 2nd ed. 1963), pp. 123–8.

6. Juvenal 11.168–9.

7. Martial 6.71.1–2: 'edere lascivos ad Baetica crusmata gestus et Gaditanis ludere docta modis.'

8. Martial 6.71.6: 'he sold her as a slave and now buys her back as his mistress.' Although this shows he took her as a lover there is no need to assume any more permanent relationship.

9. Martial 1.41.12: 'de Gadibus improbus magister.'

10. Pliny, *Ep.* 1.15.3.

11. Martial 5.78.26–30.

12. Martial 14.204, entitled 'Puella Gaditana': 'she would have made Hippolytus masturbate.' This ability to arouse the paragon of chastity, Hippolytus, is a common trope in Roman erotic poetry: cf. Ovid, *Amores* 2.4.29ff. and *Corpus Priapeum* 19.

13. Martial 14.203: 'tam tremulum crisat, tam blandum prurit.'

14. Martial 5.78.26–8: 'vibrabunt sine fine prurientes, lascivos docili tremore lumbos.'

15. T. Hobin, *Belly Dancing* (London, 1982), p. 57.

16. Juvenal 11.163–4: 'and to applause the knowing girls drop to the ground with trembling buttocks' ('plausuque probatae ad terram tremulo descendant clune puellae').

17. Statius, *Silvae* 1.6.71: 'cymbala tinnulaeque Gades.'

18. Martial 11.16.4.

19. W. Buonaventura, *Belly Dancing* (London, 1983), pp. 122–3; T. Hobin, *Belly Dancing* (London, 1982), p. 64.

20. Juvenal 11.174: 'Let him enjoy those obscene songs ...' ('Ille fruatur vocibus obscaenis ...').

21. Martial 3.63.6: 'qui movet in varios bracchia volsa modos.'

22. Martial 3.63.5: 'cantica qui Nili, qui *Gaditana* susurrat.'

23. Juvenal 11.162–3: 'Perhaps you expect they will begin to sing wanton Gaditane songs in chorus' ('Forsitan exspectes, ut Gaditana [cantica] incipiant pruire choro').

24. Juvenal 11.171–2: 'audiat ille testarum crepitus cum verbis' ('let him listen to the rattle of the castanets and their songs').

25. Daremberg–Saglio, *Dictionnaire des Antiquités* (Paris, 1877), 4.2.1106, fig. 6142.

26. On the other hand the use of the veil, a common modern feature, is less clearly attested. However, a statuette of a veiled dancer wearing a diaphanous robe has been found at Alexandria

(D. Burr Thompson, 'A Bronze Dancer from Alexandria', *AJA* 54 [1950], 371ff.), so it was used at least on occasions in antiquity.

27. Juvenal 11.168–9.

28. The hetaera Thryallis strips before belly dancing in Alciphron, *Letters of Hetaerae* 14. Given she is mentioned in a similar context in *Letter* 13, this might not just be amateur performance. For naked belly dancing in the Middle East, see G. Flaubert, *Flaubert in Egypt* (tr. F. Steegmuller, London, 1972), p. 121.

29. *Corpus Priapeum* 19: 'Telethusa ... who without any covering robe, thrusts out and moves her buttocks higher and higher and will flaunt before you her quivering loin' ('Telethusa ... quae clunem tunica tegente nulla extans altius altiusque motat, crissabit tibi fluctante lumbo').

30. *Roman Women* (London, 1962), p. 274. The bottom half of a leather 'bikini' has been found in Roman London (P. Marsden, *Roman London* [London, 1980], p. 63 and illustr. p. 65) opening the intriguing possibility that the citizens of Roman London as well as Rome enjoyed the services of the 'Gaditanae'.

31. Martial 6.71; 8.51.

32. *Corpus Priapeum* 19.

33. *Corpus Priapeum* 40.

34. See W. H. Parker, *Priapea: Poems for a Phallic God* (London, 1989), pp. 36–7.

35. *Corpus Priapeum* 27: 'Deliciae populi, magno notissima circo, Quintia, vibratas docta movere nates, cymbala cum crotalis, pruriginis arma, Priapo ponit et adducta tympana pulsa manu ...' ('The people's darling and great circus star, Quintia, skilled at wiggling her quivering rump, dedicates to Priapus her lascivious arms, her cymbals, and castanets, along with the tambourines she struck by hand . . .').

36. *CIL* 5.6134: 'quam tulerat tellus pulcherrima Tarsis.'

37. If 'Tarsis' is Gades, perhaps Claudia Tarsis (*CIL* 6.9068) and Gavina Tarsis (*CIL* 6.3500) were also 'Gaditanae'.

38. *CIL* 6.30430.2.

39. *CIL* 6.9013.

40. 'Iocosae Gades', *BRAH* 129 (1951), 97.

41. See Avienus, *Or. Mar.* 269; Valerius Maximus 8.13.4; Silius Italicus 5.339.

42. The most famous example is the opening lines of Virgil's *Copa*.

43. *The Garland of Philip*, ed. A. S. F. Gow and D. L. Page (Cambridge, 1968), Automedon 1: τὴν ἀπὸ Ἀσίης ὀρχησίδα, τὴν κακοτέχνοις σχήμασιν ἐξ ἁπαλῶν κινυμένην ὀνύχων αἰνέω.

44. 'id est, speras forsitan, quod incipiant saltare delicatae ac pulchrae puellae *Syriae, quoniam de Syris et Afris Gades condita est.*'

45. For example, A. Schulten, *Tartessos* (Madrid, 2nd ed. 1945), pp. 238–9.

46. For a discussion dismissing the possibility of a direct transmission of the 'Gaditanae's' erotic songs into the Arabic period see R. Hitchcock, 'The Girls from Cadiz and the *Kharjas*', *Journal of Hispanic Philology* 15:2 (1991), 103–16.

47. op cit., above.

48. *Gatherings from Spain* (London, 1861), p. 327.

49. *Handbook for Travellers in Spain* (London, 3rd ed. 1855), Vol. 1, p. 103.

# THE FESTIVAL FOR BONA DEA AND THE THESMOPHORIA[1]

*By* H. S. VERSNEL

Long before his obsessional wish was finally fulfilled in 146 B.C., the Elder Cato had yet other concerns than *Carthaginem delendam esse*. In his manual for the farmer, *De Agricultura* 143, he gives ample prescriptions concerning the way the wife of the bailiff (the *vilica*) of an estate should behave:

> She must visit the neighbouring and other women very seldom, and not have them either in the house or in her part of it. She must not go out to meals or be a gad-about. She must not engage in religious worship herself or get others to engage in it for her without the orders of the master or the mistress; let her remember that the master attends to the devotions for the whole household.
>
> (translation: W. D. Hooper & H. B. Ash. Loeb)

Similar instructions for women in general, often with such specifications as the prohibition to attend nocturnal ceremonies or to be initiated into foreign mysteries, are typical of republican Rome, no less than of Greece. According to the antiquarian tradition, the consumption of wine—an occasional pull of *Spätlese* excepted as we shall see—in particular, was forbidden: 'in the times of our ancestors women did not drink wine, with the exception of a few fixed days on the occasion of religious festivals', says Servius (*ad* Verg. *Aen*. 1. 737) and he adds that during the reign of Romulus a certain M(a)etennius had scourged his wife to death for having broken this rule. No less dubious from the point of historicity, but equally meaningful as a cultural signal is the theory that the kiss between relatives was invented in order to enable men to subject the female section of his family to a—admittedly rather primitive—breath test (Schneider 1919). With respect to the restrictions imposed on women, Cicero (*Leg*. 2.9.21) cites an ancient law:

> No sacrifices shall be performed by women at night except those offered for the people in proper form: nor shall anyone be initiated except into the Greek rites of Ceres, according to the custom.

## *The Festival of Bona Dea*

One—perhaps the only—exception referred to here is the festival of Bona Dea. I give a short summary of the most important features. The full evidence can be found in Brouwer 1989.

On the eve of the festive day which was held in the house of a *magistratus cum imperio* in the month of December, all the male inhabitants leave the magistrate's house. Even male animals or images of male personages are removed. Assisted by her servants the magistrate's wife decorates the house with all kinds of plants and flowers, *inter alia* arranging bowers made of vine leaves. The cult image of Bona Dea is transported from her temple and set up in the festive hall together with the image of a serpent. A *pulvinar* for the goddess is arranged as well as a table from which the goddess is supposed to take her dinner. There is a sacrifice of a sow *pro populo Romano* ('on behalf of the Roman people') and the mistress of the house performs a *libatio* over a fire in the presence of the Vestal Virgins. Then the women, including the Vestals, make merry: there are references to festive eating and drinking, music, jests, all summarized in the term *ludere* used in a number of sources. The most surprising aspect is the nature of the drinks: during this secret, exclusively female, nocturnal festival the women were allowed to drink—at the very least to handle—wine.

### *The Traditional Interpretation*

Leaving aside improbable theories that derive the goddess and her cult from Greece, practically all interpretations are typical and exclusive representatives of the fertility/vegetation model, which appears to exert a dominant influence even in the most recent text books and monographs. The picture of Bona Dea as a goddess of fertility, a kind of 'Earth Mother', whose cult focused on the protection and promotion of agricultural and female fertility, invariably involves references to a primeval antiquity. *Vice versa*, the most ancient cults are automatically assumed to relate to fertility. Going by the ubiquitous specification 'originally' this approach is particularly interested in origins. Without denying its relevance and value, it should be regretted that this frame of reference tends to monopolize the interpretation of the various elements of the ritual, including the most enigmatic ones. This is true, for instance, of a very curious fact not mentioned so far. Plutarch (*Q. R.* 20) records that in honour of Bona Dea the women offered wine as a libation which, however, they called 'milk', and Macrobius (*Sat.* 1.12.25) specifies that the wine which is introduced into the temple of Bona Dea is not referred to by its own name, but that the vessel (*vas*) containing the wine is called 'honey-jar' (*mellarium*) and the wine 'milk' (*lac*). The conventional interpretation understands these data as unequivocally referring to the oldest stratum of Roman religion. For in these primeval times people did not yet offer wine (or meat), but only milk, honey (and sacrificial cakes). 'It looks as if we may assume that milk, in combination with honey or not, had been the original offering proper to the goddess: that though the tradition was still remembered the practice of the ritual was different. Thus, the terms *lac* and *mellarium* survive when wine is poured' (Brouwer 1989). Scholars of this persuasion rarely betray concern with regard to the obvious question of *why* 'primeval' libations of milk and honey—in defiance of all codes regulating female conduct—should have been transformed into wine-offerings while retaining their original names.

That both the goddess Bona Dea and her festival were connected with human and agricultural fertility is not a matter of dispute. Difficult problems loom up, though, when it appears that this characterization provides satisfactory answers to only a fraction of the questions raised by the evidence. This is all the more disquieting if we find that the Greek Thesmophoria confronts us with the very same situation. Not only is it remarkably similar to the festival of Bona Dea but, here too, the dominant fertility paradigm has often drastically prevented both fruitful questions and productive answers. However, there is a difference: 'the most interesting contemporary analyses of Greek religion often concern the complicated relation of myth and ritual, which has been greatly illuminated from narrative, structuralist and functionalist points of view. These new approaches have been hardly applied to Roman myth and ritual' (Bremmer 1987, p. 76). Although it will appear that, here too, progress can still be made, the detour via Greece may guide us towards a more satisfactory interpretation of the Bona Dea festival. In fact I hope to show that the two festivals—closely related as to myth and ritual—contain practically identical messages on three levels, the substantialist referring to fertility, the functionalist, and the semiotic.

## *The Thesmophoria*

The Thesmophoria, the most widespread Greek festival and the principal cult for Demeter (and Kore), was held in autumn—in Athens (and a few other places) on the eleventh, twelfth, and thirteenth days of Pyanopsion—just before the sowing season. Though the evidence is not free of contradictions there is reason enough to assume that the three-day festival was reserved for married women, probably more especially women of the upper classes under the direction of two female officials, the *Archousai*. The first day bore the name 'Road Up' (*Anhodos*), probably referring to the procession to and the assembling at the Thesmophorion. The second was known as 'Fast' (*Nesteia*). On it the women abstained from food and sat on the ground. The third day was called *Kalligeneia* ('Day of Fair Offspring'), a name that refers to the concern for bearing fine children. At another festival just before midsummer, probably the Skira, women had thrown various objects related to fertility into *megara* (caverns in the ground). The chief objects were sacrificed piglets and models of snakes and male genitals shaped out of dough. The decayed remnants were recovered during the Thesmophoria by a special group of women called the *Antlēriai* ('Bailers'), who had purified themselves for this holy job by a three-day period of (sexual) abstinence. The mixture of these unsavoury ingredients was placed on altars. When scattered with seed in the field it was supposed to promote fertility of crops.

### *The Traditional Interpretation*

The core of this Demeter festival is the concern for the promotion of human and cereal fertility. Again, there is no need to revise this truism. However, this late 19th-century discovery, though revealing and productive in some respects, had damaging consequences in others: a wish to impose a neat pattern tended to explain *every* single bit of information in this perspective. In some cases this did not raise serious difficulties, but in others success could only be attained by distortion or even suppression of the facts: the paradigm tyrannized the evidence. As I noticed above, both this process and the curious pieces of evidence to which it is applied betray strong similarities with the festival of Bona Dea. I select a number of facts that seem to me most relevant and illustrative, leaving aside the few that are of minor importance. For full accounts one should consult Deubner 1932 and Dahl 1976.

First of all, during the three days of the festival the women used to camp in booths or shelters arranged in rows within the open space of the Thesmophorion. This clearly recalls the bowers of the Bona Dea festival. Quite a number of authors report that the women slept on beds (*stibades*) made of *lugos* (= *agnos: Vitex agnus castus*, withy, chaste tree, a kind of willow). This plant, generally regarded as unproductive and infertile, was supposed to work as a strong antaphrodisiac and hence to prevent all sorts of undesirable sexual impulses. No manoeuvre illustrates better how relentlessly a paradigm can impose its laws on the believer than the following argument put forward by Nilsson 1906, p. 48, and adopted by Deubner 1932, p. 56. Though perfectly aware of the connotations of *lugos* throughout the Greek world—and in spite of the fact that also other unmistakably antaphrodisiac plants were applied during the Thesmophoria—they hold that this must be a *later* inversion of its original meaning. For originally, they argue, *lugos* must rather have *stimulated* female sexuality. In support of their argument they refer to an isolated testimony on the Milesian Thesmophoria where a pine twig was inserted and hidden under the bed of willow. Indeed, pine twigs were considered to promote fertility but, as we shall see, this is, of course, not reason enough to pervert the functions of the other Thesmophoriac plants.

It is also reported that the women indulged in uttering abuse at each other and even in striking each other with a scourge plaited out of bark (*morotton*). Both types of action are all the rage in the fertility paradigm, as they remind us of Iambe's aeschrology and the 'Schlag mit der Lebenstrute' (blow with the life-giving rod) respectively. However, in this particular case more 'functionalistic' explanations have been reluctantly put forward. If this ritual ended the day of fasting, as it is supposed to do, 'it may have been in practice a very satisfying release of the pent-up irritation brought on by hunger', thus the most excessive venture into the psycho-sociological interpretation (Parke 1977, p. 86).

On the middle day prisoners were freed from their chains, a custom explained by Deubner 1932, p. 58 as a magical means to promote fertility in women: knots and chains had negative effects on everything connected with (re)production, especially confinement. However, this—in itself not impossible—idea puts its advocates into serious trouble. First: liberation from bondage is also attested for the Panathenaea and the Dionysia. And secondly: what are we to do with the complication that on the same (second) day of the Thesmophoria the law courts and council meetings were suspended as well? To the first objection Deubner responded that the custom was transferred from the Thesmophoria onto the other festivals as a 'humanitarian measure'. One wonders why, if so, the privilege was restricted to these festivals and not extended to others. The correct course of action, I would suggest, is to ask what the three festivals may have had in common and to take this common characteristic as the point of departure for further interpretation.

The second problem was not responded to at all. This occurrence is ignored even in Deubner's very complete account of the evidence. Perhaps not by chance. For it appears to confuse scholars, as may best be illustrated by one of them who thinks he has found a no-nonsense solution: the suspension of law courts and council meetings, so Parke 1977, p. 86 suggests, had to do with the disruption of ordinary life caused by the departure of the women. If I understand him correctly, men found it just a bit too troublesome to do business in such chaos.

Finally, there are two isolated, very enigmatic details that have kept their secret to the present day. We hear of two sacrifices offered by the women during or at the end of the Thesmophoria. One was called *Zēmia* ('punishment/penalty/') and Hesychius, our sole source, says: *thusia tis apodidomenē huper tōn ginomenōn en Thesmophoriois* ('a sacrifice made [to pay, compensate] for the things that happened during the Thesmophoria'). To the best of my knowledge Deubner is the only one who attempted an explanation. He thinks it must be a kind of expiatory sacrifice to pay for things that might have gone wrong—'Verfehlungen' (occasional errors)—during the festival. And this, in its turn, fosters conjecture. Before *ginomenōn*, a term like *akairōs or paranomōs* ('wrongly') should be added.

The other (secret) sacrifice was called the 'Chalcidian Pursuit' (*Chalkidikon [apo]diōgma*). A mythical aition explains that once during a war the women had prayed for victory and the enemy had fled and had been pursued to Chalcis. And that is all we know.

### *New Directions in Interpreting the Thesmophoria*

If I am now going to try and search for a more coherent and satisfactory explanation of this collection of oddities, I emphatically do not wish to reject or play down the lasting meaning of the festival as a ritual of fertility, both human and agrarian. This feature is simply too obvious for doubt. We do have the right, however, to look for another frame of reference in order to elucidate those elements which have failed to find a convincing interpretation within the old paradigm. And, in accordance with the theme of the book referred to below (n. 1), I shall start my quest in the context of the 'festivals of exception'. For indeed the Thesmophoria (as well as the festival of Bona Dea) clearly belongs in this category.

During these few days the women laid off the burden of their normal routine and of their submissiveness to male dominance, more especially their obedience to male *phallokratia*. For once, they enjoyed privileges that were unimaginable in normal life: the right to organize a women's society with complete autonomy and proper female *archontes*, to ward off male intervention (except for financial support), to leave their houses and stay outside, even during the night, to perform private and secret rituals. Detienne 1979, pp. 186ff. has drawn attention to yet another significant signal of reversal. Whereas women, being deprived of political rights, were accordingly excluded from altars, blood, and sacrifice, bloody sacrifices are on record for the Thesmophoria, both in the descriptions (and archaeological remnants) of the ritual and in the myth.

If we now consider the facts listed above in the light of reversal or exception, some of the most enigmatic reveal their secrets. First, the primitive booths or bowers have been generally explained as a token of the great antiquity of the rites, going back to the period in which people indeed lived in such primitive housing, at least in periods of agricultural activity. Diodorus Sic. 5.4 reports that the Syracusans celebrated the Thesmophoria *mimoumenoi ton archaion bion* ('imitating the old way of life'). We also read that the Eretrian women during the Thesmophoria 'did not prepare the meat on fire but by the heat of the sun': another most remarkable imitation of a very *ancienne cuisine*.

Even *if* this were an age-old heritage and not a spontaneous act of *mimēsis* (as Diodorus phrases it), *origin* is not to be identified with *meaning*. The meaning of its 'preservation' can only be explored by asking why this specific habit was maintained in so limited a number of (exceptional) festivals, whereas in other equally old-fashioned agrarian ceremonies 'it had gradually fallen into abeyance', as it is generally phrased. Now, the answer to this question is not hard to find: aspects of 'primitivism' in rituals of exception generally refer to the exceptional nature of the situation itself, signifying the reverse of normality, a temporary return to a- or pre-cultural way of life, where various aspects of disorder yield an ambivalent amalgam of hilarious *euphoria* and of disruptive 'otherness' (Bremmer 1987, pp. 76–88; Versnel 1987). And the women's festivals by their nature belong to these periods of exception. Not only the temporary residence in huts, but also the sitting on the ground and the sleeping on *stibades* can then be excellently understood as signals of primitivism.

Once we recognize this—and I am not the first to point it out—this immediately entails a most natural and, above all, *coherent* explanation of the liberation of prisoners and the suspension of court sessions and council meetings, rites that have never been understood correctly. For, as a matter of fact, they are the very expressions of the *anomia* typical of this kind of festival of reversal. Temporary liberation from chains and bondage was *the* central feature of, for instance, the Kronia and Saturnalia. Moreover, the Saturnalia shared the official cessation of all public services with some other Roman 'interstitional' ceremonies, such as the *mundus patet*. Elsewhere (Versnel 1980) I have argued that the Roman *iustitium* (literally the cessation of jurisdiction) mirrors the situation of Greek *anomia*, both being markers of 'periods of exception'—either of mourning, or of licence (or both, for instance in festivals of the turning of the year). They signify the interruption of normality through the suspension of normal law and order. And this is exactly the meaning of the same custom during the Thesmophoria. From this point of view the ribald cheers and indecent speech of the women—even if originating in fertility rites—acquire an overtone: they, too, suggest a reversal of the normal, in particular the sexual, order: women usurp 'men's language'. This becomes particularly evident when we compare modern Greek women's festivals, where the element of fertility has now practically disappeared, but indecent behaviour with imitations and manipulations of male sexual organs and dirty language, is still a standard ingredient.

The Thesmophoria, first and foremost, is a festival of fertility and a number of its most conspicuous aspects can be explained from this perspective. Secondly, it is also a festival of exception, in some respects even of reversal, a feature which helps us to elucidate other elements. Nor is this all. If origin should not be identified with meaning as I argued above, function is not identical with meaning either. In one of the most perceptive recent studies on the Thesmophoria, Zeitlin 1982, p. 131 remarks: 'There is a considerable sophistication today among the various disciplines in the study of ritual behavior which makes us dissatisfied with the more facile explanations, the purely functional social or psychological rationales, which refer every phenomenon to such superficial commonplaces as release from tensions with social solidarity as the optimum goal.' Though I do not quite subscribe to the depreciation of the functionalistic approach voiced here, I do agree that, whereas functionalism asks what rites *do for* society, one can—and should—also ask what rites *say about* society. You can read them, analyse the implied connotations, and inquire what they signify.

This third level of interpretation has been broached for the Thesmophoria in various ways by various scholars, who have considerably advanced our perception of the festival's meaning. Although their semiotic interpretations hide a common denominator, each of them detects a different (aspect of the) message. While expressing my debt to the inspiring works of especially Detienne, Zeitlin, and Winkler, which reasons of space prevent me from so much as even summarizing, let alone discussing, I shall focus on what I consider the core of the message hidden in the myth and ritual of the Thesmophoria. We shall, therefore, return to the evidence and discuss a few riddles that have so far resisted explanation.

### *Numphai Sleeping on Lugos: the Paradox of the Thesmophoria*

The beds of antaphrodisiac *lugos* confront us with a glaring inconsistency: on the one hand the festival focused on the fertility of (fields and) women: *Kalligeneia*. On the other hand, however, this 'fertility'-festival is marked by a rigorous prohibition of any sexual action that is naturally preconditional for activating the procreative potentials of women: men are excluded, both husbands and other interested males. There is a host of objects around that may provoke—or at least refer to—erotic desire, but no opportunity to implement this in sexual action. Obviously, where Demeter reigns in her temporary all-female society, Aphrodite is relegated. What is more, though men were also excluded from some other festivals, the Thesmophoria is unique in being the only certain instance of a classical Greek festival where laywomen were required to keep themselves pure in the period of preparation and during the festival. In sum, during the Thesmophoria the matrons were temporarily reduced to the status of virgins before marriage: though sexually mature they are not (yet) available for consummation. The paradox is further complicated by the fact that 'real' virgins are *not* admitted, but that Demeter and her daughter are called 'sacred-pure' (*hagnē thea*) and that her priestesses, like the Roman Vestal Virgins, must be unmarried.

It will be immediately evident now that sleeping on beds of ant-aphrodisiac *lugos* is the perfect manner to express (and effect) one side of this paradox. In a recent study on *lugos*, D. Baudy 1989 arrives at the following conclusion: 'In every ritual context this vegetable symbol warranted a "virginal", "pure" state that points already to its termination. The use of withy demonstrated (...) that the cult participants were subject to a cultural suspension of the procreative function.' This suspension of the procreative function in an otherwise overtly procreative context is exactly what I regard as the core of the 'message' of this festival, as I shall argue in more detail later on, though my frame of reference is different from that of Baudy. The fact that *lugos* is particularly associated with the virgin goddess Artemis (Calame 1977, pp. 285–9; King 1983, p. 98) adds support to this view.

Now, this ambiguity strikingly manifests itself in the unique Milesian custom of inserting a pine twig *under* these *stibades* of withies, which, seen in this light, now reveals its meaning. It 'translates' the paradox just described in a very precise manner: indeed, the festival is about fertility and this is symbolized through the pine branch, but fertility is not accorded consummation; as yet, the pine branch is 'under cover', camouflaged by the antaphrodisiac *lugos*, which forms a temporary barrier between the *bearers* and the *symbol* of fertility. This suggestion is corroborated by the fact that the pine branch is also involved in another more general, but equally ambiguous, Thesmophoriac context. According to our main witness (Schol. Luc. 276 Rabe), 'the "Bailers" fetch up "unspeakable sacred things" that are made of dough: models of snakes and male membra; they also take pine branches.' Here we have the very same paradox condensed in one sentence: overtly sexual symbols are handled by a group of women who have strict instructions to preserve a state of purity.

When we now return to the remaining riddles of our list—the two sacrifices called *Zēmia* and 'Chalcidian Pursuit'—I do not claim to offer definite solutions here, but I would at least venture a few suggestions. Again it is the specific line of approach that fosters fresh opportunities for interpretation. The first sacrifice gives rise to the question of what, actually, could be so wrong in the ritual behaviour of the women during the Thesmophoria as to justify a ritual 'punishment'. Because he could not *find* offences Deubner had to *invent* them: 'possible' ritual errors that had to be propitiated. Once more one wonders why, then, this very curious measure is attested only for this women's festival and not for (agrarian) rituals in general. And once more the natural answer should be sought in the exceptional nature of the festival itself: we do not need to look for possible flaws in parts of the ritual, for *the whole festival itself is manifestly and necessarily wrong* (as myth will unequivocally confirm). The normal codes of behaviour are suspended or reversed, women conspicuously do wrong things, they manifest subversive traits in acts of aggression or self-assertion, and as if this were not enough, during this festival for human and agrarian fertility, the male catalyst was banned, temporary sterility being the paradoxical result. Reason enough for a ritual *zēmia* for this fundamental offence and with this the sacrifice falls into the category of—mostly mythical—punishments for supposed wrongdoings.

The evidence on the Chalcidian Pursuit is less clear, since it does not offer semantic clues (such as 'punishment') in the name or the description. By way of suggestion, I would draw attention to a distant though remarkable parallel in the Roman festival of the Nonae Capratinae. There, too, women—*in casu* slave girls—are recorded as having contributed to the flight, pursuit, and annihilation of an enemy army, and it was said that the festival was founded in memory of this feat. Now, it does strike us that the Nonae Capratinae, as Bremmer 1987 has demonstrated, was a festival of reversal, in which slave girls were dressed in the outfits of, and were waited upon by, their mistresses, temporarily lived in huts (made of branches of the wild—that is infertile—fig-tree), and mocked (male) passers-by. At the least, this is a remarkable parallel, the more so since both are connected with a (pseudo-) historical war and victory. Generally, female rituals of reversal comprising temporary liberation from male dominance seem to have evoked images of female martial activity, which in their turn foster (aetiological) myths. In a way, the women thus mirror the disruptive imagery of the Amazons. Ultimately, female martial aggression may release itself against their own husbands, as is most obviously illustrated by the myth and ritual of the 'Lemnian fire' (Burkert 1970), and also in some myths concerning the Thesmophoria, to which we shall now turn our attention.

## *The Contribution of Myth*

After this analysis of the elements that, together, construct the essential ambiguity of the Thesmophoria—matrons celebrating their procreative qualities while being temporarily deprived of any opportunity of sexual fulfilment—it remains to ask what this *means*. As so often, myth will put us on the track. Unfortunately, the Thesmophoria does not abound in mythical 'commentary' but the little we have is informative.

One myth tells us that in Cyrene slaughterers (*sphaktriai*), their faces smeared with blood and swords in hand, castrated the man who came to spy on them at the festival, who was no other than King Battus himself. This is a mythical expression of the Thesmophoriac hostility to men, blown up to a gruesome picture as can only occur in narrative. Likewise, Aristomenes of Messenia, when he came too close to women celebrating the Thesmophoria, was overpowered with sacrificial knives, roasting spits, and torches, and then taken captive. These stories—apart from adding proof to the existence of female sacrificial activities—clearly reveal the tension between the sexes dramatized in the Thesmophoria. They also most clearly demonstrate that the festival is essentially *wrong*, disruptive, and, consequently in the eyes of one half of the society, threatening. Moreover, the specific threat of the Thesmophoria lies in the fact that the Demeter festival is directly connected with the overt aims and goals of the *polis*, not least in its focus on the production of legitimate citizen children. Disruption within the boundaries and even in the political centre of the *polis* may be expected to provoke a different set of responses, both ritually and in the imagination, than do Bacchic excursions *eis oros* ('to the mountain'), where reversal of cultural codes 'naturally' belongs.

Another myth is more specific. Persephone was abducted in the period in which, as a *numphē*, she was preparing herself for marriage *inter alia* by weaving clothes for her wedding and marital life. After her disappearance, her mother Demeter entrusted the basket (*kalathos*) in which these clothes had been stored to the Nymphs, but the clothes themselves she took with her when she went to the isle of Paros, where she was hosted by King Melisseus, 'king of the bees'. After her stay there she showed her gratitude by giving the bridal dress of Persephone to the sixty daughters of the king, while also revealing the secret rituals of the Thesmophoria to them. From that time on all the women celebrating the Thesmophoria bear the ritual name of 'bees' (*melissai*).

In his well-known discussion of the connotations of bees (and honey), Detienne 1981 demonstrated that in the Greco-Roman literature over fifteen centuries the *melissa* was the emblem of female domestic virtue. The bee distinguishes itself by a diligent and above all a chaste way of life, and by an extreme abstinence in sexual matters. Adultery, or, more generally, any 'indecent' form of sexual intercourse, is a sin that bees abhor and they retaliate by abandoning the place of the crime or (even attacking) the culprit himself. We may conclude that the ritual name of 'bees' exactly symbolizes the expectations concerning female behaviour during this festival of reversal: although everything may be messed up, and all sorts of extravagances condoned, the *sexual codes* should be carefully maintained. Indeed, *more* than carefully. For, apart from and beyond being the examples of chastity, bees are often regarded as preserving their virginity throughout their life-time, being notable for their asexual manner of reproduction. Here, indeed, we have the ideal virgin mothers.

Now, the little myth about Demeter at Paros contains one curious detail: the *aition* of the Thesmophoria does *not* refer to matrons, but to *numphai*, here (as usually) in the explicit sense of virgins on the eve of marriage. This is a strikingly accurate mythical translation of what we inferred from our analysis of the ritual data: during the Thesmophoria the matrons were temporarily reduced to the status of *numphai*. They become *melissai*, in the sense of virginal and sexually abstinent maiden-bees.

All this confirms our previous conclusions that the central inconsistency in the Thesmophoria is the paradox between its focus on the fertility and sexuality of the married woman on one hand, and the emphatic suppression of any opportunity to consummate this, on the other. This paradox is consistently expressed by symbols indicating the matron's temporary return to the premarital virginal existence of the *numphē*. The question remains; what is the meaning of all this?

Before pursuing our quest we shall first return to Bona Dea and analyse her myth and ritual from the same perspective. We shall find ourselves confronted with strikingly similar paradoxes and questions.

### *Back to Bona Dea*

'The female worshippers of Demeter correspond with the Roman matrons who celebrated—also with secret rites—the festival of Bona Dea', writes Simon 1983, p. 17, and by now we are able to confirm her statement. Both festivals are strictly confined to (decent or even well-born) matrons, men being demonstratively excluded, but they are both held in the political centre of the city. They refer to closely related 'fertility' goddesses and the rites aim at the promotion of cereal and female fecundity. As for specific ritual elements, both festivals reveal similar features relating to an atmosphere of 'otherness' and these take the form of a type of primitivism. Both are marked by the use of primitive bowers or huts made of leaves, while the Thesmophoria adds rites such as sitting on the ground and lying on beds of twigs, and the Bona Dea festival references to honey and milk as primitive signals. In both rites serpents play a role as do, even more emphatically, pigs. Most significantly, both are characterized by bloody sacrifices performed by matrons. Finally, besides being very serious and holy rites they also betray their nature of exception by female licence: we have noticed remarkable analogies in various elements of 'ludic behaviour', although the emphatic references to wine are only attested for the Roman festival, if we do not count Aristophanes' satirical allusions.

However, these analogies by no means exhaust the list, as we shall see from a detailed analysis of some features of the Bona Dea festival not discussed so far. Two ritual elements attract attention because of their diametrically opposite applications: whereas wine was explicitly welcomed, myrtle was banned. Our discussion will show that this very combination is immediately relevant to an understanding of the festival.

### *Wine in, Myrtle out*

Plutarch (*Q. R.* 20) says that women for the festival of Bona Dea brought in no myrtle, though they took pride in making use of all kinds of growing and blooming plants. One of the reasons he suggests is 'because they abstain from many things, and particularly from sexual pleasures, when celebrating this religious service. For they not only exclude their husbands from the houses but they also remove everything male when performing the customary rites in honour of the goddess. Now, as the myrtle is sacred to Aphrodite, they shun it on religious grounds.'

This explanation clearly hits the mark: myrtle is notorious for its erotic-sexual symbolism in accordance with its ubiquitous connections with Aphrodite-Venus. In addition, the plant was conspicuously avoided as material for the bridal crown in Rome, while it is hardly if at all attested for the ancient Greek wedding. *Silentium clamat*: the exclusion of myrtle from the bridal crown should be explained by its erotic connotations: being the *signum* of Aphrodite/Venus, it denotes erotic seduction, and for that reason should be shunned in the context of regular marriage, where Hera/Juno reigns. Incidentally, the majority of heroes, heroines, and demi-goddesses that are connected with (the name of) the myrtle are conspicuously marked by frustrated or illicit love affairs, or they concern Amazon-like types (Chirassi 1968, pp. 18–25). Consequently, the exclusion of myrtle from the Roman ritual is homologous with the inclusion of *lugos* in the Greek Thesmophoria: both signify that during the festival, in spite of the overtly sexual atmosphere, there is no place for actual erotic lust (let alone for seductive actions by males such as Clodius).

That wine was taboo for Roman women is recorded by a number of ancient sources. Noticeably, as recent research has shown, the sacrificial use of wine by women, perhaps even more than its alleged consumption, was a downright violation of Roman social and ritual codes. As a matter of fact, Piccaluga 1964 and De Cazanove 1987 have demonstrated that the prohibition of wine was not so absolute as is often assumed. Gellius (10.23.1–2) says that women of all periods abstained from the wine called *temetum*, but that they did drink *loream, passum, murrinam*, and comparable 'sweetened' wines. Now, abstention from pure, indigenous *temetum* implied exclusion from sacrifice, *temetum* being the only wine suited for sacrificial use. And there is more. According to Plutarch (*Q. R.* 85), the Sabine women, once Romanized, were officially assigned the task of processing wool and weaving, but they were denied the tasks of grinding grain and preparing meat. Now, keeping women from the kitchen is keeping them from sacrifice. There is only one exception: the Vestal Virgins did have the task of preparing the *mola salsa* for sacrificial purposes. However, as we shall see in more detail below, the Vestals were exceptional in all respects.

All this implies that women were marginalized as compared to men, whose place was in the political and cultic centre of the city. This, to be sure, was not an inference consciously expressed by the Romans themselves. When *they* reflected on the prohibition of wine, they tended to relate it to the supposed aphrodisiac effects of wine on women. Valerius Maximus (2.1.5), for instance, thus summarizes a general opinion: 'In olden days the use of wine was unknown to women, for fear that they might lapse into some disgraceful act. For it is only a step from the intemperance of Liber pater to the forbidden things of Venus.' And we have seen that in Roman legend women were scourged to death for this violation.

A comparison of the evidence on myrtle and wine reveals their correlation. If in the Roman view wine provokes aphrodisiac excesses, the festival of Bona Dea made it urgent to clarify that in this special case the ritual use of wine (*merum* = *temetum*) did *not* entail the disruptive erotic effects generally associated with it. Hence: if wine comes in, myrtle must be out. And this is strikingly analogous with the Thesmophoriac licence (perhaps, but not certainly, including wine) and the significant suppression of lurking erotic enticements by the application of *lugos* and other antaphrodisiacs. Rome, as can be expected, displayed even more rigour: ritual effected a duplication of the 'warning'. For only now do we fully understand the curious detail that women called the wine 'milk' and the wine vessel 'honey-jar', to which we may add an additional fact handed down by Arnobius (*Nat.* 5.18), that the wine vessel was present but covered with a cloth. If wine is permitted to women—surprisingly and exceptionally—it must be covered, disguised, and made harmless by an innocent incognito. These pseudonyms, in their turn, carry several layers of significance. Milk and honey are the markers *par excellence* of utopian golden times (Graf 1980), and as such, even as mere denominators, help to determine the 'exceptional' nature of this festival of reversal. On the other hand, the mimicry may also have functioned as fuel for 'laughter of the oppressed', as Winkler 1990, pp. 188ff. characterized the women's festivals: 'say, dear, would you be so kind as to pass on the milk?'

All this is gratifyingly illustrated by myth, but before turning to this, we have to pay attention to one special section of the merrymakers.

## *Ambiguous Virgins*

Side by side with the Roman matrons the Vestal Virgins played an important part in the Bona Dea festival. The notorious ambiguity manifest in their two co-existent and apparently contradictory roles, that of virgins *and* that of matrons, has been convincingly elucidated by Mary Beard 1980. She vindicates the ambiguity as an essential and structural feature in that it designates sacredness, the ambiguous object or person being drastically set apart and distinguished from any normal category. There are also male aspects involved, since some of the Vestals' privileges (the *lictor*, the right to give evidence in court, the right to bequeath property in their own right) are otherwise almost exclusively associated with men. By their partaking of several sexual categories the Vestals are placed on the brink between these categories. This interstitial position, Beard argues, is symbolized by their bridal nature (as for instance recorded by Festus 454 L). So she concludes: 'Like the girl on the day of her wedding, they are seen as on the brink between virginal and marital status, but perpetually on the brink, perpetually fixed at the moment of transition from one category to another.'

Instead of following Beard's more specific interpretation of the supposed equally ambiguous status of the fire tended by the Vestals, I would rather concentrate on the analogy with the women attending the festivals under discussion, who, as we have noticed, betray the very same ambiguity in their sexual status: despite being matrons they are temporarily reduced to the status of virgins. We even inferred that this ambiguity comprised the central paradox of the Thesmophoria. In choosing to follow this track I feel encouraged by the fact that the festival of Bona Dea is the *only certain* Roman ceremony in which matrons and Vestals were associated.

## *The Contribution of Myth*

According to Plutarch (*Q. R.* 35), Bona Dea, Faunus' wife, after having been found out drinking wine in secret was beaten by her husband with myrtle twigs. (Cf. Arnobius, *Nat.* 5.18; Lactantius, *D.I.* 1.22.9–11.) Quite a different story, however, is handed down by Macrobius (*Sat.* 1.12.20–9). He first notes that Bona Dea is the same as Fauna or Ops or Fatua and then continues: 'It is said too that she was the daughter of Faunus, and that she resisted the amorous advances of her father who had fallen in love with her, so that he even beat her with myrtle twigs because she did not yield to his desires though she had been made drunk by him on wine. It is believed that the father changed himself into a serpent, however, and under this guise had intercourse with his daughter.'

It will be immediately apparent that these two related but diverging versions of a mythical theme, refer to the most remarkable elements of the ritual and the cult of Bona Dea: wine, myrtle, serpents, female modesty blemished. These stories of excess and punishment constructed after the model of the well-known Maetennius story (above p. 182) strongly corroborate our views of the interrelated meanings of wine and myrtle.

The first version reflects the general taboo on wine for women and pictures the consequences when this code is violated. The sole additional element, viz. the fact that the matron is beaten with *myrtle*, cannot but signify that myrtle in this context bears strongly *negative* connotations. And so it is applied: as an aetiological explanation of its exclusion from the festival. Lactantius, who makes Faunus *regret* the death of his wife and deify her so that she becomes Bona Dea, may refer to the exceptional situation of the Bona Dea festival: what is not allowed in daily life is allowed to the goddess and her servants.

The other version, however, is both more enigmatic and more instructive. First, there is an unequivocal linkage of wine drinking, myrtle, and excessive erotic desire. Faunus uses both wine and myrtle as instruments to stimulate his daughter's erotic appetite. The symbol of the serpent also fits in. But, of course, the shocking part is the act of incest performed by father Faunus. Passing in silence possible models in Hellenistic stories, we can regard this version as an extreme 'blow up' of the most threatening expectations concerning the relation of wine and erotic myrtle in the context of Bona Dea. However, I would draw attention to one striking—and to my mind meaningful—coincidence: in this unique version presenting an extreme erotic excess the *matron* of all other versions has disappeared, yielding her place to a *virgin*(al daughter).

### *Twin Festivals in Greece and Rome*

When we survey this section on the myth and ritual of Bona Dea the remarkable parallelism with the Thesmophoria strikes the eye. Women violate the normal codes of behaviour, but, just as in the Thesmophoria, there are warning signs: if wine is in, myrtle, symbol of *erōs*, must be out. And just as in the Thesmophoria, the female sexuality and fertility, which are in the centre of things, are curiously frustrated: no men are admitted to bring it to completion. And, again comparably to the Greek festival, there is a marked emphasis on virgins, both in ritual (Vestal Virgins) and myth (Faunus and his daughter), who assist or take the place of the matrons as soon as the situation seems to require this.

So, in the end, the two closely related festivals of Greece and Rome confront us with the same paradox: matrons celebrate their basic procreative qualities by rites that focus on sexual symbolism. At the same time they are rigorously prevented from satisfying erotic desire by antaphrodisiac symbolism. Matrons become virgins. Why? The answer to this question should be sought in the fundamental tension hidden in these two ambivalent festivals. In terms of the dominant ideology of Greece and Rome, the ceremonies are *beneficial and necessary* from a socio-biological point of view but *wrong and undesirable* from a socio-cultural point of view. Matrons are in the centre of things, both literally and figuratively. Their specific procreative potential is celebrated as essential for the continuity of the community *and* this takes place in the centre of the community: *Kalligeneia* close to the Pnyx, pig's sacrifice *pro populo Romano* in the highest magistrate's house. The matrons enjoy a licentious excursion from reality, but do so right in the centre of the city. Hence these festivals affect the prevailing codes in two respects. First, they focus the attention on the women's sexual import by references to erotic aspects through licentious behaviour, dirty language, sexual symbolism, drinking of wine, etc. And secondly, they present women taking over (part of) men's predominance while expelling the men from the centre of things and adopting their dominant roles. The first is intolerable in terms of the family codes, the second unthinkable in terms of the codes of the community.

Now, I would suggest that there is only one way of coping with the intolerable and of depriving the unthinkable of its extreme disruptive effects. The incompatibility of matrons doing un-matronlike things should be mitigated. So, *if* for some indisputable reason matrons must act as they do, they cannot remain matrons: for the time being they must give up this status and adopt another, that of the unmarried maiden. This, at any rate, is what both myth and ritual unequivocally express. A short glance into Greek and Roman views on virgin-maidens, matrons, and the function of marriage can, finally, teach us why.

### *Gunē-parthenos: on the Fatal Ambiguity of the Female Race*

'Emotional, self-indulgent, inebriate, gluttonous, irrational, weak-willed: these form the common-place description of women in the writings of fifth- and fourth-century Athens', writes Just in the most recent discussion of the 'construction' of the female in classical Athens (Just 1989, p. 166). In the eyes of the 'club d'hommes', as Vidal–Naquet baptized the citizenry of Athens, the female race was marked by excessive expenditure on food, drink, clothing, or any other bodily comfort or pleasure, and, more especially, by excessive sexual indulgence. 'To be a slave of pleasure is the behaviour of a licentious woman, not a man', thus the 4th-century Anaxandrides (fr. 60) sums up a ubiquitous judgement. In the background of these specific weaknesses is women's lack of self-control, a deficiency common to women, slaves, and children. There is, then, a clear dividing line between the free male citizen and all other human beings: the line between autonomy and dependence.

Side by side with this there is another: the distinction between women who enjoy the freedom to indulge in their natural passions, and those whose natural inclinations are restrained and subjugated to cultural control. The borderline, in other words, between 'natural/wild' and 'cultural/tamed' women. The first quality is either associated with mythical and other imaginary women in a marginal landscape or with the virgin maiden in a premarital state. Both are *numphai*. Myth presents us with women such as Artemis, Kore, Atalanta, and the countless anonymous nymphs of forests, rivers, and mountains, who are all pictured as virginal creatures of the wild. 'Shunning contact with males, living far from men and the life of the city, the *kore* (maiden), like Artemis, the virgin huntress, mistress over wild animals and uncultivated land, shares in the life of the wild', says Vernant 1982, p. 139.

*Numphai* of this type cannot be tamed: gods or demi-gods they keep outside the borders of culture: awe-inspiring, threatening, a terror especially to men, as the Amazons—wild women, warriors, *and* barbarians—most distinctly illustrate. *Human numphai*, on the other hand, can—and must—be subjugated. Unmarried maidens are consistently referred to as fields to be cultivated, ploughed, sown, animals to be broken in, mounted, domesticated. Women, especially in their premarital state, are part of nature, part of the wild, which men must 'cultivate' (Just 1989, p. 231; Gould 1980, p. 52). The domestication of young horses, being the symbols of unbridled violence (Ghiron-Bistagne 1985), is especially rife in the imagery of marriage, terms like *pōlos* being as common metaphors of the young (fe)male as are yoking and taming of marriage (Calame 1977; Loraux 1985 ch. 2). Jenkins 1983, esp. p. 142, views the mythical sacrificial death of virgins in the perspective of their marriage: both denote a radical and definitive subjugation, just as, on the other hand, the notion of the girl as a wild thing to be captured and tamed through marriage (…) is one of the perceptions expressed in the well-known erotic pursuits of vase paintings (Sourvinou-Inwood 1987).

The only way to incorporate women in society—that is to mould them from a natural into a cultural being—is through marriage. The negative and wild aspects of the female race are conceived as being operative and virulent only in—and necessarily restricted to—the premarital period. Loraux 1981, pp. 86ff. makes the salient observation that the first woman, *kalon kakon* Pandora, who combines all these negative features with the seductiveness of her beauty, is presented in the appearance of a *parthenos aidoiē*, a respectable *maiden* in Hes. *Th.* 772. In *Th.* 513–14 it is exactly her double nature of *gunē-parthenos* that makes the first woman so alarming: in the mythical universe there is no character more ambiguous than the *parthenos*, who unites in her person every frightful inclination denied to the adult woman, in particular the works of Aphrodite.

Consequently, the *parthenos* must be tamed, yoked, domesticated, cultivated, through marriage. The transition is marked by rituals like the ones of Brauron or by the ceremonies of the wedding itself, where, as Detienne 1972, p. 216f. has shown, a child, wearing a crown of thorny plants entwined with acorns, offered bread from a winnowing basket to all the guests saying, 'I have fled from evil and found what is best', which the Greeks interpreted as referring to the transition from the 'thorny' life' (*bios akanthōdēs*) to the 'cultivated life' (*bios hēmeros*) or from the 'wild life' (*bios agroikos*) to the 'life of milled corn' (*bios alēlesmenos*). Both transitions, the one from virgin to matron and the other of mankind from a pre-agricultural to an agricultural age, involve the domestication of nature and a shift from the province of Artemis to that of Demeter.

However, this subjugation never loses a taint of precariousness. Women remain a potential source of disorder and the risk that they will run wild can never be completely ruled out. The result is a lasting ambiguity between women's natural characteristics that are peripheral to the male dominated body politic—woman as outsider—and their vital significance for the existence of the state through her progeny—woman as insider. In other words, marriage retains a certain duality in that the sexual-erotic facet (especially attributed to the 'female intruder') belongs to nature and thus affects its character as a social and cultural institution. King 1983 thus phrases the essential tension: '"Woman" is thus both excluded and included, alien and familiar. For the Greeks woman is a necessary evil; an evil because she is undisciplined and licentious, lacking the self-control of which men are capable, yet necessary to society as constructed by men, in order to reproduce it.' And she observes once more that as the positive values of 'woman' tended to be centred on the concept of the reproducer, the *gunē*, so the negative values shifted to the unmarried girl.

Additionally, the only phase of life in which the female can be equated with the male—at least in some respects—is the period in which she is still a *parthenos*. Not only are terms such as *pōlos* in use for both boys and girls, but as especially Schmitt 1977 has noted, in myth the *parthenos* often leads a life comparable to that of the *ephēbos*. Atalanta, Artemis, the Amazons by applying themselves to hunting, use of arms, even war, usurp male/ephebic functions. 'Artemis inverts the classical picture of the domains of female and male', and 'these *parthenoi* have turned themselves into ephebes'. In this respect too marriage is an essential instrument in drawing boundaries and delineating culture: while transforming wild animals into respectable women marriage also represents a definite state in the evolution from barbarism to civilization. (Some) barbarians are promiscuous, (all) Greeks are monogamous. And promiscuity may effect political equality among the sexes or even the superiority of the females in non-Greek cultures (Pembroke 1967).

Finally, if women's membership of the *polis* is always derivative, dependent on their association with the men, problems loom up as soon as a structural and professional feminine authority is required in a domain that is independent of male dominance. This occurs especially, if not exclusively, in the domain of cult. Significantly, women performing structural sacral roles were, as a rule, not selected from the matrons but from virgins (or widows). This is conspicuously so in the case of the priestesses of Demeter and of the Vestal Virgins—as argued above—but, for instance, also in that of the Pythia, who was an old woman dressed up as a maiden (Beard 1980; Sissa 1987, pp. 59–65). Much more could be said on these issues but this must suffice for our purpose.

## *Conclusion*

The above short impression can now serve as a grid that can help us to 'read' the curious paradox hidden in our two festivals. During their celebration Aristotle's famous dictum that the rule of a husband over his wife is 'political', but in contradistinction to democratic practice, *permanent*, is set at nought. The solution of the problem that women's *psychē* was by nature *akuron* (inoperative, without command) by placing them under the *kurieia* of the husband is cancelled during the women's festivals. They temporarily recreate a liberty that was incompatible with the status of the matron. Moreover, by their emphasis on the matrons' natural predominance in the process of procreation they suggest men's superfluity in this sector.

Matrons did things that were unimaginable in terms of the normal codes of family and society. They usurped man's political roles (dominant functions in the centre of the state), man's cultural privileges (sacrifice, wine), man's language (sexual jokes), and discarded their own specifically female roles (care for the house) and sexual codes (chastity by staying in the house and submission to the phallokratia of their husbands). In sum, during the festivals the ever lurking threat of matrons 'running wild' materialized. This necessarily evoked other stereotyped components of the complex of 'nature' in women's life and behaviour. Female 'wildness' was as inextricably interwoven with—or rather sublimated in—the representation of the *parthenos/numphē*—including its Amazonian 'masculine' independence—as was incest with parricide or cannibalism as negative signals, and marriage with Olympic sacrifice or agriculture as positive signals of culture. Expose one item in myth or ritual, and others will be automatically attracted. Women who exceed the boundaries of social codes to such an extent as was the case in these festivals, fundamentally violate the definition of matronship. As I have argued in Versnel 1990, pp. 1–35, there are various strategies to cope with extreme tensions caused by cultural paradoxes and ambiguities. One can try to cover, that is hide from sight, one of the conflicting elements, for instance by calling wine 'milk', expelling myrtle when introducing wine, covering pine-branches under *lugos* beds, calling women 'bees' when they indulge in obscene language. One can also resort to strategies of negotiation or adjustment: if matrons must return to nature they *cannot* do so *as matrons*. Then the web of associations closes: in breaking the fetters of social and marital codes women inevitably return to nature; in returning to nature they inevitably return to the premarital status of the virgin. Apart from all other natural—and naturally negative—connotations implied in the adoption of the virginal status, one should be singled out. The disjunction of 'sex/sensuousness' and 'maternity/motherliness', which is so typical of many cultures and most emphatically of the Greek and Roman, and which is evidently jeopardized in the fertility festivals, is thus safeguarded. In his illuminating analysis Friedrich 1978, esp. pp. 181–91, writes: 'In probably the majority of cultures sex and sensuousness are associated with wildness, evil, lack of control, both external and internal, and, more generally, with an animal or primitive order of being' (p. 187). To this 'order of being' then, the women return during their festivals and pay for it by becoming *numphai*. And it is this return from culture to nature that is mirrored with great precision in the concomitant symbolism for the return from cereal culture to the natural wildness of precultural primitivism.

Finally, one last question: if this interpretation should prove correct would this mean that other interpretations have lost their value? By no means. I am convinced that the sexual abstinence of the matrons had its roots in an ideology of fertility—our first level of significance—for instance intended as a state of purity conditional to agricultural productivity (as scholars of an earlier generation argued) or as 'an antithetic preparation which seeks fulfilment in procreation and birth' as Burkert 1985, p. 244 has it. Nor would I exclude the possibility that the obligation to sleep on *lugos* originated in this primeval context as well. I also argued that the references to a state of 'primitivism' are most illuminatingly explained when viewed from the perspective offered by our second level of significance, the functionalistic one with its focus on aspects of social reversal during the festivals. But this does not imply that the evolution of meaning must have come to an end in those stages. With the development of civilization, growing complexity of political systems, changing positions of women and men in society, the function and meaning of the women's festivals must have undergone drastic alterations. And it is on the third level, that of the 'meaning' of various cultural elements in the context of historical society, that I hope to have found a new meaning in elements that may have had a place already long before.

Greece and Rome in a united Europe. The 'fertility paradigm' had its roots in Germany with the works of Mannhardt, but attained its full development in Frazer's Great Britain. The functionalist approach to the social aspects of religion had its cradle in France with Durkheim, but reached maturity in the Anglo–Saxon school of structural-functionalism. For the application of semiotic hermeneutics as explored in the (initially) structuralist approach of myth, many of us have attended the 'École de Paris'. Is it a stroke of pedantic perversion or the wish to remain on good terms with everybody that makes a representative of Europe's Tom Thumb argue that none of his big brothers could claim the exclusive truth but that the great protagonists have all contributed to an elucidation of different aspects of the truth? I am not sure but I do hope to have drawn attention to the potential polyvalence of myth and ritual.

## BIBLIOGRAPHY


Baudy D., 'Das Keuschlamm–Wunder des Hermes (Hom. H. Merc. 409–13). Ein möglicher Schlüssel zum Verständnis kultischer Fesselung?', *GB* 16 (1989), 1–28.

Beard M., 'The Sexual Status of Vestal Virgins', *JRS* 70 (1980), 12–27.

Bremmer J. N. and Horsfall N. M., *Roman Myth and Mythography* (*BICS* Suppl. 52, London, 1987).

Brouwer H. H. J., *Bona Dea. The Sources and a Description of the Cult* (Leiden, 1989).

Burkert W., 'Iason, Hypsipyle and New Fire at Lemnos: a Study in Myth and Ritual', *CQ* 20 (1970), 1–16.

—— *Greek Religion. Archaic and Classical* (Oxford, 1985).

Calame C., *Les Choeurs de jeunes filles en Grèce archaïque* I (Rome, 1977).

Cazanove O. de, '*Exesto.* L'incapacité sacrificielle des femmes à Rome (à propos de Plutarque *Quaest. Rom.* 85)', *Phoenix* 41 (1987), 159–73.

Chirassi I., *Elementi di culture precereali nei miti e riti greci* (Rome, 1968).

Dahl K., *Thesmophoria: en graesk kvindefest* (Opuscula Graeco–latina, Copenhagen, 1976).

Detienne M., *Les Jardins d'Adonis* (Paris, 1972).

—— 'Violentes Eugénies'. In M. Detienne and J.-P. Vernant, *La Cuisine du sacrifice en pays grec* (Paris, 1979), pp. 183–214.

—— 'The Myth of "Honeyed Orpheus"'. In R. L. Gordon (ed.), *Myth, Religion and Society. Structuralist Essays by M. Detienne, L. Gernet, J.-P. Vernant and P. Vidal–Naquet* (Cambridge–Paris, 1981), pp. 95–109.

Deubner L., *Attische Feste* (Berlin, 1932 = Darmstadt, 1959).

Friedrich P., *The Meaning of Aphrodite* (Chicago–London, 1978).

Ghiron–Bistagne L., 'Le Cheval et la jeune fille ou de la virginité chez les anciens Grecs', *Pallas* 32 (1985), 105–21.

Gould J. P., 'Law, Custom and Myth: Aspects of the Social Position of Women in Classical Athens', *JHS* 100 (1980), 38–59.

Graf F., 'Milch, Honig und Wein. Zum Verständnis der Libation im Griechischen Ritual'. In G. Piccaluga (ed.), *Perennitas. Studi in onore di A. Brelich* (Rome, 1980), pp. 209–21.
Jenkins I., 'Is there Life after Marriage? A Study of the Abduction Motif in Vase Paintings of the Athenian Wedding Ceremony', *BICS* 30 (1983), 137–45.
Just R., *Women in Athenian Law and Life* (London–New York, 1989).
King H., 'Bound to Bleed: Artemis and Greek Women'. In A. Cameron and A. Kuhrt (edd.), *Images of Women in Antiquity* (London–Canberra, 1983), pp. 109–27.
Loraux N., *Les Enfants d'Athéna. Idées athéniennes sur la citoyenneté et la division des sexes* (Paris, 1981, repr. 1990).
——*Façons tragiques de tuer une femme* (Paris, 1985).
Nilsson M. P., *Griechische Feste von religiöser Bedeutung* (Leipzig, 1906 = Stuttgart, 1957).
Parke H. W., *Festivals of the Athenians* (London, 1977).
Pembroke S., 'Women in Charge: the Function of Alternatives in Early Greek Tradition and the Ancient Idea of Matriarchy', *JWI* 30 (1967), 1–35.
Piccaluga G., 'Bona Dea. Due contributi all'interpretazione del suo culto', *SMSR* 35 (1964), 195–237.
Schmitt P., 'Athéna Apatouria et la ceinture', *Annales ESC* 32 (1977), 1059–73.
Schneider K., 'Ius osculi', *RE* X 2 (1919), 1284f.
Simon E., *Festivals of Attica. An Archaeological Commentary* (Madison, 1983).
Sissa G., *Le Corps virginal. La virginité féminine en Grèce ancienne* (Paris, 1987).
Sourvinou-Inwood Chr., 'A Series of Erotic Pursuits: Images and Meanings', *JHS* 107 (1987), 131–53.
Vernant J.-P., *Myth and Society in Ancient Greece* (London, 1982 = 1974).
Versnel H. S., 'Destruction, *Devotio*, and Despair in a Situation of Anomy: the Mourning for Germanicus in Triple Perspective'. In G. Piccaluga (ed.), *Perennitas. Studi in onore di A. Brelich* (Rome, 1980), pp. 541–618.
——'Greek Myth and Ritual: the Case of Kronos'. In J. N. Bremmer (ed.), *Interpretations of Greek Mythology* (London, 1987), pp. 121–52.
——*Ter Unus, Isis, Dionysos, Hermes: Three Studies in Henotheism. Inconsistencies in Greek and Roman Religion* I (Leiden, 1990).
Winkler J. J., *The Constraints of Desire. The Anthropology of Sex and Gender in Ancient Greece* (New York–London, 1990).
Zeitlin F. I., 'Cultic models for the Female: Rites of Dionysus and Demeter', *Arethusa* 15 (1982), 129–57.

## NOTE

This contribution started as a very abridged prepublication of a chapter of my *Transition and Reversal in Myth and Ritual. Inconsistencies in Greek and Roman Religion* II (Leiden, 1993), 228–88. As I refer to the ample evidence and argumentation there, this is the only footnote in the present article. For an introduction into the central issues of inconsistency in the study of religious history see my *Ter Unus. Inconsistencies in Greek and Roman Religion* I (Leiden, 1990), pp. 1–35. I also seize the opportunity to express my gratitude to the editors of *Greece & Rome* for having invited me to contribute to their European volume (1992) and for having corrected my English.

# SUBJECT INDEX

# INDEX OF PASSAGES

A000018392821